THE
MILLIONAIRE
WAS A
SOVIET MOLE

THE
TWISTED LIFE OF DAVID KARR

HARVEY KLEHR

Encounter BOOKS

New York • London

First American edition published in 2019 by Encounter Books,
an activity of Encounter for Culture and Education, Inc.,
a nonprofit, tax-exempt corporation.
Encounter Books website address: www.encounterbooks.com

Manufactured in the United States and printed on
acid-free paper. The paper used in this publication meets
the minimum requirements of ANSI/NISO Z39.48–1992
(R 1997) (*Permanence of Paper*).

FIRST AMERICAN EDITION

LIBRARY OF CONGRESS CATALOGING-IN-PUBLICATION DATA
Names: Klehr, Harvey, author.
Title: The millionaire was a Soviet mole : the twisted life of David Karr /
by Harvey Klehr.
Other titles: Twisted life of David Karr
Description: New York : Encounter Books, [2019] |
Includes bibliographical references and index.
Identifiers: LCCN 2018060271 (print) | LCCN 2018061389 (ebook) |
ISBN 9781641770439 (ebook) | ISBN 9781641770422 (hardcover : alk. paper)
Subjects: LCSH: Karr, David, 1918–1979. | Spies—United State—Biography. |
Businesspeople—United States—Biography. | Espionage, Sovie—United
States—History—20th century. | Public relations consultants—United
States—Biography. | Journalists—United States—Biography. |
Pearson, Drew, 1897–1969—Friends and associates. |
Hammer, Armand, 1898–1990—Friends and associates. |
United States—Politics and government—20th century. |
Communists—United States—Biography. |
Espionage—United State—History—20th century.
Classification: LCC E840.8.K27 (ebook) | LCC E840.8.K27 K55 2019 (print) |
DDC 070.92 [B]—dc23
LC record available at https://lccn.loc.gov/2018060271

To Layla, Sawyer, Solomon and Hudson

CONTENTS

ACKNOWLEDGMENTS

It often feels like David Karr has become an inescapable presence in my life. He has been around for nearly thirty years, sometimes part of my work virtually every day; sometimes hovering in the background. So, it is a bit unnerving to prepare to let him go.

When a research project goes on as long as this biography has, friends and family have a habit of asking awkward questions about why you haven't finished it, whether you are blocked, or just plain lazy. In the case of David Karr, the reasons are more complicated, but may actually have made this a more complete book.

Not entirely complete, because some of the secrets of his life remain buried in closed archives—primarily in Russia, but also in Israel—that may never see the light of day. Others may be in the possession of family members who declined my requests for information. But some archival material, once closed, has been opened since the fall of the Soviet Union and some former spies have been willing to tell some of his story.

I first became aware of David Karr in the mid-1980s, while doing research for the book that would be published in 1996 as *The Amerasia Spy Case: Prelude to McCarthyism*, co-authored with Ron Radosh. One of the defendants in that spy case, Andrew Roth had leaked information to Karr, who was then working for Drew Pearson. As I learned a bit more about Karr and his remarkable career, I was fascinated. The *Amerasia* book was delayed by a dispute with the original publisher, and casting about for a new topic, I decided to see if I could accumulate enough information about Karr to write a biography, or at the very least, an article.

I filed a Freedom of Information request to get his FBI file, a process that took several years. I put notices in the *New York Times* and *New York Review of Books* asking people who had known him to contact me. I began to visit archives that held material about him and traveled to interview friends and enemies. I wrote to family members. It was apparent that one of the keys to his life was in the Soviet Union; I wrote to an archive likely to hold material about his business dealings and was informed that it held material that I could see if I came to Moscow. Obtaining a grant and hiring a reliable translator and aide, I made plans to visit the Soviet Union in the spring of 1992. Between the time I planned the trip and when it took place, the Communist coup against Mikhail Gorbachev failed, and Boris Yeltsin gained power and dissolved the Soviet Union.

When I arrived in Moscow, the archive that had promised access suddenly claimed it held no material on David Karr. I later learned that a Russian journalist had published an article denouncing Western politicians who had cooperated in some way with the KGB, specifically naming Senator Ted Kennedy, and quoted from a KGB document naming Karr as an intelligence source. The topic had become too politically sensitive. I was, however, able to conduct an interview with Karr's closest Soviet colleague, although it produced little of value.

The trip, however, pushed David Karr out of my research plans for more than two decades. Yeltsin had banned the Communist Party and seized its property, including its main archive. Suddenly open to researchers, the Russian Center for the Preservation and Study of Documents of Recent History, as it was then known, contained the records of the Communist International. I was the first American, and one of the first Westerners, to rummage in those files. The archivists themselves had no idea what was in the files, many of which had never been examined by anyone. I discovered explosive material about Soviet espionage in America and was allowed to make copies of KGB memos marked "Top Secret" that were later "resecretized."

That material began a more than twenty-year research enterprise, during which my collaborator, John Haynes, and I published six books (two with Fridrich Firsov) dealing with various aspects of Soviet espionage in America. During that period, the National Security Agency and CIA declassified the Venona files, a former KGB archivist defected to Great Britain with a treasure trove of material, and another former KGB officer, Alexander Vassiliev, worked with us, using his notebooks filled with copies and summaries of intelligence documents. It was an extraordinary opportunity and all-consuming. David Karr receded into the background.

As I began to near retirement, I vowed to finish my David Karr project. Going back to my notes, documents, and interviews from more than two decades ago, locating some people close to Karr whom I had not been able to find earlier, and discovering additional material, I was also chagrined to think of the questions I wish I had asked some people, now deceased, or the leads I wish I had followed before being drawn into other research. On the other hand, I hope that this project has benefitted from a longer perspective and deeper knowledge of both espionage and a tumultuous era in American history.

I am deeply grateful to the dozens of individuals, many now deceased, who wrote and talked to me about David Karr: Arnold Forster, Arthur Derounian, Jack Anderson, Luvie Pearson, Charles Simonelli, Denise Karr, Samuel Pisar, Louis Nizer, Alan Cranston, Armand Hammer (with whom I held a bizarre phone conversation in February 1989), Norman B. Norman, Sir Charles Forte, Dzhermen Gvishiani, Hervé Alphand, Jean Guyot, Max Youngstein, Jacques Elis, Feenie Ziner, George Biderman, Christopher Cross, Daniel Bell, Felix Rohatyn, John Marsh, Arthur Schlesinger, Chester Berger, Theodore Marss, Lee Falk, Leo Bogart, Oscar Brand, and Russell Rourke.

Many of the interviews are cited in the text. A handful of people who spoke about David Karr's Soviet connections insisted on anonymity; similarly, two people who knew about Eliezer Preminger's ties to Israeli intelligence did not want to be named. I am particularly appreciative of the willingness of Karr's second wife, Buffy Cooke, and their son, Frank Karr, to speak frankly with me about some painful memories, and to Preminger's son, Aner, for his help. I am also grateful to Evia Karr, David's last wife and widow, and Douglas Karr, David's grandson, who talked about his family's dynamics.

Among my colleagues and journalists who shared information, Mark Kramer, Gideon Remez, Isabella Ginor, Amnon Lord, Diana Henriques, Robert Nedelkoff, Jeff Gerth, Michael Johnson, Dan Mulvenna, Hayden Peake, Eric Fettman, John Haynes, Laurence Cott, Svetlana

Sevranskaya, Thomas Remington, David Katz (of Tel Aviv University and not related to David Karr, despite sharing his birth name), and Kenneth Stein were all helpful. Roy Rowan's portrait of Karr after his death in *Fortune* remains the gold standard for anyone trying to understand his complicated world. Jeff Gerth sent me some of the material he had accumulated for his article on Karr in the *New York Times*.

Research assistants Alona Dolinsky in Israel, Nicoly Silin in Russia, Laura Kennedy, Gina Stamm, Elena Goldis, and Kurtis Anderson in Atlanta, Eli Klehr in New York, Marilyn Farnell in Boston, and Jorge Santos in Connecticut, saved me long trips by patiently scouring archives for relevant documents.

Archivists at the Drew Pearson papers at the LBJ Library in Austin, the Sargent Shriver papers and White House files in the John F. Kennedy Library in Boston, Westbrook Pegler papers at the Herbert Hoover Presidential Library, American Heritage Center at the University of Wyoming, Department of State, Office of Passport Services and Central Foreign Policy Records, Harry S. Truman Library, the Dwight David Eisenhower Library, the General Charles Lanham papers at the Seely G. Mudd Manuscript Library, Princeton University, James Wechsler papers at the Wisconsin Historical Society, Gerald Ford Library, J. B. Matthews papers at Duke University Library, Henry Wallace papers and Gardner Jackson papers at the FDR Library, Henry Wallace papers at the University of Iowa, Clinton Anderson papers at the Library of Congress, and the Feenie Ziner papers at the University of Connecticut all responded to my requests gracefully and helpfully. The FBI processed Karr's extensive file, and the CIA retrieved and made available a small number of documents. The Securities and Exchange Commission claims to have lost its files dealing with Karr. The record of the settlement of Karr's estate can be found in a mountainous and largely unorganized file at the Surrogate's Court, Borough of Manhattan, in New York.

This project would never have gotten off the ground without grant support from the long-patient Lynde and Harry Bradley Foundation. I owe particular thanks to Hillel Fradkin. Emory University provided a number of small grants that enabled me to travel to archives and to interview people.

For reading all or parts of the manuscript, I am grateful to David Evanier, Jonathan Brent, John Haynes, and Mark Kramer. They are, of course, not responsible for any errors or misjudgments; all that is entirely on me. After so many years of obsessing about David Karr, I owe a debt of gratitude to my agents, Lynn Chu and Glen Hartley, for their assistance. I would also like to thank Katherine Wong and Ian Gibbs for their meticulous production and copyediting of the manuscript.

My friends and family have patiently endured my stories about David Karr and his fantastic life over and over again for decades. My family is probably happier to see this project end than I am. My brother and sister and brothers-in-law and sisters-in-law never quite believed that it would ever be finished. I am indebted to one of them, Gerry Benjamin, for carefully explaining details of Karr's probate records to me. My late wife, Elizabeth, told me that it was my best shot at a mini-series and accompanied me on several of my research trips. My children—Ben, Gabe, Josh, and Aaron—have heard tales about David Karr since they were children, and their wives—Annsley, Alice, Lauren, and Brittany —were not considered part of the family until they heard the Karr saga. My wife, Marcie, kept telling me to make sure to emphasize the sex so that people would be interested. My grandchildren—Layla, Sawyer, Solomon, and Hudson—could not have cared less but I am blessed to be able to dedicate this book to them.

INTRODUCTION

David Karr was the Zelig of twentieth-century American life. He popped up at key moments and important places, next to such significant figures as Alan Cranston, Drew Pearson, Armand Hammer, John Tunney, and Sargent Shriver. He preoccupied J. Edgar Hoover, and hobnobbed with Aristotle Onassis, Henry Wallace, and political movers and shakers in France and Russia. His sister, who admitted "very intense" positive and negative feelings about him, thought he had an "uncanny yearning to be an insider because he was an outsider."[1]

To more suspicious observers, Karr was a Svengali who bewitched and corrupted those who were sometimes naïve, sometimes greedy, who worked at newspapers, in public relations, or in government propaganda agencies. In this narrative, Karr later decided he could do more damage to American interests as a capitalist and used his access to business tycoons to weaken American companies and benefit the Soviet Union. Westbrook Pegler, the acerbic conservative newsman, devoted dozens of columns to denouncing his machinations, complaining that "planting plugs, intimidating Government officials by threats" and surveilling the unsuspecting were his "vocation."[2]

To still others, his life epitomizes a peculiarly American journey—that of constant reinvention of self, a young man on the make, ever alert for the main chance, and careless about the roadkill left behind in his meteoric, unprincipled rise from obscurity. Jack Anderson, who succeeded him as Drew Pearson's chief "legman," insisted that Karr was the model for *How to Succeed in Business without Really Trying*, the hit Broadway show that celebrated the astonishing rise of a window-washer up the corporate ladder to boss.[3]

Some who knew Karr swore by his probity. Hervé Alphand, a French statesman, thought he was "always very nice and very kind. I never saw him offend anyone." Arnold Forster, the former head of the Anti-Defamation League, called him "one of the good guys." But many more people loathed him. One of his ex-wives wrote that "David makes people feel disposable—like a piece of Kleenex." George Biderman, who worked with David Karr in the 1950s, regarded him as "an exploiter and opportunist. Very devious and shifty. Not honest." A onetime business partner, Ronnie Driver, thought, "it might be a little harsh to categorize" his tactics "as blackmail, but that was undoubtedly the area in which he operated." Daniel Bell, the famous sociologist, thought he was "slightly pathological, slightly slimy."[4]

Everyone who knew him could agree that he was driven. Senator Joseph McCarthy thought it was ideology that motivated him. He charged that Karr was "the connecting link between Drew Pearson and the Communist Party. He is the man who assigns to Pearson the important task of conducting a character assassination of any man who dares to stand in the way of international Communism." Others regarded him as a chameleon, intent only on advancing his own interests. To his sister, he was consumed by a need to dominate; "his capacity to reduce everyone around him to ashes of one sort or another...accounts for his successes, as well as his failure...he only permits one posture, I must be on my knees, worshipping his successes."[5]

However one interprets his life, David Karr is one of the more fascinating characters of the middle of the twentieth century. Never a household name, he was a familiar presence in a world where journalism, government, and business intersected, well known to Washington insiders for more than three decades. He knew or met with every American president from FDR to Gerald Ford. Readers of *Fortune* and *Business Week* magazines were treated to regular updates about his activities during the 1960s and 1970s. He played a role in any number of national controversies, ranging from finger-pointing during World War II over who was to blame for the assassination of Italian-American anarchist Carlo Tresca, and charges by Congressman Martin Dies about Communists on the government payroll, to accusations by Senator Joseph McCarthy that he was a Soviet intelligence mole, to hand-wringing later in the 1950s about hostile business takeovers weakening American capitalism, continuing to the age of détente to mutterings about shady Western business dealings with the Soviet Union and unethical practices surrounding contracts for the Moscow Olympics. His various exploits not only got chewed over in newspaper stories but were commented on in the halls of Congress and subjected to frequent government investigations.

His personal life was almost as tumultuous. Married four times, he was in the process of divorcing his last wife at the time of his mysterious death. His second wife described him as "dynamic, intellectually fasci-nating and an exciting husband in every regard." He cheated on all his wives. His five children loved him but were damaged by their relation-ship with him. When they visited, "he treated them to horrendously luxurious living that was unrealistic" and would "spoil them rotten" but he would then "never help with medical bills for the kids or tuition." He enjoyed playing his two daughters against each other, telling one she looked beautiful and then disparaging the other's looks.[6]

He left a trail of angry and embittered former friends, but he com-manded the deep loyalty of several powerful men. Charming and knowl-edgeable, he was also capable of gratuitous acts of cruelty and lacerating rudeness, delighting in parading his affluence and importance in front of family and friends.

When he died, his last wife halted his burial with a court order for an autopsy, convinced that he had been murdered. She named as suspects the KGB, CIA, Israeli Mossad, and the Mafia. No hard evidence ever turned up, but every one of them did have a plausible reason for desiring his silence. Probating his will took nearly a decade as children, ex-wives, a widow, and former business partners sparred over his complicated and messy financial affairs.

Even after Karr's death, scandalous accusations about his activities persisted. Journalists flung around claims that he ran guns to dicta-tors, spied for the Soviet Union, even colluded in Robert Kennedy's assassination. As a man of mystery, he could be inserted in any number of conspiratorial plots, his fingerprints glimpsed at a variety of crime scenes.

The most explosive part of his life is also one of the murkiest. There is no doubt that as a young man, he was close to the Communist Party of the United States. He wrote for its newspaper, consorted with several of its members, and shared many of its views. Everything else about David Karr and Communism, however, remains disputed territory. Karr himself spent decades apologizing for and explaining away his youthful flirtation. He vehemently denied ever being a Party member and periodically attested to how much he detested Communism. His legions of enemies were less charitable, insisting that he had belonged to the CPUSA, had never surrendered his youthful beliefs, and, in fact, had worked diligently over the years to advance Communist causes, not only while employed by the United States government during World War II, but also as a newspaper correspondent for Drew Pearson, for whom he acted as a conduit to carry out subversive tasks. Even after his death, periodic leaks and charges that he had been a KGB agent continued to surface, including incriminating documents from Russian archives.

Born to immigrant Jewish parents in New York, David Katz died in a fashionable Paris apartment as David Karr. His remarkable American journey encompassed many different worlds from Communist newspapers to the Office of War Information (OWI), from muckraking columnist to public relations flack, from corporate raider to corporate executive, from moviemaker to hotel executive, from business fixer to Olympic Committee confidant. According to some sources it also included arms smuggler, corrupt businessman, visionary deal-maker, protector of Jewish emigrants from Russia, behind-the-scenes political fixer, and Communist spy. His strange journey is not just a unique, fascinating American life—how many future CEOs of powerful defense companies were once accused on the floor of the United States Senate of being the KGB controller of a major media personality? It also illuminates significant episodes of twentieth-century American history.

Several themes that have fascinated historians are illuminated by David Karr's tumultuous life. Was he the prototypical ideological and political leftist who moves from trying to transform the world into manipulating it to enrich himself? The crusading idealist who parlays a bulging Rolodex into positions of power? The canny opportunist who cheerfully uses fair and foul means to scramble over old friends and climb the greasy pole?

There is no doubt that Karr played half a dozen ends against the middle. So many people thought they knew who he was and what his views were. As a young man, he tried to befriend Nazis to expose them. He told the FBI that his flirtations with Communists were designed to gather information to weaken them. He boasted to people that he had worked for the FBI. He fervently declared his sympathies for Henry Wallace and his left-wing views up until 1948, even while cozying up to Republican presidential candidate Thomas Dewey. At the same time, he feverishly worked to counter Soviet influence in Western Europe. He was friends with many men accused of involvement in Soviet espionage. When the State Department withheld his passport, he offered an affidavit in which he savaged a number of leftists suspected of espionage or Communist Party membership. He told his mother he had been on secret missions for the Israelis. The Russians clearly believed they had recruited him. American counterintelligence officials were inclined to agree. He may not even have known exactly for whom he was working. It is possible that Karr had agreed to cooperate with Israelis, or the Russians, or both. He was enough of an egotist to think that he could keep many balls in the air at the same time.

What kind of ideological journey did David Karr make in his life? Was he a Communist who burrowed into the American government, or a democrat who burrowed into the Communist world? Was he a businessman who saw the Soviet market as an opportunity to make money, or an ideologue who saw Soviet-American trade as a chance to advance Communist interests? Was he a proud Jew inspired by Israel's achievements and anxious to assist its interests, or a deracinated Jew willing to sell Soviet arms to such Arab dictators as Muammar al-Qaddafi, or befriend a PLO operative implicated in the massacre of Israeli athletes at Munich? How much did his business associates and political allies know about his shadowy and controversial past? What did his Soviet contacts think he was up to?

And how did this brash young man from Brooklyn, who never went to college, claw his way up the corridors of power to become a confidant of presidents and millionaires, in spite of a coterie of powerful people in the press and government convinced that he was a dangerous subversive?

Not every question about the many lives of David Karr can yet be answered. Some of the most important remain distorted by the wilderness of mirrors that still surrounds aspects of the intelligence world—others are shrouded by the reluctance of surviving members of his family to reopen wounds he inflicted on those closest to him. Unlike some biographers uninhibited by the absence of evidence, I am reluctant to spin fantasies about my subject. But this man of mystery left enough of a paper trail to track the main contours of his life. Without leaping into fiction, I can at least report and judge the often-fantastical theories of those who imagined his hidden hand behind the assassination of Robert Kennedy or supplying arms to Idi Amin. The truth about David Karr is strange enough.

1

YOUNG RADICAL
ON THE MAKE

Nothing about his childhood or early years suggested that David Karr would mingle with powerful politicians or industrialists, let alone become a man of mystery. Nor was there much surface evidence that he would be attracted to Communism. He was born as David Katz on August 24, 1918 in Brooklyn into a prosperous Jewish family. His father, Morris, had emigrated to America in 1892 from Bucharest, Romania, where he had been born in 1886, and settled in Brooklyn. His mother, Sophie Guttman, had been born in 1895 and arrived in New York in 1899 with her parents from Riga, Latvia. Morris began working as a clerk in a jewelry store as a teenager. He and Sophie married in 1917. By the time David was born, Morris had become a jewelry manufacturer and importer. His business prospered and the growing family, which included a sister, Florence, born in 1921 and the youngest brother, Mortimer, arriving in 1923, enjoyed an upper-middle-class lifestyle in a brownstone in Crown Heights, Brooklyn. The 1925 New York State census listed the three children and a maid in residence.[1]

The family also had a summer home in Crompond, a small town in Westchester County, east of Peekskill, where Lake Mohegan provided recreation. The area was home to several colonies of bungalows built by New York radicals. The Mohegan Colony, founded by Jewish anarchists in the 1920s, was the oldest, but Communists and other leftists established small communities in succeeding years, along with some New Yorkers just looking to escape the heat and humidity of the city.

Morris Katz was most likely just looking for a summer retreat since, unlike militant Communists, or even many anarchists and socialists, the Katz family retained some ties to the Jewish faith. Morris belonged to a synagogue, sent David to Sunday school and Hebrew school, and had him bar mitzvahed at the Brooklyn Jewish Center. Morris had, however, strayed from the Orthodoxy of his youth. He was a mainstay of the Ethical Culture movement, a secular, universalist body, most of whose members were Jews anxious to escape from the tribalism and particularism they associated with traditional Judaism. And, unlike many Jewish socialists, Morris had sympathies for the effort to build a Jewish homeland in Palestine. While he was not an active Zionist, in later years he endowed a chair in adult education at Tel Aviv University.[2]

David was a sickly child, forced to miss a great deal of school because of ear infections. Deprived of playmates, he became a voracious reader of newspapers and was determined to become a reporter, no doubt influenced by the success of *The Front Page*, written by Ben Hecht and Charles MacArthur. It debuted on Broadway in 1928, dramatizing and glorifying the lives of beat reporters. After he endured twelve operations for mastitis between the ages of six and ten that left him deaf in his right ear, his mother moved with him to San Antonio, Texas, in 1928 to escape a harsh New York winter. For some reason, she enrolled him at the Peacock Military Academy, where he was certain to be a fish out of water. According to Karr, after an intelligence test determined that he had a genius-level IQ, the *San Antonio Light* published a photograph of the school's founder measuring his head with a pair of calipers.[3]

Back home in New York the following year, David's intelligence was not reflected in his academic prowess. Overweight and unpopular, he skipped school whenever possible and barely scraped by academically. School authorities conducted numerous conferences with his parents to explore why a boy with his abilities performed so poorly. He attended Boys High in Brooklyn from 1931 to February 1936, when he was booted out for being overage. Returning a year later, he managed to graduate in June 1937 with a 65 average, ranking in the bottom 20 percent of his class with no extracurricular activities, except serving as manager of the ice-hockey team. He attributed his dismal performance to a "craving desire to escape into the world from the cloistered existence of a semi-invalid."[4]

His father later explained that he "had many misgivings about David's future until he came out of his teens." Morris Katz attributed his interest in adult education to the realization, forced on him by David, that a set academic curriculum was not appropriate for all children. Some people like David required "learning from life for life."[5]

His less-than-stellar high school career was marked by two rebellious incidents. Standing with a group of tardy students to get late passes, he suggested they all not fill out the required forms, and just play hooky. Promptly hustled into the principal's office, he had to call his mother to effect his release. Better illustrating his burgeoning political sympathies, during the Communist-inspired Peace Strike of 1934 he was taken out of class and ensconced in the principal's office to prevent him from participating in the demonstration.[6]

According to Karr, both of his parents "were conservative in outlook politically." That claim, however—made to the State Department in an effort to gain a passport—certainly distorted the political milieu in which David started to swim. Particularly after the onset of the Depression, the world of New York Jews leaned left, and summers in Crompond no doubt contributed to his burgeoning radicalism. But it was his entrance into the field of journalism that first nudged him into the wider left-wing world.[7]

Karr's undistinguished high school career was marked by only one passion, his dream of becoming a sports reporter. He covered school sports for the *New York World-Telegram* and the *Daily Mirror*. The passage of the National Labor Relations Act had inspired a wave of union organizing across the country. Heywood Broun, a close ally of the Communist Party, had founded the American Newspaper Guild in 1935 and the Guild was diligently attempting to establish a foothold in the industry. Karr eagerly pitched in, making an abortive effort to organize a unit of the Newspaper Guild at the *Mirror*, but he was "rebuffed by the other employees who considered him to be an upstart since he had been working for the paper such a short period of time." When a unit was formed, Karr joined in 1937 while still in high school. He showed up at picket lines in Long Island and Brooklyn, sometimes going from strike duty to school. He even voted to authorize a strike at the *Mirror*, but negotiations produced a contract.[8]

With few evident skills to show after finally getting a high school degree, Karr earned a living with menial jobs, scrambling to find a niche. He later claimed to have written for several other newspapers, but since few had any record of his employment, it is most likely that he was a freelancer who occasionally sent in contributions. After his high school graduation he worked in the shipping department of the Mannheim Company, which bought diamonds from his father, who no doubt had procured the position for him. He bought merchandise at auctions, loaded it into his father's car, and peddled it to retailers, pushcart owners, and Coney Island concessionaires, clearing five to ten dollars a day. For several months in 1938 he was a salesman for the Fuller Brush Company. He briefly worked as a part-time press agent for jai alai contests at the New York Hippodrome, earning five to ten dollars a week for writing publicity releases; once he even got Babe Ruth to appear as a publicity stunt.

Not until the spring of 1938 did Karr finally discover a calling. In 1937, around the time he graduated from high school, David Katz had changed his name to Karr, presumably to avoid anti-Semitism. It was a growing menace in the United States and particularly notable in New York. Fritz Kuhn, a German immigrant who had become an American citizen, had been elected leader of the German American Bund in 1936. Originally financed by the German government, the Bund worked to bolster the Nazi regime's image in the United States. Under his leadership, it sponsored training camps for young German-Americans, demonstrations in support of Nazi Germany, and boasted a corps of uniformed storm troopers. Karr later claimed that he had become interested in the issue of Nazi subversion as a result of a conversation with a woman working for the U.S. Attorney's Office, and that he did some investigating and wrote a story about Kuhn. Although the *Mirror* refused to publish it, a colleague sent it to several other Hearst papers, one of which, the conservative *Chicago Herald Examiner*, ran it. Far from immediately advancing his career, however, the article caught the attention of William Randolph Hearst, who ordered the *Mirror* to have nothing more to do with him.[9]

Bill Mahoney, a Communist on the sports staff of the paper who edited Karr's contributions, suggested that he should talk to Lowell Wakefield, a writer on the CPUSA's organ, the *Daily Worker*. At a lunch in August, Wakefield urged him to continue his investigations, and agreed to print whatever Karr wrote about Nazi activities. Anxious to break into journalism, worried about Nazi propaganda in America, impressed by Wakefield, and, he later claimed, young and naïve about Communism, Karr eagerly agreed: "Mr. Wakefield offered me an opportunity to realize this ambition and I accepted his offer."[10]

While Karr, like most New York Jews, was undoubtedly worried by the growing prominence of the Bund, this tale of how he initially connected with Communists may have been told to try to minimize his affinity with Communism. His first contribution to the Communist paper was more prosaic than a look at American Nazis; on September 11, 1938 his first piece was titled "Ambulance: How to Call One Fast," followed on October 2 by "City Owned Water System Costs but One Cent per Day." On October 9, "Nazi Spy Here Equals 1917 Sabotage Says Expert" got to the ostensible reason Karr had approached Wakefield. Only one of his other five contributions to the *Daily Worker* dealt even tangentially with the Nazi issue he later said had led him to approach Wakefield. Three concerned the fallout from a sensational fraud case, the McKesson & Robbins trial, while his last article, published on January 15, 1939, was about the boycott of goods made in fascist countries. One review of the Flatbush Players, a drama troupe of a Young Communist League club in Brooklyn, rhapsodized that they had raised more than $600 for "the party fund" and included Communist rhetoric about "the rats and parasites that fatten upon America's youth."[11]

In addition to freelancing for the *Daily Worker*, Karr traveled to the Yorkville area of Manhattan to buy Nazi propaganda, for which Wakefield reimbursed him, attended Bund meetings, and sat in on the McKesson & Robbins trial. Wakefield also brought Karr along to a spy trial held in New York in late 1938 (four Nazi agents were convicted), asked him to cooperate with *Life* magazine for a pictorial exposé for which Karr was paid, and sent him to the American League for Peace and Democracy to give speeches at public meetings as an expert on the Nazi menace in the United States, for which he was also paid.[12]

In just a few short months, David Karr had gone from being a part-time writer of local sports stories to a consultant to a major media institution and a paid speaker for a prominent left-wing organization— all as a result of his connection to the *Daily Worker*, the official organ of the CPUSA. For a young man with few discernible talents or prospects, it must have been a heady experience. Lowell Wakefield, his benefactor, was a veteran Communist who had been expelled from the University of Washington for leading a student protest against the ROTC. He was serving as the southern organizer of the International Labor Defense in Tennessee in 1931 when his dispatches from Scottsboro, Alabama, first gave prominence to what became the Scottsboro Boys case. Back in Washington State in 1932, he became a leader in the state Communist party and founded and edited *Voice of Action*, its newspaper. By 1938 he was a *Daily Worker* correspondent; his coverage of the Nazi trials was turned into a pamphlet, *Hitler's Spy Plot in the U.S.A.* Wakefield surely found the enthusiastic and ambitious Karr a useful researcher, and, most likely, pointed him toward investigating Nazis. In Karr's later telling, Wakefield knew he was not a Communist and discouraged him from joining the Party. He recalled that Wakefield sent him to a man named Berman who was in charge of dispatching Communist infiltrators into the Bund in late November or early December. When Berman learned Karr was not a Communist, he urged him to join the Party; Wakefield "told me not even to think of joining the Communist Party and I did not join the Party."[13]

Early in January 1939, Karr claimed he was summoned to the ninth floor of Communist Party headquarters where V. J. Jerome, one of the CPUSA's ideological commissars, called him to task for the absence of "a class angle" in his review of a movie that had appeared on December 27. When Karr seemed perplexed by the charge, Jerome asked what Party unit he belonged to and abruptly terminated the interview after hearing that Karr was not a Party member. Within days Wakefield called him at home, arranged to meet away from the *Daily Worker* office, and explained that he had been "hauled up on the carpet for using a non-Communist who was likely also a Hearst spy." He had been ordered to terminate all connections with David Karr.[14]

But Wakefield disobeyed Party orders—or at least ignored them, if Karr is to be believed. That same month, he introduced Karr to Albert Kahn, executive secretary of the American Council Against

Nazi Propaganda, who hired him to investigate right-wing subversion at a salary of between twenty-five and thirty-five dollars a week. Kahn wasn't just another well-meaning liberal opponent of fascism, like many of the Council's members and leaders, which included former American Ambassador to Germany William Dodd. Scion of a distinguished and wealthy family, Kahn had joined the Communist Party in 1938 under the influence of its support for the Spanish Loyalist faction (which was dominated by the Communists) and was forced out of the family firm. Under his direction, the Council was a thinly disguised Communist Party front that published *The Hour*, which specialized in exposés of alleged Nazi and fascist individuals and groups working in the United States.[15]

Karr's job at the American Council was to investigate fascist and Nazi groups and write stories about them. An interview with Anastase Vonsiatsky, the American head of the Russian National Revolutionary Labor and Workers Peasant Party of Fascists, Karr said, had helped launch a government investigation that ended with Vonsiatsky's conviction for espionage. In 1939, Karr interviewed the Grand Dragon of the Ku Klux Klan, and wrote articles about William Pelley's Silver Shirts and other fringe groups that appeared in the magazines *Fight*, *The World*, and *Equality*. In January 1940, *Equality* published Karr's attack on Martin Dies, chairman of the Special Committee on Un-American Activities, forerunner of HUAC.[16]

This record later provided plentiful fodder for critics who said that Karr had been a member of the Communist Party and might still be one. Publishing in the Party's flagship newspaper and associating with Communists over a number of years seemed to present a prima facie case for Party membership. But throughout his life, Karr insisted that his relationship to the Party in the 1930s was, at most, poor judgment, and at best cooperation with those who shared his hostility to fascism and anti-Semitism. The evidence is equivocal.

Like many Jews in the 1930s, the Katzes worried about anti-Semitism and the Nazi regime in Germany. Particularly in the last half of the decade, as the Communist party modified its previously revolutionary stance and proclaimed its commitment to anti-fascism and "Americanism," David was sympathetic and attracted. No one ever proved he was a card-carrying member, but friends and acquaintances

assumed he was at least a close sympathizer. Daniel Bell, the future sociologist, knew him in the late 1930s and believed he was a Communist.
Arthur Derounian, who gained fame for exposés of fascist activists in
the United States under the name of John Roy Carlson, met Karr when
he wrote for *The Hour*; he assumed from the company David kept that
he was in the CPUSA. Leo Bogart, a future public opinion analyst who
dated Dave's younger sister Florence, recalled Karr as a very bright,
very impatient presence, seemingly out of *Front Page*. Already writing
for several papers, to Leo he seemed very sophisticated. He wore a
black fedora, cultivated an aura of mystery, and was quite open about
his pro-Communist views.[17]

Oscar Brand, the future folksinger, knew David in the late 1930s
when he was engaged to the woman who later became Karr's first wife
and was also friendly with Florence Katz. Brand thought that Madeline
Baratz, who married Karr in 1942, grew up in a Communist family and
was probably in the Young Communist League, so he assumed David
was also a Party member. He recalled an occasion when the two of them
attacked him for his less radical political views. They opposed American
aid to Great Britain after the Nazi-Soviet Pact and regarded the Pact as a
mere act of *realpolitik*. Although David had Communist opinions, Brand
considered him less zealous than Madeline and said that at some point,
he stopped echoing the Party line. Brand didn't know whether David
had actually had a change of heart or had decided to conceal his views.[18]

Both Madeline and David always strenuously denied Communist
affiliations. Her family, however, had ties to Communism that the more
financially successful Katz family did not. Her father, Samuel Baratz,
owned a small business that imported and exported costume jewelry.
Madeline, born in the Bronx in August 1921, recalled years later to a
lawyer that her mother, Rose, had occasional trial subscriptions to the
Daily Worker and the *New Masses*. After visiting her family in Russia
around 1934, Rose had returned enthusiastic about the Bolshevik
regime, and praising the opportunities it had created for young Jews,
but Madeline said she became less dewy-eyed after learning that one of
her brothers had been persecuted for possessing American dollars she
had sent him. Madeline attended several non-Communist Jewish camps;
one Camp Boiberek, sponsored by the Sholem Aleichem Folk Schools,
was hostile to the CPUSA. Madeline did go to Young Communist

League–sponsored dances and movies over the years—on New Year's Eve 1938, she and David went to a *New Masses* dance—but she later insisted that she never joined either the CPUSA or the YCL. Her most extensive connection with Communist causes came as a result of the Spanish Civil War; she attended numerous meetings but could not recall who had sponsored them and she was certain that her name would never have been included on a committee or letterhead. Like David she had joined the American League Against War and Fascism, made monetary contributions, and attended meetings. After the Pact, she claimed that disgusted by the alliance with Nazis, she had quit, but during World War II, she joined the American-Soviet Friendship Council.[19]

Personal recollections aside, whether a non-Communist could even write for the Party newspaper is unclear. Howard Rushmore, a Communist journalist turned government witness, knew Karr on the *Daily Worker*. He testified that he gave Karr assignments and "he had to show me his party card to get these assignments." He also said that Karr had told him he rewrote articles for the *Party Organizer*, an internal Party publication. Yet Lowell Wakefield offered an affidavit in 1951 backing up Karr that he was not formally a Communist. Wakefield had left the CPUSA after the Nazi-Soviet Pact to return to Washington state, where, in 1946, he started a fish and canning company for Alaskan king crab. Wakefield Seafoods pioneered the process of freezing the crab at sea and marketing them as a luxury item; by the mid-1950s it had captured 85 percent of the American market. When he died in 1977, the onetime Communist organizer was a well-known expert on fishing issues, a philanthropist, and a prominent citizen of Alaska.[20]

Nineteen thirty-eight was the high point of the Popular Front. Sympathetic non-Communists clustered around the *Daily Worker*. Some young Communists plausibly might have been happy to advance their own interests as well as the Party's but balked at actually joining. While some Party members might privately hold some objections to the Party line, Wakefield's introducing Karr to Albert Kahn makes little sense if Wakefield had been ordered to cut ties to a presumed Hearst spy. It would have cost him dearly if either Kahn or Jerome learned of his defiance. If not formally a member, Karr was a member in all but name. He associated with Communist Party members, sympathized with its positions, and was hostile to its critics.

By introducing Karr to Kahn, moreover, Wakefield was, no doubt unwittingly, inserting him into a more complicated and devious world than that of the open CPUSA. While *The Hour* was devoted to the public exposure of Nazis and had established a relationship with the Anti-Defamation League, which sought to track and expose fascists, Kahn also had other goals. Kahn used his contacts and information to feed information to Jacob Golos, a high-ranking CPUSA official and a conduit to the NKVD. Elizabeth Bentley first identified Kahn in 1945 as one of Golos's sources, particularly on American Ukrainians, and Kahn was identified in the Venona decryptions as a KGB agent code-named "Fighter."[21]

Throughout the rest of his life, Karr continued to insist that he had not followed the Communist Party line, had never joined the Communist Party, and had never been on the staff of the *Daily Worker*. He would offer a variety of explanations for these early associations ranging from naïveté to ambition and from a shared interest in combating anti-Semitism to working as an FBI informant. But by the end of 1940, Karr understood that his activities were potentially troublesome. The Nazi-Soviet Pact may have played a role; it is possible that it disillusioned Karr about the Soviet Union's commitment to anti-fascism. A book published in 1940 attacking "fifth columnists" in the United States thanked Karr for providing information; while almost exclusively focused on Nazi sympathizers, it included critical comments on Communists as well. Karr later cited it as evidence that he had not supported the Nazi-Soviet Pact, although all it proves is that he was friendly to a fellow journalist who did not. Also, in 1943, the FBI interviewed someone who had known Karr who reported that he had worked actively to reelect FDR in 1940, at a time when the CPUSA denounced FDR as a warmonger.[22]

Karr was still close enough to the Communist movement, however, to continue writing for a Communist-aligned magazine, *Equality*, even after the Pact. The managing editor until February 1940 was Abraham Chapman, who was succeeded by Harold Coy. Both were Communists, as were many of its board members and contributors. Karr had published two articles there, in May 1939 on Silver Shirt leader William Pelley, and in December on the German Bund. The September 1939 issue had included an appeal for collective security against fascism. By October, responding to the Nazi-Soviet Pact, an editorial denounced "this fascist-imperialist orgy of destruction" and demanded America stay out of an imperialist war. Not only did Karr write for the December issue, he accepted a request from Abraham Chapman to write a critical article about Martin Dies for the January 1940 issue of *Equality*. Karr later told the Dies Committee that it was not until a year later that he learned that Chapman wrote for the Communist Yiddish daily *The Freiheit* under the name of John Arnold and realized that the magazine was a Party front. He must not have been paying much attention. Chapman was a high-ranking CP official active in Jewish affairs. Even if Karr had no idea who he was, Chapman's selection of Karr to write the article on Dies indicated some level of confidence that Karr was not hostile to the Party after the Pact. In 1950, Chapman suddenly fled to Mexico and then Czechoslovakia with his wife and two daughters, not to return to America until 1963. Ann Kimmage, Chapman's daughter, suspected but could never learn from her father whether he had connections to Soviet espionage agencies. But the magazine did include a number of non-Communists among its writers; the same issue that contained Karr's attack on Dies also included pieces by Ernest Hemingway and Walter White of the NAACP.[23]

Tellingly, as late as February 1940 Karr wrote to John Spivak, who made no secret of his Communist sympathies, on an *Hour* letterhead. He reported on his effort to interview a right-wing businessman close to Father Coughlin. He also mentioned that "we were changing the emphasis of our work," going more heavily into "peace and civil liberties" and investigating British activity, all part of the shifting Communist emphasis on opposing any American involvement in anti-fascist activities. And, he disparaged an aide to Mayor LaGuardia of New York as "quite a red-baiter."[24]

While working for *The Hour*, Karr had also been doing part-time work for Transradio Press Service. Transradio sent dispatches to radio stations around the country. Karr was hired full-time in June 1939. An indefatigable networker, he parlayed this job into a temporary position that gave him access to a number of important and connected figures in mainstream American politics. After only about a year at Transradio, he was given a six-week leave of absence to work for the National Committee of Independent Voters for Roosevelt-Wallace (sometimes known as the Norris-LaGuardia Committee) on its radio operations. Thomas Corcoran, "Tommy the Cork," FDR's notable fixer and one of Washington's most famous lobbyists, persuaded Karr's boss at Transradio, Herbert Moore, to temporarily loan him to the campaign. Karr worked under Nelson Poynter, who later became the publisher of the *St. Petersburg Times*. This position put him in friendly contact with such Washington insiders as David Niles, a White House aide, George Vournas, a prominent Greek-American attorney, and Gardner Jackson, a legendary radical activist. Among Karr's accomplishments was arranging for R. J. Thomas, president of the United Auto Workers and Congress of Industrial Organizations (CIO) leader, to appear on a national radio hookup, where he delivered a Karr-written speech attacking John L. Lewis. An isolationist, Lewis was a Communist hero for opposing FDR's support for Britain and France. This may support Karr's claim that he had become disillusioned with the Communist Party after September 1939—or he may have concluded that open loyalty to Communism would stymie his career. After the campaign, Niles and Jackson suggested to Herbert Moore that Karr would be more valuable to Transradio in Washington, and he was shifted to the capital in 1940.[25]

Karr's relationship with Gardner (Pat) Jackson indicates that after the Nazi-Soviet Pact, Karr distanced himself from the CPUSA. Jackson, the scion of a wealthy Colorado mine owner, was a non-Communist radical with a long pedigree of activism who often cooperated with Communists but occasionally found himself fighting them. He had cut his radical teeth in the 1920s while covering the Sacco-Vanzetti case for a newspaper. Sacco and Vanzetti were two famous anarchists convicted for a Boston robbery during which people were murdered, believed by many to have been framed. Jackson had thrown himself into doomed efforts to save the pair from execution. Recruited by two covert Communists working in the Agricultural Adjustment Administration (AAA), Lee Pressman and Nathan Witt, he joined the New Deal in 1933. Along with Pressman and Witt, Jackson was purged in 1935 when Henry Wallace ousted most of the left-wingers in the agency. Jackson remained in Washington to work for the interests of small farmers and continued to cooperate with Communists in the CIO and its Labor's Non-Partisan League. But, angered by the Nazi-Soviet Pact, Jackson broke with John L. Lewis in 1940 over his isolationism.[26]

Karr met Jackson soon after the latter had split from Lewis. The two quickly formed a close bond. When Karr moved to Washington in January 1941, he stayed with the Jacksons at their Chevy Chase home for three months and vacationed with them on Cape Cod in the summer of 1941. Jackson wrote letters of introduction for Karr's then-girlfriend, who wanted to break into the theater world, sent political intelligence to Karr, and received some in return. Although their surviving letters do not explicitly discuss Communism or the Pact, in one undated note, Karr promised to bring Jackson material on Lewis's relationship with a pro-German oil importer, an indication that he shared Jackson's hostility to his old boss, or at least was willing to help discredit someone the Communist Party was supporting.[27]

His correspondence with Jackson also displayed Karr's calculating and unctuous personality. Karr had introduced Sandra Waring, his girlfriend, to the Jacksons and asked that Pat write letters recommending her to both Hallie Flanagan and Herman Shumlin, well-known figures in the theater world. Jackson did so but warned Karr that Sandra might be the wrong woman for him. Karr agreed, explaining that he himself was "thoroughly unsophisticated," knew "her faults" and liked her mostly because "I stole her away from a very handsome lad at a very nice affair, right under the lad's nose." He had been taken in by her claims of being an orphan and, "being motivated like yourself by a deep sense of appreciation of the fact that there are a lot of underprivileged people in the world," he had been too nice. "I was intrigued more by a case history than by a mortal being with a thin gloss of very bad tinsel." Karr assured Jackson that he had begun dating other women.[28]

Jackson also introduced Karr to his future employer, Drew Pearson, for whom the old radical served as a tipster. Visiting the famous columnist in 1942 to give him a story, he took Karr along. Pearson invited Karr to provide information and Karr began feeding him items. Karr's relationship with Gardner Jackson lasted only a few more years. Jackson didn't like the fact that Karr was friends with Jackson's ex-friend Lee Pressman, a Communist who remained loyal to John Lewis, though Karr claimed he was only friends with Pressman because he was an especially good source for anecdotal and "background" material. Karr later slimed Jackson as a drunkard and loudmouth, and retailed gossip that Jackson had been accused of showing lewd pictures to children. Karr's friendship with Jackson broke in 1946.[29]

Karr moved to Washington, D.C., permanently in January 1941 for Transradio. Just before he left New York, an FBI agent phoned. Someone had told the Bureau that he might have information of interest and that he had been bragging about cooperating with the FBI. Getting ready to move, Karr agreed to meet once he had settled in the capital. He later claimed that he met with FBI Special Agent George Dorsey three or four times in Washington to pass along tips and information, and that Dorsey had also given him information he had used for his employer's "Confidentially Yours" feature. FBI files tell a different story. Karr did meet with someone at the FBI late in February, but the agent thought he "had no information of value to the FBI and was seeking more to receive information than to impart the same." The agent warned that any future contacts with Karr should be "handled in a cautious and discreet manner inasmuch as it is believed that Karr is the type who would not hesitate to 'double-cross' anyone."[30]

In Washington, Karr knew no one except those he had met on the Norris-LaGuardia Committee. He quickly remedied that situation and soon had a wide circle of friends and acquaintances. His major task for Transradio was to cover the Office of Production Management and the War and Navy Departments as both a reporter and a rewrite man. One of the stories he followed was the mysterious death of KGB defector Walter Krivitsky in a Washington hotel room in February 1941. He also did some writing for "Confidentially Yours," a Transradio program appearing daily on the Mutual Network, retailing gossip and inside stories. In September he enrolled for classes at George Washington University, but the hyperactive Karr had no taste for the contemplative world of books and study, lasted less than one semester, and received no credit. On weekends he often took the train to New York to see Madeline Baratz.

Following Pearl Harbor and American entry into World War II, another contact from his days investigating Nazis soon offered Karr a chance to join the government. Alan Cranston, a future United States senator from California, had worked as a foreign correspondent in the late 1930s. Angered by an abridged English-language version of Hitler's

Mein Kampf that omitted a number of anti-Semitic passages in what he saw as an effort to sanitize the Nazi movement, Cranston published a complete edition with the aid of a New York newsman named Amster Spiro, and it sold half a million copies. They were quickly sued for violating copyright and forced to cease publishing. In the course of discussions with Spiro about starting a new paper, Cranston met Karr and was impressed by him.[31]

Early in 1942 Archibald MacLeish, newly appointed head of the Office of Facts and Figures, later transformed into the Office of War Information, hired Cranston to head the Foreign Language Division and he, in turn, asked Karr to join him as a senior liaison officer, "servicing the foreign language press," at a salary of $4,600 a year, a steep upgrade from the $60 a week he was making at Transradio. Cranston later explained the purpose of his unit as developing "the understanding of these people who depended upon foreign languages of their responsibilities in the American war effort, in understanding why we were fighting and we sought to cement down or nail down their loyalty to this country." Critics charged that it promoted censorship or had as its "real purpose...to instigate and sponsor loyalty to Russia."[32]

David Karr's application for employment explained his background as a reporter investigating subversive propaganda, boasted of his contacts and expertise, and included David Niles and Herbert Moore, publisher of Transradio, among his references. It also brazenly lied about his qualifications, noting that he spoke and read Spanish and French and could also speak German. In fact, as he later sheepishly admitted to the Dies Committee, he neither spoke nor read any foreign languages. No one bothered to verify his language expertise because Karr began work for the federal government on February 3, 1942. Ten days later, the FBI received a normal administrative request for a security check, since he would have access to confidential material.[33]

At the same time as it began to check on Karr, the Bureau received an anonymous letter from "A Loyal Citizen" upset by his appointment. Claiming to have "known him for some time," the writer thought he was and might still be a Communist, who had contributed to the *Daily Worker* and spoken before Communist groups. "Having spoken with him recently," he went on, "I know that his viewpoint is unchanged, and his sympathies are definitely communistic." The FBI's investigation, however, turned up little concrete evidence besides his writing for the Communist press. Two people at Transradio agreed that as a young man Karr "had many foolish ideas but was now a hundred percent." One insisted that his collaboration with Communists and fascists was part of his job and that his real ideology was "to get money and progress." Several people praised his character and "Americanism." The FBI examined his articles for radical periodicals but concluded that he was "a moral young man of good appearance and personality whose character and reputation are not criticized. Also that his loyalty and patriotism are unquestioned."[34]

Still, the report of Karr's ties to Communism triggered some unease in the Office for Emergency Management, under whose authority the Office of Facts and Figures resided. It decided to interview Karr to get his side of the story; because of the press of business, which had him travel-ing almost immediately after his employment, Karr's sworn testimony was not taken until July 14. His description of his relationship with the *Daily Worker* differed significantly from the version he later told the Dies Committee in 1943 or proffered to the Passport Division of the State Department in the 1950s. At this time Karr noted that during his work with Wakefield, he had collaborated with John Spivak, a well-known writer on fascist groups, who had published several exposés of figures such as Father Coughlin and William Pelley. Despite his public deni-als, Spivak was a covert member of the Communist Party, did security investigations for its underground apparatus, and had extensive ties with Soviet intelligence for much of the 1930s and 1940s. His specialty was passing along information to discredit and disrupt the activities of Trotskyists and native American fascists. Karr admitted to working with him and Wakefield on at least a dozen stories.[35]

In his testimony, Karr made no mention of being summoned by V. J. Jerome to Party headquarters. He said Sam Don and Howard Boldt, two other Party members, objected to his presence at the *Daily Worker*, saying they felt he could not be trusted since he was not a Party mem-ber. He did not mention that Wakefield advised him not to join the CPUSA; rather, Wakefield "was interested in helping me to become a newspaper man and perhaps, for all I know, a Communist." Karr said that Don's hunch that he, Karr, could not be trusted was true; he knew Karr "had turned over a number of tips given me by Wakefield over to the

Federal Bureau of Investigation" from his work on the *Daily Worker*. Karr claimed that he continued to provide the FBI with information when he joined the American Council Against Nazi Propaganda, and that, in Washington, he had helped the FBI investigate the American Youth Congress, a Communist Party front group. He had obtained credentials for an AYC convention that he turned over, and given the FBI photos of attendees, indeed, had been an undercover op for the FBI, bravely infiltrating the Communist movement the better to expose it! All with his employer, Transradio's full consent. Karr emphatically denied any Communist sympathies. He had written critical reports about the CPUSA before the Nazi-Soviet Pact, he said, and was "as vigorously opposed to Communism as I am to Nazism." He said he had dropped his membership in the Newspaper Guild when he realized it was dominated by Communists and rejoined it after the Communists were forced out. As soon as he learned that *Equality* was not a religious magazine, he "had dropped it." For the moment his brazen lies about his past ties to Communism went unnoticed.[36]

Karr hit the ground running in his new job. Within two weeks of starting work, he was on the road, reporting from the Midwest that few people had any clear idea of how serious the war situation was, of the grave sacrifices that would be required, or of how seditious the activities of appeasers and pro-Nazis, who could be found everywhere, were. He faulted government propaganda and condemned the *Chicago Tribune* and other newspapers that were "following the straight Berlin line."[37]

On trips to Illinois and Michigan, Karr worked to set up an organization called "Americans All," designed to celebrate the ethnic diversity of America and their unity in the face of war. Convinced it was a good idea, he feared it might work against the New Deal, or be ineffective. Karr helped it to sponsor a large rally in Detroit, arranged speakers, and got newsreel coverage, explaining to Cranston that the chorus of more than twelve hundred people from twenty different national choirs "warmed the cockles of the hearts" of attendees and pitched expanding the program to other cities with the involvement of the Office of Facts and Figures. Karr drove himself and others hard; in April he was briefly hospitalized. His first efficiency rating signed by Cranston gave him an almost perfect score of 2 on a scale running from 1 to 9, with no weak categories.[38]

His coworkers admired Karr's buoyancy and inventiveness. Cranston recalled that Karr would take an idea and run with it. Lee Falk, whom Cranston had brought in to run the OFF Radio Foreign Language Division, called him "inventive" and "brilliant," with a quick mind. One of his ideas was sparked by the Nazi destruction of the Czechoslovak town of Lidice on June 10, 1942. Two weeks earlier, Czech partisans had blown up the automobile carrying Reinhard Heydrich, Nazi overseer of Bohemia and Moravia and one of the most powerful and brutal men in Nazi Germany. Heydrich died of his wounds on June 4 and Adolf Hitler ordered horrific reprisals. Lidice was chosen as the site for a demonstration of Nazi brutality. An Einsatzgruppen unit massacred some two hundred men from the village. Nearly the same number of women were transported to Ravensbruck concentration camp where most died; several pregnant women were first aborted. Seven village children were randomly selected to be Aryanized and another eighty were gassed at Chelmno, bringing the death toll to 340. Lidice itself was burned and then bulldozed, including the town cemetery. The Germans filmed the destruction and boasted about it publicly.

Karr came up with the idea of renaming a town in Illinois for Lidice. He flew to Chicago, consulted with Mayor Kelly, and telegrammed Cranston on June 16 that the *Chicago Sun* had agreed to sponsor the memorial. A committee of 150 prominent individuals from numerous ethnic groups did fundraising. A newspaper article reported that on July 13, 35,000 people turned out for a ceremony in a little town near Joliet called Stern Park at which Wendell Willkie spoke. Contrary to reports that the official name was changed to Lidice, it appears that only a neighborhood was so named and a memorial erected.[39]

Lee Falk was Karr's closest friend in the OFF office. He, too, was controversial and talented. Also recruited by Alan Cranston, whom he had met in Europe before WWII, Falk was placed in charge of the radio division. Born Leon Gross in St. Louis in 1911, while still a student at the University of Illinois, he had developed the idea for a comic strip named *Mandrake the Magician*. He sold it to King Features Syndicate and it debuted in 1934, beginning a decades-long run. A few years later he created another iconic character, The Phantom, a masked adventurer who predated Superman and Batman. He also did radio shows and, less successfully, wrote plays.

For several months after starting his job, Karr lived with Falk, who recalled that Karr regarded him as a more sophisticated older brother. Falk credited himself with teaching the innocent and naïve Karr how to dress and dine with style. Falk served as best man when Karr married Madeline Baratz on September 5, 1942 and later claimed that he had to tutor his virginal friend who had approached his wedding night with trepidation. Their friendship did not, however, survive the war. Falk enlisted in the Army as a private in 1944 and the Signal Corps shifted him all around the country, declining to send him overseas. Drew Pearson mentioned this in one of his broadcasts, and Falk blamed Karr for making him look bad. Their break lasted several years.[40]

The Office of Facts and Figures became part of the Office of War Information, headed by Elmer Davis, in July, and Karr became Assistant Chief of the Foreign Language Division. His job inevitably pulled him into controversies over Communism. The OWI had to navigate some treacherous disputes among the ethnic groups whose publications it monitored and tried to manipulate in order to build support for the American war effort.

During the 1920s and the first half of the 1930s the CPUSA had been an organization of mostly foreign-born Americans. In ethnic communities ranging from the Finns and Bulgarians to the Italians, Greeks, and Slavs, communities of Communist loyalists had their own newspapers, fraternal organizations, and self-help groups. Internal conflicts between conservative and religious immigrants and Communist enclaves were endemic. These different groups not only fought bitterly over domestic issues, they supported different political parties and resistance groups in their European homelands.

During the war, the OWI tried to arbitrate disputes within ethnic communities that were sharply divided over what support the United States should give to different partisan groups fighting the Nazis, and the postwar shapes of their homelands. Conservatives and some liberals complained that the OWI pressured them into alliances with Communists. Non-Communists complained that the OWI linked them to fascists if they objected to cooperation with Communists. Karr got involved with the American Slav Congress, a coalition of Croats, Serbs, Poles, Bulgarians, Slovaks, and others dominated by the Communist Party. There he worked closely with Leo Krzycki, vice president of the

Amalgamated Clothing Workers Union, and a close Party ally, organizing a large demonstration in Chicago. The OWI barraged the Polish-language media with Soviet propaganda that the Nazis had committed the Katyn Massacre of thousands of Polish officers, which was in fact carried out by the Soviet Union. In the interests of war unity, the OWI sought to discourage the press from blaming the Soviets. This enraged Polish Catholics and Polish organizations who knew the truth and who were determined to prevent a postwar Communist takeover of Poland.

Testifying before a Senate Committee in 1949, Paul Nadanyi, editor of *Amerikai Magyarsag*, recounted his battles with Communists in the Hungarian-American community during the war. He complained that Cranston and Karr came to his office "and practically held a club over my head to tone down all differences with the Communists. My publisher and myself resented his attitude and told him so." Jewish socialists enraged at the murder by the Soviet Union of Bundist leaders Viktor Alter and Henryk Ehrlich, on false charges of being Nazi spies, likewise bristled at the OWI's efforts to avoid criticizing America's ally.[41]

None of these contretemps, however, caused David Karr to become a public figure. His first taste of fame came in January 1943, less than a year after he had begun working for the OWI. Karr learned that attacking politicians invites payback. Congressman Martin Dies of Texas, whom Karr had savagely accused of consorting with fascists in print in 1940, turned his gaze on Karr for consorting with Communists.

Dies had chaired the House Special Committee on Un-American Activities since its creation in 1938. Ironically, the impetus for the committee was supplied by Congressman Samuel Dickstein of New York, a liberal who was actually on the NKVD's payroll as an informant under the code name "Crook." In return for supplying Soviet intelligence with information, Dickstein was receiving a regular stipend. Anxious for information about White Russian and Trotskyist activities in the United States and expecting that as the sponsor of the resolution creating the committee, Dickstein would become its chairman and be able to direct its investigations along paths he preferred, the Soviets had supported his initiative. Instead, Dies got the nod. While Dies did investigate Nazi and fascist activities, the bulk of his attention was directed at Communists; he also provided a platform for a number of witnesses who tried to link the New Deal with the CPUSA. Dickstein, meanwhile, with less access to information desired by the KGB, and increasingly expensive, was dropped from its payroll.[42]

After the outbreak of the war, the Dies Committee continued its investigations of Communists and fascists, but by the middle of 1940 largely abandoned public hearings. Nevertheless, in mid-1941 Congress included an appropriation for the Committee to provide the FBI with a list of suspected subversives employed by the government. By August, Dies was publicly denouncing individual bureaucrats. In October, he sent the attorney general a list of more than 1,100 individuals with questionable ties, and soon after singled out Gardner Jackson for his long list of Communist associations. While Pearl Harbor inspired Dies to launch broadsides on Axis subversives, he returned to the Communist danger at the end of March 1942 with an attack on several employees of the Board of Economic Warfare for their Communist affiliations (although he singled out one, Maurice Parmalee, for a book he had written on *Nudism in Modern Life*). Insisting that he would continue to expose individuals with Communist records in government, on January 2, 1943 Dies released a report that drew criticism from several liberal Democrats in the House, who objected to his procedures and complained that the charges of Communism were thinly supported.[43]

Dies prepared to defend himself on the House floor. In late January Dies' aide, Robert Stripling, came across an old book review in the *Daily Worker* written by a David Karr. Stripling telephoned Karr at the OWI and asked if he was the same person; Karr acknowledged he was. Knowing that he was now in Dies' gunsight spurred Karr to action. The next day, Drew Pearson's legman, Tom McNamara, visited Stripling and accused him of going after "little Davey Karr" because he had once criticized Dies. The following day Karr telephoned three times, told Stripling he wanted to explain his behavior to Dies, and insisted he had been an FBI informant, saying that Lou Nichols in Hoover's office at the FBI could confirm his claim. Nichols was out of the office but wrote a memo saying that Karr had "furnished information" a few times but "never at any time" been asked for specific information, and "by no stretch of the imagination could Karr be classified as an informant." Rabbi Paul Richman, head of the Washington, D.C., office of the Anti-Defamation League, had introduced Karr to Nichols. Nichols said he had talked to Karr only because he was a roommate of Gardner Jackson and employed by Transradio, whose owner, Dixon Stewart, had been helpful to the Bureau. Nichols told Stripling that "anything we wanted to do was quite all right with them." Stripling accordingly told Dies that Karr had never been an FBI informant.[44]

Karr apparently had second thoughts about his claims, because just a few days later he called Nichols protesting that while he wasn't too worried about Dies, he was concerned that he might have made a mistake in claiming to be an FBI informant. Nichols told Karr that he'd told Stripling he wasn't. It was a matter of how the Bureau classified "informants." Karr was just a guy who occasionally voluntarily provided information. There were numerous references to Karr in FBI files, but he was not working "under the direction of the Bureau securing and furnishing information." In fact, Nichols always had the feeling that Karr was trying to get information from him. While he was willing to tell anyone who asked that Karr had furnished background information, J. Edgar Hoover was adamant that "Karr was not a 'confidential informant' of the FBI and that is that." Other FBI files indicated that Karr had periodically given Bureau field agents information about fascist organizations but also "information dealing primarily with Communists." Nichols noted that none of his information "was of great importance."[45]

Dies spoke on the House floor on February 1 to denounce thirty-eight government employees for their Communist connections. After a while, he got around to David Karr, former staffer on the *Daily Worker*, of whom he observed that "there is not the slightest doubt that all members of the *Daily Worker* staff were required to be members of the Communist Party." He also noted his writings and work for other Communist-front groups. Dies concluded by demanding that Congress withhold appropriation for the salaries of all the officials he had named. Within days, the House of Representatives had voted to block the salary of William Pickens. To everyone's embarrassment, Pickens turned out to be African-American, opening the door to charges of racial discrimination; the House responded by voting on February 9 to create a special subcommittee of the Appropriations Committee, named after its chair, John Kerr (D-NC), to investigate Dies' charges. Among the appointees were future United States Senators Albert Gore, Sr. and Clinton Anderson.[46]

As the Kerr Committee began its investigation, Karr once again contacted Lou Nichols on February 19. Sure that he would be called to testify, Karr wanted to know what he should say. While Nichols told him to tell the truth, he added that, "of course, he should not say that he was an informant." He agreed that Karr had occasionally furnished the Bureau with information and listened as Karr insisted the Civil Service Commission (CSC) had cleared him and that Dies' statement was "a deliberate lie."[47]

Attorney General Francis Biddle asked the FBI to investigate all those named by Dies, and on March 2, Hoover, not realizing that Karr now lived in Washington, directed the New York Field Office to undertake a probe "to determine whether he might be engaged in activities inimical to the best interests of the Federal Government." The Kerr Committee, in turn, requested that it be furnished with the investigative reports in the case.[48]

As the FBI was investigating, Karr testified before an executive session of the Dies Committee on April 6, where J. B. Matthews, once the most prolific joiner of Communist fronts in America, but now a fierce anti-Communist, questioned him. Karr went over his employment history, vigorously denying that he had been a Communist or a staff member of the *Daily Worker*. His affiliations all stemmed from his stalwart anti-fascism. Likewise, he hadn't realized that some of the magazines in which he had published were Communist-controlled. In addition, he denied ever serving as publicity director of the American League for Peace and Democracy; he insisted that the Reverend Thomas Harris, its head, had appointed him without his knowledge, and he had declined to serve. Karr also vehemently objected to any implication that he was a Communist because he had associated with Communists. He complained that the "entire tenor and the effect of the statement…does impugn my patriotism and Americanism." When Karr conceded that most of Dies' facts were correct, Joe Starnes of Alabama asked if he had not done precisely the same thing in his articles by linking Dies with Fritz Kuhn and other Nazis; Karr sheepishly agreed that he had. When first questioned about his relationship with the FBI, Karr said he had made his earliest reports to the FBI while writing for the *Daily Worker*, implying that he had informed on Communists. While reticent about exactly what he had told the Bureau, he claimed that his goal had been "to expose both Nazi activities and the workings of some of the Communist people in New York." But, when pressed by Congressman

Starnes he went further: "I have helped them develop a number of cases...I don't know how much of that material the F.B.I. would be willing to make accessible to the committee, but I am sure that you will be satisfied in that connection if you inquire. I have checked with Mr. Hoover's executive assistants, and they said that Mr. Hoover would be glad to substantiate that information for you."[49]

If Karr had wanted to irritate J. Edgar Hoover, he could not have picked a better way to do so. Nor did he stop trumpeting his ties to the FBI. In late April, Nichols got a call from Frank Waldrop, a reporter from the *Chicago Times-Herald*, who said that Karr had boasted to him about all the assistance he had given to the FBI and that if his case was taken up by the Kerr Committee, Hoover himself would testify on his behalf. Nichols responded that he would be surprised to see that happen. At the bottom of the memo, Hoover wrote, "I don't like his loquacity."[50]

The FBI's new examination of Karr did not turn up anything significant; he was interviewed under oath on April 21 and acknowledged that the FBI "never paid a single penny in any way, manner, shape or form...My cooperation was voluntary." Two days later he again called Nichols to tell him he had contacted the Attorney General's Office and asked that his Kerr Committee hearing be expedited, since he was about to be inducted into the Army and wanted everything cleared up to facilitate his admission to Officer Candidate School. The Bureau sent its reports to military intelligence. Karr was rejected from the Army, but the FBI reports probably had less to do with it than his classification of 4-F, on May 12, due to deafness in his right ear, a consequence of his childhood ailments.[51]

Having failed to get into the Army (although he probably knew his ear ailment would disqualify him), Karr tried to get a job as a military correspondent. He stopped by FBI headquarters on May 10 and told Nichols that he had received an offer from Generoso Pope, a New York publisher, to go to North Africa. If he could interest Transradio, his old employer, to hire him also, he might go. Karr asked if he should take the job and if he'd be able to get an exit visa. Nichols replied that he was in no position to answer either question.[52]

Amid this personal turmoil, Karr still had his official duties to perform. The publicity about him couldn't have come at a worse time for the OWI, whose seeming infiltration by Communists suddenly, in early

1943, had become front-page news, with no assistance from David Karr. The trouble originated from the shocking murder of one of the most famous radicals in the United States and the efforts of Lee Falk and Alan Cranston to use it to the OWI's advantage.

The politics of the Italian-American community were fraught with peril for building wartime unity. The most widely circulated Italian-language newspaper in America was *Il Progresso Italo-Americano*, published in New York and edited by Generoso Pope. Pope had been an ardent supporter of Mussolini and fascism until 1941; he also had close ties to such Mafia figures as Frank Costello. He was anathema not only to Communists, but also to scores of other left-wing organizations among the large Italian population of New York. There was a small but active Italian-American Communist group, but a larger number of anarchists, syndicalists, and socialists who were admirers of Carlo Tresca, a fiery speaker and writer who had waged numerous battles, both verbal and physical, with fascists, Communists, and gangsters over the prior decades.

Karr had already gotten into disputes with some Italian-Americans. Luigi Criscuolo, editor of a weekly newsletter, *The Rubicon*, objected to a Cranston speech warning foreign-language publishers of the dangers of echoing Nazi propaganda. He wrote Cranston saying that "he was spreading unnecessary hysteria." This prompted a telephone call from David Karr demanding that he present himself in Washington forthwith. Criscuolo was unimpressed and "told this young man that we had been a citizen since before he was born, and we knew our way around." Karr refused to placate Criscuolo or assuage his concerns. In fact, the editor muttered that Karr was impertinent, "some people would say 'snotty.'" Criscuolo complained about Karr to Elmer Davis, now heading the OWI; Cranston explained to his boss that Criscuolo was "a very noisy Italian in New York City who for a long time has made Fascist propaganda."[53]

Criscuolo's irritation, whether based on fascist sympathies or outrage at government interference with the press, highlighted the OWI's dilemma. Its mission of encouraging the foreign language press to support the war effort easily shaded over into efforts to pressure ethnic Americans into accepting or endorsing certain government policies. And, since no organization was beating a louder drum for wartime unity than the CPUSA, the OWI often sided with Communists against those who mistrusted them and wanted nothing to do with them.

In late 1942, the OWI was drawn into a conflict with Tresca that showed the pitfalls of working with ethnic groups harboring totalitarians of both the right and left. A group called Victory Conference of the Foreign Language Press planned to convene in New York in January 1943. Chaired by Louis Bromfield, a Pulitzer Prize–winning novelist, its letterhead included several Communist fellow travelers. Its chief organizer was Abner Green, head of the Communist-dominated American Committee for the Protection of the Foreign Born. Among the stated goals of the conference were "to coordinate more effectively the contribution" the groups could make to the war and take steps "to guard against the publication of any fifth column propaganda." Ten foreign-language papers objected—particularly to Green, and accused the conveners of having "an ulterior objective." Their alternative conference, labeled the "Common Council for American Unity," also took place in January 1943 and attracted opponents of the U.S.S.R., of the Roosevelt Administration, and a number of anti-Semites. While not endorsing such sentiments, the Common Council said they would not work with either Cranston or Karr.[54]

Cranston and Falk met in early January 1943 with Carlo Tresca to press him to agree to include an Italian Communist group in a proposed Italian-American Victory Council as well as former fascist sympathizers like Pope. Tresca was adamantly opposed to cooperating with either the Communists or Pope, and he implied to a friend that he knew Falk had been in the CPUSA under another name. In fact, there is no evidence for that claim. On January 11, Tresca was gunned down on a New York Street in a murder that has never been officially solved. Both Cranston and Falk suggested in interviews soon afterward that he had been prepared to accept Communist participation. This was a clear misrepresentation of Tresca's views—one friend indignantly reported that he was "not 100% against admission of Communists, he was 1,000% against it"—and it ignited a firestorm of criticism from socialists such as Norman Thomas and labor leader Luigi Antonini, who insisted that the OWI bureaucrats were lying, and that the Communists had killed Tresca. Falk insisted that the press had misquoted him saying the very opposite of what he had said. According to Elmer Davis in a letter to Norman

Thomas, Falk had said Tresca had *not* agreed to Communist participation. The messy argument was swept under the rug by early February, but a New York branch of the Italian-American Victory Council was never formed due to the anger over Tresca's killing.[55]

As Martin Dies launched his attack on David Karr, Elmer Davis was increasingly engaged in damage control—assuring newspapers and Congress that his organization wasn't honeycombed with Communists or forcing anyone to cooperate with them. But in fact, the OWI's foreign-language divisions employed a number of Communists. A few emigrated, or returned, to Eastern Europe after the war to take positions in the new Soviet governments. One, Giuseppe (Joseph) Facci, worked in the Italian section. Several others have since been identified as Soviet spies. Yet in a 1945 report to the president about the OWI's work during the war, Davis complained that many of the charges "originated with bush-league Fascists just beyond the range of indictment, or with the copperhead press; but they came also from sources ostensibly more respectful, though equally gifted in invention; and in some degree no doubt from honest men who considered anybody to the left of their own position as Communists." He admitted that the OWI should not employ Communists whose loyalty was "dependent on the vicissitudes of Russian foreign policy," but wanted to make exceptions for people who had repented of their previous alliances. The difficulties in drawing those distinctions or enforcing them, he admitted, arose from the large number of investigations that were required, the length of time they took to complete, and the often conflicting or equivocal nature of the evidence. It was as if he were describing David Karr.[56]

Cranston also wrote a memo to Davis explaining the OWI's thinking about the Italian-American Victory Council. He said the OWI had not been able to ignore pro-fascists like Pope, because other federal agencies had cooperated with them, and because the anti-fascists were so splintered. So the OWI had agreed to include them but had tried to limit their influence. He denied ever pressuring anyone to include Communists and said he had been misquoted in the newspapers about Tresca. All the OWI wanted was unity in the support of the war "on an American basis." The two organizations he cited as embodying this vision were "Americans All," in Detroit and the Communist-dominated American Slav Congress.[57]

Even if Davis and Cranston believed Karr's explanations about working with Communists, Karr was still obviously becoming a liability. They probably encouraged him either to get a clean bill of health from Congress or leave the agency. His efficiency rating at the end of March 1943 was significantly lower than the previous year; Karr was now ranked "good" as opposed to "very good," and judged "weak" in promoting high working morale.[58]

Karr kept trying to clear his name. In May he submitted an affidavit from Dixon Stewart, the general news manager at Transradio, insisting that he had written critical stories about American Communism even before the Nazi-Soviet Pact. Since the material was used in radio scripts, it was not easily recoverable, but Stewart was willing to let FBI agents dig through the company's files to obtain them. According to one FBI report, none of the stories aired in 1939 was anti-Communist. One correspondence file indicated that some listeners had objected that the broadcasts Karr wrote for were in fact pro-Communist.[59]

Yet another government report on Karr was produced for a Select Committee to Investigate the Federal Communications Commission. Transmitted to the Committee's chair, Ed Cox, on July 10, 1943, it incorporated large portions of an FBI report, including material blacked out when Karr's file was released under the Freedom of Information Act in the 1980s. It included more unverified claims about Karr's affinity for Communism. One confidential informant said that Karr had told him in January 1941 that he had joined the CPUSA but had dropped out after the Hitler-Stalin Pact. Another confidential informer reported meeting Karr while he worked for the OWI and was working on forming Victory Councils in New York. As they argued over whether Communists should be included, Karr favored adding Communist branches of the International Workers Order and "in his language and speech used typical Communist Party expressions." Still another informant had never met Karr but, in asking why German Communist groups were overrepresented in the German-American Victory Council, was told it was Karr's doing.[60]

While Karr continued to press the FBI, he now hoped the Kerr Committee would clear him. Clinton Anderson, a Kerr Committee member, drafted a memo to his colleagues in June 1943 with suggestions about "a way to work ourselves out of a job." The Committee had gone through all of the investigative files and held hearings on some individuals. Anderson recommended that most of the forty-four people reviewed be cleared, though three men, William Dodd, Jr., Robert Morss Lovett, and Goodwin Watson, were found unfit for government service. (Dodd was, in fact, a Soviet agent.) Several others had already resigned, including Gardner Jackson, making their cases moot. Anderson's judgments were breezy and, in retrospect, wildly off the mark. Five of those investigated and cleared were more than Communist Party members; they were active Soviet agents, including Jack Fahy in the Interior Department, Alice Barrows in the Office of Education, Leonard Mins in OSS, and David Wahl and T. A. Bisson in the Board of Economic Warfare. But Anderson was not terribly impressed by most of the evidence of pro-Soviet ties. Of Bisson, Anderson wrote that "he was unusually well qualified for the work he is doing," a sentiment with which his Soviet military intelligence employers would doubtless have agreed.[61]

Karr was one of five employees from the OWI who were looked at by the committee. Only Joseph Facci was investigated in more than a cursory fashion. It only required a half-hour hearing to review the minimal evidence against the others. Karr was given "a streamlined consideration." On Anderson's initiative, Karr skated by without triggering a closer look, and Kerr concurred. The next week, the Committee informally cleared David Karr.[62]

Karr may have known Anderson. In May 1942, Karr had asked Gardner Jackson whom to lobby on a medical student matter and he had suggested "Congressman Anderson of New Mexico, who is a very intelligent and competent person." There is no evidence of any actual prior contacts, but after Anderson's airy dismissal of Dies' charges without a hearing, Karr wrote Anderson a brief thank-you note on July 1. Karr later said he thought his testimony and Dixon's affidavit had persuaded Anderson; he also denied harboring hard feelings for Dies, since it led to his "official encounter with Congressman Anderson," resulting in "a warm friendship." At the end of July, Karr resigned from the OWI and claimed to be working as a Washington representative at the American Jewish Committee (AJC). At that time Anderson wrote the AJC that there was nothing in the material he had examined "which would handicap him in the slightest of being employed by the Government... There is no evidence of subversive activities that I was able to find." Years later Karr boasted of his close ties to Anderson in his affidavit to obtain a passport. A private investigative report in the archives of the ADL, however, held a more jaundiced view of the Karr-Anderson relationship. It claimed that at the 1948 Democratic Convention, Karr and Anderson "had a big time—having several parties, involving ladies of the evening and that Karr had paid all the bills." Allegedly Anderson was "known as a 'ladies' man' and as a Don Juan and that Karr has enough information on him to control him."[63]

Like so much in his life, the circumstances of Karr's resignation from the OWI and later employment were murkier than he pretended. Karr did send a letter of resignation to Elmer Davis on July 29, 1943, effective that day, claiming to be leaving "in order to undertake work which I feel will be of an even greater value in the effective persecution [sic] of the war," and thanking the OWI director "from the bottom of my heart" for defending him from the false charges made by Dies. Davis did not respond for nearly a month and when he did, he praised Karr's work and denounced the "obvious absurdity" of the charges. Yet in his passport affidavit years later, Karr said he resigned because he felt his "usefulness to OWI was seriously impaired by reason of the publicity" he had received.[64]

The Civil Service Commission did not think the charges were so absurd. Its June 25, 1943 report recommended that Karr be fired because he had "formed a close association with the Communist Party, joining it before he was hired" by the *Daily Worker*. Senator Joseph McCarthy read the Commission's report into the *Congressional Record* in December 1950. Because Karr had "admitted to several FBI agents and informants" that he had done "rewrite work for the *Party Organizer*," an internal CPUSA publication, this was evidence that he was "of necessity a trusted and powerful member of the Communist Party." The CSC's conclusions were based on its witnesses and FBI files, and on its finding that Karr's ambiguity appeared only to echo Communist policy. It found "the activities, affiliations and associations of David Karr" were "communistic, and a finding of ineligible is considered necessary in this case," recommending that "he be barred" from performing any duties and "that his immediate removal from the service be requested."[65]

It is not clear if either Karr or the OWI knew of the CSC findings or even if the Commission took a final vote—the document was labeled

"Status of Karr Case." A CSC investigator asked the OWI for further information about Karr on July 31 and was told he had resigned. Given the congressional interest, Karr's superiors knew weeks before his "resignation" that he had to go. When Karr applied for reinstatement, the CSC resumed its probe in November. It asked the FBI about Karr. In a formal response in February 1944, Hoover repeated that although Karr had given some information to the FBI, none of it had been of much value and he declined to comment on Karr's "truth and veracity," except to note that "he has been prone to exaggerate his cooperation with the Federal Bureau of Investigation, and he does this in a very subtle manner which might lead a person to believe he had furnished far more information to the FBI than he actually has." By this time Karr had abandoned his effort to get back his old job; the Commission's response was to flag Karr's file so that if he tried to reenter the federal government, he would undergo further scrutiny.[66]

For the rest of his life Karr insisted that Congress had cleared him of all charges. In the early 1950s he used Congressman Anderson's November 5th letter to obtain a passport, claiming to the State Department that he was eligible for rehiring by the government (when in fact he was not). That was not the only fib he told. His federal personnel file contains a letter from the American Jewish Committee dated March 24, 1944 that details how in applying for a job in its public relations department, Karr told them that he had served as Chief of the Foreign Language Press at a salary ranging from $6,000 to $7,500. The AJC asked for verification and was duly informed that he had been a Senior Liaison Officer making $4,600 a year. Karr later complained that the AJC suddenly dropped him from a job in 1944 without explanation; it may have been related to the false information he had submitted. Even more curious, Karr applied for reinstatement to the OWI before the end of 1943, suggesting that he had difficulty in landing a job after leaving the OWI (although there is some indication he might have briefly worked for the Overseas Press Bureau).[67]

Although he never referred to it in any testimony or signed statements, Karr worked at least several months in late 1943 and early 1944 for Vice President Henry Wallace but was not paid with government funds. Karr had first met Wallace during the 1940 presidential campaign and was friends with his chief assistant Harold Young. While working at the OWI, he had drafted letters of greeting for Wallace to various ethnic rallies and advised Young in memos on the internal politics of ethnic American groups, and on what factions the administration should support.[68]

In August and September 1943, Karr traveled to the Midwest on Vice President Wallace's behalf to meet local politicians and orchestrate favorable publicity—including arranging for him to throw out the first ball at a World Series game. Young also used Karr to investigate critics and supporters of Wallace. He asked him to check the bona fides of Helen Alfred, a New York editor of a small magazine called *Peace News*, who was irate about FDR's decision to shift control over several wartime economic agencies from Wallace to Commerce Secretary Jesse Jones and urged the vice president to head a new American People's Party.[69]

Karr negotiated Wallace's speaking schedule with local politicians. In October 1943, Quentin Burdick, a lawyer in Fargo, North Dakota, and future United States senator, wrote Karr about a planned rally in Bismarck the next month at which Karr had promised to produce Wallace. Harold Young was forced to write Burdick back that Karr, a "young man who admires Mr. Wallace greatly, has been telling you and other people" that Wallace was coming for a rally, but in fact there were no such plans. In February 1944 in Minneapolis on a cross-country tour, Wallace finally caught up with Burdick who later thanked Young for the connection and asked him to convey his greetings to "that effervescent Mr. Carr [*sic*]."[70]

Karr accompanied Wallace on that tour in which Burdick finally met the vice president. Congressman Fred Busbey of Illinois was not pleased with the tour. He denounced Wallace as the "Grand Exalted Smearer of all Loyal Americans who disagree with his pet theories," noting Karr's presence in his "entourage," and placed lengthy excerpts from Karr's Dies Committee testimony into the *Congressional Record*.[71]

Wallace had to fight for his political life that spring and summer. Franklin Roosevelt was in increasingly frail health and many of the power brokers in the Democratic Party desperately wanted to replace Wallace on the presidential ticket, regarding him as too eccentric and left-wing to inherit the presidency if FDR died in office. In early July Roosevelt formally announced that he would not insist that Wallace be on his ticket but would let the delegates to the Democratic National

Convention decide his running mate. In the interim Wallace had traveled to Russia and China, a disastrous trip during which he visited a
gulag slave labor camp in Siberia and naïvely accepted his hosts' assur-
ances that it was a model rehabilitation center. By that time David
Karr had a job as a reporter with the *Washington Post* but continued to
write speeches for Wallace. He also organized a large demonstration of
support for Wallace at the Democratic Convention that proved futile.
Harry Truman was selected to run for vice president.

2

INVESTIGATIVE
JOURNALIST

David Karr's youthful infatuation with Communism had cost him dearly, bringing him damaging notoriety. Unlike most young Americans who flirted with or even joined the Communist Party in the 1930s, he had been denounced on the floor of the United States Congress, been made the subject of several government investigations, and been scrutinized by the FBI. This record would dog him for the rest of his life.

The next phase of his life began in mid-1944. Barred from a government job, he landed at the *Washington Post* City desk. (Later, he told the State Department that Drew Pearson had offered him a job at $150 a week, but he feared he didn't have the experience, so he started at $75 a week at the *Post* to gain experience—but no one who knew Karr believed this story, or that he would ever be so humble and self-effacing.) At the end of May, assigned to write a story on listening devices, Karr dropped in on Lou Nichols at FBI headquarters. He claimed to know that Hoover had told Drew Pearson off-the-record that the Bureau had a device that could hear conversations nine hundred feet away so that it would be "possible to ride along in a car in front of the White House and monitor a conversation going on inside." Nichols verified that Hoover had never had such a conversation and "told Karr he should tell his City Editor to stop smoking marijuana."[1]

Karr's stint on the City desk was brief. He was fired, but quickly landed on his feet. Drew Pearson hired him as a legman in June 1944. Karr's energy, chutzpah, and doggedness, essential traits for an investigative reporter, were augmented by a cheerful unscrupulousness. Some admired his "pixieish charm," but most who ran up against Dave Karr did not retain fond memories. He never hesitated to exaggerate his connections with the FBI, or to deceive Communists and fascists alike about his loyalties, or to brazenly lie about his qualifications and salary to get jobs. An indefatigable networker, he knew hundreds of people in Washington and wasn't shy about name-dropping, even if the connection was only imagined. These talents perfectly suited Pearson, one of the most famous and influential journalists in America and one of the most controversial.[2]

Son of a Swarthmore College professor, as a fledgling reporter for the *Baltimore Sun*, Pearson was known more for being the son-in-law of Cissy Patterson, a wealthy, eccentric, conservative newspaper magnate, than for his journalistic prowess when veteran reporter and foreign correspondent Robert Allen approached him in 1931 to collaborate on a sensationalistic exposé of the Hoover administration. The resulting book, published anonymously as *Washington Merry-Go-Round*, became a bestseller. After the authors were identified, they were both fired by their respective newspapers. They quickly produced a sequel and, in 1933, started a syndicated column bearing the same name as the book. It flourished, adopting a strongly liberal line and specializing in inside gossip and leaks from administration figures. (Unbeknownst to Pearson, Allen also sold information to the KGB for a few years in the 1930s.)[3]

When World War II started, Allen joined the Marine Corps and Pearson carried on the column by himself. He also had a popular Sunday evening radio show. The pressure of deadlines and the need to produce scoops and inside gossip were ferocious, and Pearson began the practice of hiring legmen to do the work on which his columns were based. Karr covered the White House, Departments of State, Treasury, Justice and Interior, and many of the wartime government agencies. Since scoops were his stock-in-trade, Pearson relied on Karr and his other assistants to turn up juicy tidbits or secrets, which he then published or broadcast without much of an effort at verification. Tipsters could inoculate themselves from bad press, savage their enemies, and promote their agendas by judiciously leaking to Pearson or Karr. Equally loved and hated, Pearson played a key role in Washington political life. His column was a must-read for political insiders and an important venue where politicians settled scores or leaked policy initiatives either to advance or defeat them. Guarantees of anonymity allowed Pearson to make or break reputations. With hundreds of newspapers across the country in his syndicate and a nationwide radio broadcast on Sunday evenings, he had enormous reach and influence.

Neither Pearson nor Karr was particularly scrupulous about how they got their information. Jack Anderson, Karr's successor as Pearson's chief aide, later recalled that Karr was "sort of unethical;" he would often obtain off-the-record information that other reporters had developed and pass it off as his own or buy material from sources. He could stand in front of someone's desk and read letters or documents upside down. Arthur Schlesinger, Jr. recalled Karr regaling a group of friends "with stories of the way he covered the State Department. He used to go to the men's room, sit in a stall and eavesdrop on conversations between State Department officials as they used the facilities and washed their hands."[4]

Almost as soon as he started working for Pearson, Karr delivered a scoop that showed how he would do almost anything for a story, including lying about his bona fides. The fate of Poland was one of the most contentious issues in the American-Soviet relationship in 1944. Most Polish-Americans supported a London-based government-in-exile and bitterly opposed Soviet plans to annex large portions of eastern Poland, which the much smaller pro-Communist forces of the American Slav Congress, chaired by Karr's old friend Leo Krzycki, supported. Two previously obscure Polish-Americans, Father Stanislaw Orlemanski and University of Chicago economics professor Oscar Lange, had thrown their support to the pro-Communist forces and been invited to Moscow by Stalin to discuss the issue in April and May 1944. Lange met with the exiled Polish prime minister in Washington after his return and reported on his meeting to the American government, stressing how reasonable Stalin planned to be. (Lange, in fact, had agreed to work with the KGB in 1943 and been given the cover name "Friend." In 1945, he renounced his American citizenship and became a high-ranking Polish Communist diplomat.)[5]

With speculation rife over what Stalin had told Lange and Orlemanski, Karr called Lange's office in Chicago on June 26 and told Dorothy Sheinfeld, his secretary, that he was from Vice President Wallace's office. Wallace was about to leave for China and Russia, where he was to have a secret meeting with Stalin and he needed to learn what the Soviet leader had told Lange. Karr informed her he would come by that afternoon to examine Lange's report. She was dubious, but Karr reassured her, discussed Wallace's secret travel plans with her, and insisted that it was imperative that the material reach Wallace immediately and that it could not await Lange's return to Chicago. Assuming that it was a matter of some importance, the secretary did not call her boss, but agreed to show the report to him. Karr arrived and made detailed notes, commenting that the report "would create political dynamite" if published. He reiterated that it would be kept confidential. Before leaving, he promised to send Sheinfeld a signed picture of the vice president.[6]

When Lange learned what had happened, he immediately became suspicious. He telephoned Karr and asked if he was acting for Wallace. Karr "refused to answer and became rather arrogant over the telephone." He soon called back and told Lange that "it was customary for him to collect information for the vice president on his own initiative." Lange warned him not to let anyone but Wallace see the material, since it was prepared confidentially for the State Department and President Roosevelt. Karr assured him that his notes were in Wallace's office and Lange could "rest assured about the secrecy of the matter." Karr boasted about his close relationship with Wallace. Still not reassured, Lange wrote to Secretary of State Stettinius and "disclaimed any responsibility" if Karr "should misuse the information obtained by posing as a representative of the Vice President."[7]

Lange's fears were well founded. Just days later, on July 2, the "Washington Merry-Go-Round" had a detailed description of Lange's account of his conversation with Stalin. It included the Soviet dictator's dishonest reassurances that he wanted a strong, independent Poland; that an agreement had been reached on Polish borders at Tehran; that conditions for Poles living in Russia would be improved; and that Polish intelligence sources within Poland were misleading the government-in-exile about its popularity. A second column on the report was promised for the next day. Upset, Lange wired Harold Young warning that responsibility for the security breach lay with "Carr [sic] and [the] Vice President who employs him." Young quickly disclaimed any responsibility, telling Lange that Karr "did not, and never had worked for Mr. Wallace. He had been about on some occasions and was good at carrying suitcases." Young promised to talk to Karr and Pearson. A follow-up telegram reiterated that Karr "had no authority of any kind to use the Vice President's name."[8]

It was too late to stop the second column from appearing. The furious Lange told Young that Karr had caused "great damage to my reputation and, I am afraid, also to the Vice President, in whose company he was seen frequently and by many persons." He was "a public menace" who had violated the law by "impersonification [sic] of a public official" and his "theft of information" had "come close to espionage." Lange contacted the FBI and demanded an investigation, warning Young that Wallace's reputation was at stake. At the time, of course, no one noted the irony of a man, Lange, secretly working on behalf of the Soviet Union berating another man, Karr, secretly working on behalf of a muckraking journalist.[9]

The Justice Department asked the FBI to investigate whether Karr had violated the Federal Impersonation Statute, but wanted Wallace questioned first. The vice president was interviewed on July 28. He told the agent that he had known Karr for about a year and a half through his activities at the OWI and as a Pearson employee, but had never hired him himself. He supposed it was possible that Young had some arrangement to pay Karr for information. (Karr told the FBI that Young had paid his expenses since July 1943.) Karr had traveled with him and had actively supported Wallace's futile bid to remain on the Democratic ticket at the Chicago convention. He admired Karr because of "his whole-hearted espousal of liberalism." He professed absolutely no knowledge of Karr's purloining Lange's report and had never seen it. He had heard about the incident from Harold Young, who had been very upset, but Wallace himself "took a humorous view of the incident, considering it just another way for an aggressive reporter to get news."[10]

Attorney General Biddle decided that prosecution was not warranted—in a letter to J. Edgar Hoover, Lange had expressed relief that Pearson's column had missed some of the more sensitive portions of his report and that the leak had "proved less damaging than I had feared"—but suggested that Karr be interviewed to "make him realize the seriousness of what he is doing and probably slow him down." It would take a lot more than an FBI agent to slow down David Karr, however. When he talked to an agent on August 16, Karr was unapologetic. He explained that on his way to Chicago to cover the Republican Convention, he had asked Harold Young if Wallace would be interested in seeing Lange's report and Young had responded, "You're damn right." He vehemently denied misrepresenting himself as a member of Wallace's staff. He claimed that he had given Young the report on July 27; no one else had received a copy. Pearson had asked him what he had been up to in Chicago and he said he had obtained Lange's report for Wallace. The columnist then supposedly said he had already gotten a copy. The FBI blanked out the names of people whom Karr said also had copies of the report.[11]

Knowing that Pearson would not reveal a source, Karr had no compunctions about lying or contradicting Lange, Lange's secretary, and his assistant, to say nothing of Young. He proudly told the FBI agent that he had pulled a number of "fast ones" in his reportorial career, even quoting another reporter who had credited him with "getting around as quick as an octopus on roller skates," but adamantly denied doing so in this case. He even threatened to sue Lange for libel. Years later, in an affidavit, Karr admitted that he had obtained Lange's documents for the columns.[12]

And that was the end of the incident, which did not seem to hurt Karr's relationship with Young, who continued to send him clippings and ask for favors, although Young seems to have become more discreet around his old friend. As for Wallace, Karr continued his close association with him until well after the Cold War began.

Nothing better symbolizes the FBI's frustration in dealing with Karr than his nifty footwork in obtaining confidential information, deflecting objections, and avoiding legal problems while retaining the affection and friendship of those whose names he took in vain. An FBI wiretap just before the 1944 Democratic National Convention picked up two men whose names are blacked out discussing Karr, who they recalled as having been fired from the OWI. When one noted that he was working for Pearson, the other laughed. They then discussed his closeness to Wallace. One said: "He's a commie" to which the reply was "Oh, no question about it, but he's a very entertaining fellow."[13]

Karr nailed other scoops from individuals associated with Soviet intelligence. He also had a peripheral connection with the famous *Amerasia* spy case of 1945. Like the Lange incident, it involved purloined documents thought to have been stolen from the American government by Communists. There is no evidence in either case that Karr knew that the people he was dealing with were Soviet agents, nor is it likely that political considerations would have curbed his digging for inside information. Still, Karr's close associations with so many people who proved to be Soviet spies troubled the FBI as it untangled the intricate web of Soviet subversion over the years. Karr was simply part and parcel of a community, many of whose members were either secret Communist Party members, or close sympathizers.

During the summer of 1944 Karr had obtained a cache of classified letters written by William Phillips, the American Ambassador to India, expressing support for Indian independence and criticizing British colonial policy. An Indian nationalist politician, Obaidur Rahman, had obtained copies from a source in the State Department and was shopping them around Washington in hopes that their publication would embarrass the British government and pressure Washington to openly endorse Indian independence. Karr got ahold of a set and Pearson published their contents. Before publication, Karr also told one of his sources, who was mixed up in an espionage plot that never quite got off the ground, about the letters.

Lieutenant Andrew Roth, stationed in the Office of Naval Intelligence in Washington, was conducting a guerilla campaign against what he saw as the government's "soft" policy on postwar Japan. Roth advocated deposing the emperor and breaking up the big business cartels that he blamed for Japan's militarism. Although not a Communist, he was sympathetic toward the Party's goals. Back in New York before the war, Roth had worked for *Amerasia*, a small-circulation magazine specializing in American-Asian relations with a decided tilt to the Communist left. Its editor, Philip Jaffe, was a financial contributor to the Communist Party of the United States, a personal friend of Party leader Earl Browder, and a devoted supporter of Mao Tse-tung's Chinese

Communist forces. Roth had met Karr at a party in late 1944. Learning that he worked for Pearson, he invited him to lunch where he criticized General MacArthur's alleged plans to work behind FDR's back and have the United States keep the Japanese emperor on his throne after the war. Karr expressed interest in tips and information from Roth, and the two men met a number of times over the next few months. Karr also introduced him to Pearson and gave him copies of the Phillips letters.

An indefatigable collector of documents, on a visit to Washington, Jaffe pressed Roth for a copy of the Phillips letters, and Roth copied them out in his own handwriting. Jaffe and Roth were both arrested and charged with conspiracy to commit espionage in May 1945. Roth's handwritten copy of the confidential Phillips letters found in Jaffe's office was one of the key bits of evidence in the government's arsenal, along with a wiretap of Jaffe's hotel room in which Jaffe told Roth that a Soviet agent had asked to help him get material out of the Far Eastern Division of the State Department. In a wiretapped conversation with Jaffe on May 29, 1945, Roth mentioned that Karr obtained "a lot of information on Far Eastern matters" from the Treasury Department, particularly from Harry Dexter White, whom Karr contacted at least once a week. Although the *Amerasia* spy charges eventually fizzled due to problems with how the evidence had been obtained—illegal wiretaps—the Bureau remained convinced that Roth and Jaffe were guilty of trafficking in stolen documents. Karr gave a speech in San Francisco shortly after the case had collapsed, in which he congratulated Drew Pearson and Walter Winchell for exposing "the frame-up." Of course, the case was not a frame-up; the prosecution had only failed due to technical defects in the collection of evidence. Nevertheless, Pearson assiduously pushed the line that the *Amerasia* arrests were not about Russian spies, but about conservatives in the State Department who were trying to muzzle the press and stop leaks. To the FBI, Karr's friendship with Roth was telling. Notes from an interview in preparation for a lawsuit indicate that Karr admitted Roth gave him documents, which "he shouldn't have done," and that Attorney General Herbert Brownell told senators in 1953 that if the wiretaps from the case had been admissible in court, Pearson could have gone to jail.[14]

In 1944 and 1945 Karr also met with Samuel Krafsur, an American Communist and Soviet source working for Tass. In a partially decrypted message sent to KGB headquarters in Moscow in June 1944, KGB agent Vladimir Pravdin mentioned information Krafsur obtained from David Karr. This Venona cable was only partially decrypted, so whether Karr was innocently sharing information with a fellow journalist, or knowingly tipping a Soviet agent, remains unclear.[15]

Karr was accredited as a journalist to the founding conference of the United Nations in San Francisco in May 1945. While he was there, he met with a host of West Coast Communists and left-wingers: Joe Starobin of the *Daily Worker*, Leo Krzycki of the American Slav Congress, Claude Cockburn, British journalist and Comintern propagandist, Samuel Krafsur, American representative of the Tass News Agency (and a KGB source), Louis Dolivet, a shadowy front man for Comintern activities, Robert Kenny, the attorney general of California, and Henry Kaiser, the powerful industrialist. Karr knew many of the government employees whom Elizabeth Bentley had named as Soviet spies in 1945, among them, Harry Dexter White, David Wahl, Larry Duggan, and Duncan Lee. Karr later said that White was a friend, and a very good source. In an affidavit to the State Department, Karr denied knowing Lee after he left Washington, but this was false. A 1946 FBI wiretap had recorded Karr informing Lee about a mine workers' strike in which the two discussed John L. Lewis's goals and actions. This wiretap had arisen from an investigation of the Silvermaster spy ring that had been exposed by Elizabeth Bentley.[16]

Of course, any left-wing journalist in Washington knew lots of people, including some who later proved to be spies. As a journalist, Karr was always on the lookout for a tip or a good story, and therefore met with many people. He naturally gravitated to other left-wing journalists and leaders of Popular Front groups anxious for a Drew Pearson broadcast platform. But his activities continued to raise red flags to the FBI. His protestations that he was a firm opponent of Communism and had cooperated with the FBI to combat it were almost too frequent. While spies purloined documents or offered secrets to foreign agents, there was a fine line between leaking information and espionage. When Philip Jaffe told Andrew Roth of his wish to help Soviet intelligence get information out of the State Department, Roth advised him that leaking classified information to a reporter for publication would do the same thing but be much less risky.[17]

The FBI regarded both Karr and Drew Pearson as even more suspicious after Adolf Berle's testimony on the Alger Hiss spy case before the House Committee on Un-American Activities in 1948. Whittaker Chambers had first revealed details about Soviet spy rings in the government in 1939 to Berle, naming Alger Hiss. In several columns during the war, Pearson had criticized Berle for blocking oil shipments to the U.S.S.R. Berle no doubt took some pleasure in telling HUAC that "there were pretty consistent leaks whenever anything went through that office [Hiss's]. Usually we would know about them because they would come out in Drew Pearson's column and one of the legmen was pretty intimate in that office." Despite the sly innuendo that Karr was the pipeline between Hiss and Pearson, no evidence has ever surfaced tying the two men.[18]

Throughout this period Karr walked a fine line in his public comments about the FBI. Just before he went to work for Pearson, in June 1944, he contacted the Bureau about a fugitive named Larry Kelly, who had been accused of embezzling union funds. He told the FBI he had been ordered by his editor at the *Washington Post* to ask the FBI why it had not been able to arrest Kelly, even though he was serving on a Merchant Marine ship. The subsequent *Post* article was critical of the FBI, but Karr told the FBI he thought the story unfair and that it was among the reasons he left the *Post* to work for Pearson. Pearson called the *Amerasia* arrests a "frame-up" in a radio broadcast from Los Angeles in May 1945, but exonerated the FBI, stating that Hoover had been forced to conduct the investigation against his will.[19]

The FBI regarded all this as a barely disguised effort to conceal Karr's real leanings. It was not surprised to learn in January 1946 that Karr had favorably reviewed Albert Kahn's latest book defending the Soviet Union, including the Soviet purge trials of the 1930s, *The Great Conspiracy*. Kahn had been made head of the Jewish People's Fraternal Order, a unit of the Communist-controlled International Workers Order. In an effort to impress acquaintances, Karr also continued to throw Hoover's name around. The FBI director was not amused. On January 23, 1946, a visitor concerned about Communist infiltration of the CIO told Hoover that David Karr had just informed him that Hoover had urged Drew Pearson to blame the recent strike wave on Communists. The visitor assumed that it was a ploy to arouse hostility in the labor movement to the FBI, since he suspected that Karr leaned left. Hoover flatly denied making any such request. As one FBI agent later said, "Karr is the type who would not hesitate to double-cross anyone."[20]

Karr wielded considerable power in Washington as Drew Pearson's chief aide. He could threaten to embarrass, or offer to advance, a person's career. Nor was Pearson himself above such blackmail. He used his columns to force federal agencies to hire his friends, lest he trash them in a column. He ignored his sources' peccadilloes while savaging his enemies for the very same offenses. He pressured politicians for special deals for himself. He sanctioned illegal break-ins to get evidence while excoriating government officials for such behavior. And for a man so quick to extravagantly denounce others, he was fiercely protective of his own name; his biographer noted that "considering the way he shredded the reputation of others, Pearson was incredibly thin-skinned."[21]

Pearson was involved in at least 275 libel suits during his years of publishing. He lost only one. He was willing to go to extreme lengths to win such battles. Sued for $1.75 million by General Douglas MacArthur—who was encouraged by FDR—Pearson located his discarded Eurasian mistress, copied MacArthur's love letters, and blackmailed one of the most powerful military men in the United States to drop the suit. He gave as well as he got, suing critics like an Alaska newspaper editor who called him the "garbage man of journalism." Yet he persisted for years in labeling a Romanian-American businessman an anti-Semite, despite private assurances from the Anti-Defamation League's Washington representative that his target was not hostile to Jews; Pearson's response was to pressure the ADL, a longtime source of information, to fire the offending staffer and to stretch out the lawsuit until his exhausted victim dropped it.

Pearson's approach was tempered by a deep streak of pragmatism. He embarked on crusades but was always willing to cut a deal or appease a politically powerful foe when conditions warranted it. Despite his criticisms of the FBI over the years, he accepted tips from J. Edgar Hoover to discredit isolationists and fascists. He asked the FBI for help in tracking down his wife's first husband, who had fled the country with their son. He cut short his campaign against "Lyin' Down Lyndon" Johnson in return for LBJ's agreement to oppose the nomination of Lewis Strauss, a longtime Pearson bête noire, to the Cabinet.[22]

David Karr was a perfect fit for this amoral environment. He would do anything to get a story, he could lie with a straight face with charm, and he could bluff his way out of tight spots secure in the knowledge that he was on the side of the angels. One of his jobs for Pearson, an admiring profile explained, was "to gather unpublishable but useful information that the columnist could employ in persuading Congressmen to cooperate with him." Like Pearson, his politics were instinctively left-wing and they both liked money. Pearson, the product of a middle-class Quaker family, had amassed considerable wealth by the 1940s, fueled partly by his journalism and broadcasting, and partly from his first, failed marriage to the daughter of Cissy Patterson, the wealthy newspaper publisher, who left a tidy sum to his daughter. Despite his comfortable circumstances, Pearson was notoriously cheap, paying his staffers low wages and encouraging them to earn extra money from side ventures, which Karr undoubtedly did himself. By 1946, Karr was actively involved in Pearson's efforts to build up his newspaper syndicate, extend its reach—the "Washington Merry-Go-Round" was being carried in some six hundred newspapers across the country—and obtain and keep advertisers for the weekly radio broadcast.[23]

After World War II, the "Washington Merry-Go-Round" specialized in exposing corruption among the hustlers and Missouri cronies around Harry Truman. Pearson was sympathetic to the idealistic New Dealers like Harold Ickes and Henry Morgenthau whom Truman had pushed aside, and critical of the growing rift with the Soviet Union. Unlike Henry Wallace, however, Pearson eventually surrendered his naïvety about Soviet intentions; his radio broadcast had first alerted the public to the defection of Igor Gouzenko and the existence of widespread Soviet espionage directed against the United States and its allies, and he enthusiastically supported the Marshall Plan.

Nevertheless, it took a few years for both Pearson and Karr to shed their illusions about the Soviet Union. In April 1946, Karr accompanied former Vice President Wallace, now Secretary of Commerce, to a Los Angeles rally. Wallace was about to make a decisive break with the Truman administration on foreign policy. Increasingly worried that the president's tougher line on Russia was leading to a preventable break with our wartime allies, Wallace gave a defiant speech at Madison Square Garden in September 1946, at which Karr was present.

Truman then fired Wallace on September 20, but Karr kept working with Wallace. Almost two months later Karr wrote to Norman Corwin that Wallace would need Corwin "to assist him in saying what needs to be said so urgently" in his planned anti-Truman offensive set to begin on January 3. That fall, Karr accompanied Wallace on a trip to meet with sympathizers upset over Truman's abandonment of "FDR's Old Uncle Joe" Stalin.[24]

Throughout 1947, Karr's correspondence with friends remained highly critical of the Truman administration, sympathetic to Wallace, and despairing about American politics. Wallace had accepted a largely ceremonial job as editor of the *New Republic* as he mulled challenging Harry Truman for the presidency in 1948. Karr advised the magazine to send out press releases about the crowds Wallace was drawing for his speeches to every Democrat in office, just as he was, "where I am sure they will do the most good." And he reassured Robert Kenny in July that "now that you've taken [an] oath for God, country, Roosevelt and Wallace, I'm for you in the day time and night time." In August 1947, he told one friend in Europe that things were in "a rapidly deteriorating state here." "We're heading straight down the road for war and Fascism...the monkeys in the State Department are just plunging forward without rhyme or reason." In September he wrote Bartley Crum that their mutual friend Robert Kenny was hopeful about the Wallace boom in California and "I think we'll all be on the same side when the chips finally get down."[25]

In 1947, a prominent Greek-American who was a close friend of Pearson's ran into problems getting a passport. George Vournas was a successful Washington lawyer and owned a neighboring farm near Pearson's weekend retreat in Potomac, Maryland. Vournas had represented the Spanish Loyalist government in the late 1930s, a cause also dear to Pearson's heart. He also had helped to found and served as president of the American Hellenic Educational and Progressive Association (AHEPA), one of the largest Greek-American fraternal organizations in the country. During World War II, Vournas had served in the OSS in Cairo, where he criticized the British government for aiding the monarchist resistance. As Greek Communist guerillas threatened to overthrow the Western-backed government in 1946, Vournas opposed the Truman administration's decision to provide military aid to the monarchist government. Pearson wrote several columns attacking the decision.[26]

Pearson asked the State Department to accredit Vournas as a correspondent for his press syndicate, to accompany a presidential mission headed by Paul Porter to study the Greek situation. It was scheduled to leave Washington in early January 1947. When Vournas's passport request stalled, on Friday, January 10, he met with John Maragon, a shadowy White House assistant to Major Harry Vaughn, Truman's military aide. Vournas complained that the mission was leaving Monday, but the State Department had refused to issue him a passport. In addition to his press duties, he explained that he was carrying a letter addressed to Marshall Tito of Yugoslavia. He appealed for Maragon's assistance but was told that if he had bothered to comply with departmental regulations, he would have had no problem.[27]

According to Maragon, David Karr went ballistic over Vournas's failure to get a U.S. passport. Phoning him, he demanded that he intervene with Vaughn. When Maragon refused, "Karr in [a] threatening tone gave me forty-eight hours to produce Vournas's passport." Karr then called Charles Ross, Truman's secretary, complaining that "at the express request of the White House," Vournas had been blocked, presumably for opposing U.S. government policy, and thundering that Vournas had better get his passport. When asked if he was making a threat, Karr replied, "Yes," adding that if it didn't happen, they would be flayed on Pearson's radio broadcast that week. Karr later insisted that he had made no threats, and in 1949 called Ross to get his recollection of the incident in response to a column by Westbrook Pegler. Ross had White House advisor Lloyd Cutler listen in on an extension and write a memorandum on the conversation. Ross acknowledged that Pegler's version was incorrect, but then recollected that indeed, there had been threats. Karr had told him that Vournas was a solid citizen, a friend of Sam Rayburn's, and that his passport request should be granted. Ross also recalled being told that Karr and Pearson "could not understand why General Vaughn was meddling in passport matters, that they had a good bit of material about the relations between Vaughn and John Maragon, and that they would use it if Vaughn did not lay off Vournas."[28]

Pearson soon began attacking Maragon, an immigrant from Greece who had parlayed a friendship with Vaughn—a mediocrity who owed his position to his longtime acquaintance with Truman—into a role as a Washington fixer. Not only did Maragon lack any qualifications for working in the White House, his background included a stint as an undercover FBI agent during World War I, from which position he had been fired for consorting with prostitutes. He had a record as a petty crook and had been investigated for, but not charged with, murder. Three years later, in 1950, he was convicted of perjury in an investigation of the "5% boys," Washington influence peddlers.

The Vournas case did not go away. In the summer of 1949 it was the centerpiece in a campaign launched by Westbrook Pegler, an acerbic conservative columnist and longtime enemy of Pearson. Pegler, labeled "journalism's angry man," a master of nasty put-downs and cheerleader for vigilante justice, had developed into a rabid FDR hater by 1943. Harry Truman was more to his liking, an attitude shaped by his friendship with Maragon. Pegler also had a history of conflict with Drew Pearson, who had sued him for, by Pegler's standards, rather mild slurs accusing him of being a fake reporter and a smear artist. That conflict had been resolved by grudging apologies all the way around. When their war of words was resumed, David Karr was caught squarely in the middle as Pegler's prime exhibit for Pearson's Communist sympathies.

It was not simply friendship that had inspired Pearson and Karr to defend Vournas or intervene on his behalf. The lawyer also shared their opposition to Truman's foreign policy. In May 1947, responding to a diatribe from Vournas denouncing American militarism and aid to Greece, Karr recalled meeting with the letter-writer in Washington and noted his agreement with many of his views on foreign policy. Nor was Vournas just an apolitical lawyer anxious to end the bloodshed in his native country. His brother, a suspected Communist, had been sentenced to prison in Greece in the 1930s on charges of espionage and subversion. Vournas himself was allied with left-wing forces in Greece that included the Communists. One purpose of his proposed trip to Greece with the Porter mission in 1947 had been to deliver a letter to Josip Tito, dictator of Yugoslavia and a fervent supporter of Greek Communist rebels. As part of that effort Vournas had contacted Louis Adamic, a left-wing writer who had been supporting the Yugoslavs in their dispute with the U.S.S.R. Tito's government, however, was widely unpopular in the United States, having recently shot down several American aircraft, killing five aviators, and inflaming both the American government and public opinion.[29]

Karr's interest in Greek affairs also had a personal connection. His wife, Madeline, served as Washington correspondent for the left-wing *Nation* magazine, and also held press credentials at the White House and the State Department, representing the *National Herald*, a small, Greek-language newspaper published in New York. Pegler aimed his fire not only at David Karr but also at Madeline. Madeline's politics were not dissimilar from David's. Like him, she had flirted with several Communist front groups in the 1930s but claimed to have been disgusted by the Nazi-Soviet agreement in 1939. She remained a resolute leftist, however, joining the American-Soviet Friendship Council during the war.

Dave and Madeline had first met at a dance in 1938 in Crompond where both their families summered. They dated occasionally that fall but did not become serious about each other until the summer of 1939. David visited her regularly after he relocated to Washington, but the relationship cooled in the summer of 1941, a time when David was dating other women. A year later, however, they resumed contact. As she finished her senior year at Brooklyn College, from which she received a BA in 1942, she taught high school history and dramatics. They were married on September 5, 1942 and she moved to the capital.[30]

In January 1943, Madeline Karr went to work for the Board of Economic Warfare as a secretary; by the time she resigned from the agency in October 1943 she was a junior economic analyst. Her next job was to write memos on issues of Jewish concern arising in the Congress for George Mintzer of the American Jewish Committee, an acquaintance and sometime-employer of her husband, but she quickly secured a reporting job for the *National Herald*, a Greek-American daily newspaper published in New York. Basil Vlavianos, its publisher, a lawyer, had first approached David, at loose ends following his resignation from OWI, but he declined the offer and suggested his wife instead. Locked in a battle for circulation with the pro-monarchist *Daily Atlantis* on the right and the pro-Communist weekly *Greek Tribune* on the left, Vlavianos hoped to bolster his paper's credibility with a Washington correspondent. Madeline also wrote for WMCA radio in New York, became a Washington correspondent for the *San Diego National Journal*, run by David's friend Clinton McKinnon, wrote for Orson Welles' radio show, and in the fall of 1947 went to work for the left-leaning *Nation* magazine. Madeline flew to Athens, Greece, in April 1946 to cover the Greek elections and spent six weeks in Europe. Her work for Vlavianos and hostility to conservatives, views shared by George Vournas, no doubt played a role in validating Karr and Pearson in their attacks on the Truman administration policies. Madeline later told a lawyer that she had helped in first exposing Maragon.[31]

By April 1947, Karr's stock with the Truman administration had hit bottom. In response to a request from the general manager of a New York radio station to get Truman to help memorialize boxer Benny Leonard, Karr ruefully noted that "frankly my connections there are less than one percent of what they were last year."[32]

Karr kept up his relationships with others on the pro-Communist left. He wrote a cordial letter to Vito Marcantonio, the radical congressman from New York, seeking a favor for a friend; he deplored how old friends had abandoned Harry Dexter White's widow after his death amid charges he had been a Soviet agent. One old acquaintance, the folksinger Oscar Brand, who had briefly been engaged to Madeline, recalled years later that he had met both Karrs during the 1948 Henry Wallace campaign, in which he was sure they were active. David asked him to sing at a Madison Square Garden rally; he agreed, and Karr introduced him to Wallace. He thought the "Karrs were practically running the whole event" and that it was a sign that his political commitments had not changed. But no documentary evidence linking Karr to the Progressive Party campaign in 1948 exists. None of the accounts of the Party mention him, and his correspondence does not reflect contacts or sympathies with it, so Brand's recollection is most likely incorrect. However, it would not have been out of character for Karr to keep a lifeline out to someone he was not publicly supporting.[33]

The political winds were dramatically shifting in Washington, however, and, like many on the left, Drew Pearson was becoming more concerned about Communist threats to the stability of Western governments, and less enthusiastic about liberals forming coalitions with Communists. Pearson enthusiastically endorsed the Marshall Plan, an enormous program of American assistance to the distressed nations of Europe to rebuild their shattered economies. Designed to counter the surging Communist parties of Western Europe, the brainchild of Secretary of State George Marshall, first proposed in June 1947, was widely credited with launching Europe's economic recovery. David Karr came up with a typically flamboyant plan to dramatize its goals and publicize the effort. Although the Friendship Train, as the project was dubbed, was not formally connected with the Marshall Plan, it played on the same concerns and generated enormous amounts of charity in the United States and goodwill in Europe.

In a column appearing on October 11, 1947 and in a broadcast thereafter, Pearson suggested collecting food and clothing to send to impoverished Europeans. Quickly generating widespread enthusiasm, the Friendship Train left Los Angeles on November 7 and traveled across the country, stopping in numerous cities to pick up donations. The initial goal of eighty trainloads was easily surpassed; more than seven hundred boxcars were eventually shipped abroad—more than $40 million worth of goods.

Karr was central to the effort. As soon as Pearson's suggestion started to generate interest, he dispatched Karr to meet with Italian and French officials in Washington to learn what foods were most needed and could be easily shipped and distributed. It was then on to the Department of Agriculture to discuss issues of what could be shipped and how. Officials there warned that the Friendship Train would have to be strict about how donations could be made; sugar in small packages to facilitate distribution, wheat only in bulk, flour in 25-, 50-, and 100-pound sacks for easy repackaging, etc. No glass containers could be accepted due to breakage and neither could homemade products. Pearson was warned that without strict rules and limits on what was taken, mass confusion, anger, and waste of manpower would imperil the success of the effort. Karr also negotiated with the railroad companies to donate use of the cars and coordinate schedules. In addition to overseeing the administrative nitty-gritty, Karr enlisted a roster of distinguished Americans to serve on the Friendship Train Committee, chaired by Harry Warner of the Warner Brothers movie studio.[34]

Less than a month after conception, the Friendship Train received a rousing send-off in Hollywood. As it moved across the country newspapers and radio stations urged contributions and drummed up publicity. Mayor William O'Dwyer keynoted the occasion in a culminating ceremony in New York on November 19. The exhausted Karr wrote to a friend that he now hoped "to go back to being a newspaperman again and cease flacking for a while," but Pearson was growing concerned that his brainchild might be derailed either by Communist opposition in France or distribution problems that would generate bad publicity. He decided at the last minute to bring Karr to Europe with him, pleading with Ruth Shipley, head of the Passport Office on December 9, to expedite a passport for Karr so he could leave the next day.[35]

The original plan, worked out with the State Department, was to have American relief agencies oversee the distribution of the food. One-quarter each was allocated to the National Catholic Welfare Center, the Jewish Joint Distribution Committee, Church World Services, and American Aid to France, but that caused "no end of initial trouble." There were additional worries that strikes in France and Italy might cause delays, or that Communists might riot and impede the effort. But dockworkers in Le Havre unloaded the shipments gratis, and the Friendship Train's reception in both countries was overwhelmingly positive. Pearson told one person that Communists in Paris had "set fire to the warehouse where food was unloaded and completely destroyed it," but this must have been only one small blip in an otherwise popular and successful program. Karr and Pearson eventually concluded that the distribution should be without any reference to religion, and the initial agreement was altered. To avoid any chance that some of the food would be diverted to the black market, it was distributed directly to needy recipients. The French Minister of Health and Education submitted a list of cities suffering from food shortages and 90 percent of the goods were shipped directly to orphanages or schools for lunches. The remainder went to the elderly. Italians were so enthusiastic that the trains had to stop at small towns not slated to receive shipments just to hear speeches expressing thanks to the Americans. American newsmen accompanied the various trains as they made their way across France and Italy to ensure that all went well and to publicize this effort in personal diplomacy.[36]

While he largely stayed in the background, Karr was the key organizer, soothing egos, coordinating schedules, and cajoling dignitaries and bureaucrats alike to ensure success. Not the least of his abilities was his charm, which was used frequently and to good effect with prominent figures. He carefully wrote effusive and effective thank-you letters to key players, assuring such men as Harry Warner of Hollywood that one of the great pleasures of the Train was "watching you work calmly and devotedly under almost impossible conditions, without thought to your own health or welfare," and that his employees reflected his wise style of leadership. Both he and Pearson praised Warner's acumen and asked for the chance to pick his brain. Karr was an indefatigable networker, who knew how to praise, flatter, and interest the powerful, a trait that eased his rise from lowly reporter to business tycoon (although it never worked with the FBI).[37]

The growing anti-Communist consensus in 1947 and 1948 had an impact on both Pearson and Karr, forcing both of them to tack more to the center and distance themselves from alliances with Communist forces. It wasn't just the Marshall Plan. For Pearson, the Communist issue on his own staff began to loom larger. Pearson had been a constant critic of the House Committee on Un-American Activities and had broken the story in 1948 exposing J. Parnell Thomas's use of kickbacks among his staff that had sent the HUAC chairman to federal prison. Karr's own alleged Communist background had been a frequent and unwelcome issue that emerged whenever a critic sought a cudgel with which to beat Pearson. But, in 1947, after learning that one of his employees, Andy Older, had been a CPUSA member from 1940 until at least 1944 and had remained sympathetic to Communism, Pearson consulted with J. Edgar Hoover and Ed Tamm of the FBI. Pearson, increasingly uneasy about Soviet intentions, warned his staff, and Older in particular, about his evolving views, soon after returning from the Paris Peace Conference in late 1946. When Older remained obdurate, Pearson fired him in 1947.[38]

As an admitted Communist, Andy Older was of course particularly vulnerable to controversy and attacks and in the new postwar climate of opinion, Pearson had fewer incentives to defend him. Karr was in a different category; he had always strenuously denied Party membership and had ready, if sometimes strained, answers for his former activities, some of which were ambiguous enough to admit of innocent explanations. Privately, Pearson mused that "Dave, like a lot of other youngsters, might have had Communist leanings or even been a party member. But if I am any judge of human nature, he was cured of this long ago. And even if he was, a lot of us would be out of luck if all the sins of our youth were held against us." Still, Karr continued to be a lightning rod. He was also, however, an essential part of Pearson's media empire, which encompassed not only the daily newspaper column in hundreds of outlets and the weekly radio show, but also a private tip sheet, *Personal from Pearson*, that went to private subscribers.[39]

Around the same time he told Pearson about Older, J. Edgar Hoover also spoke to the columnist about Karr, warning that although there was no evidence he had ever been a CPUSA member, he had close associations with Communists, and with the Party. In early March 1948, the Bureau produced a forty-three-page summary of Karr's "questionable" contacts, most of which was redacted when released under the FOIA. Karr became still more cautious as the year went by. Not only did he apparently keep at a distance from the Communist-inspired and -supported presidential campaign of his old friend Henry Wallace, he also took pains to assure the FBI of his high regard for them, bad-mouthing even his own wife in order to do so.[40]

Whether motivated by opportunism or pragmatism, Karr seemed to have accepted the need for America to confront the Soviet Union in Europe—in contrast to Wallace's calls for appeasement. He was unimpressed by the alleged desire of the Soviet Union for peace. Late in the summer of 1948 he and his wife spent a month in Europe. On a visit to Berlin he talked with General Lucius Clay and an old friend, J. Anthony (Joe) Panuch, who had been ousted from the State Department for too vigorously pushing to fire suspected Communists. To them, Karr was an enthusiastic supporter of the American airlift to supply goods to the Russian-blockaded city, writing upon his return that it was "sickening to see the indignities to which our people and our flag are subjected by the Russians" and that "to think that our great United States is forced by the Red Army to meekly and humbly ask for the right to feed a million people is something shameful in itself." Karr even believed that the U.S. should have used an armored train to break the initial blockade.[41]

Far from pining about the collapse of the New Deal coalition or bemoaning the end of left-wing unity, Karr busily prepared for what he assumed would be the impending Republican administration. He met with aides to Republican candidate Thomas Dewey in October, and effusively thanked them, while praising the "high standards and mental caliber so intimately associated with the soon-to-be President-elect." He was so convinced Thomas Dewey would win that on October 25, he wrote his chief counsel with a rough draft of a speech the governor could give on education and a warning not to go overboard on loyalty witch hunts. Karr suggested that Dewey appoint a blue-ribbon commission to study the issue of subversives in government and make recommendations; he proposed Henry Stimson, Robert Patterson, Jimmy Byrnes, and Dwight Eisenhower—none very sympathetic to the left—as potential members. And he wrote one of Dewey's confidants in October with advice for staffing the new administration, warning of the "pratfalls" in Washington. Once in place, the Dewey team would not have time to think; the press of business, the intrusiveness of the press, and the growing complexity of government all required "pre-war planning." He reiterated his belief that they needed to appoint Dewey loyalists and warned that where there was intense political pressure to appoint an outsider, they should surround him with loyalists. He told him: "Rest assured of our earnest desire to cooperate with you."[42]

Many of Karr's old left-wing friends were furious at what they saw as his political about-face. When in 1950 an investigator for Drew Pearson preparing for a libel suit met with "left-wing information specialists," one of them denounced Karr in the "most violent language as a rotten character and wound up his tirade with the assertion that if for no other reason than that he employed Karr, Pearson was a despicable and dangerous man."[43]

To demonstrate his confidence in the FBI, Karr was even prepared to take its side against his wife, albeit privately. Madeline Karr published an article in *The Nation* on May 1 about federal loyalty investigations that included a derogatory comment about the FBI. She reported that a recent Bureau report had referred to its subject as the sort of person "who permits his Negro maid to come and go by the front door." Hoover was enraged—whether by the charge or that it was published—and at his request Lou Nichols interviewed Madeline. She refused to identify either the case to which she was referring, or her source. A month later David told Nichols that Madeline's source "was not too reliable" and that he would try to obtain the information. He spoke to Madeline and called Nichols on July 2 to report that she "was pretty 'green' as a journalist" and did not know the name of the person who had supposedly made the comment. He later added that she "was very foolish to publish the article" since her source was unreliable, and she did not even know that person's name. He apologized on her behalf and indicated that she would try to make amends.[44]

Karr began making plans to leave Washington early in 1948. Pearson's conversations with Hoover may have caused him to fear that Karr was now a liability. Or Washington's growing conservatism may have made it a less inviting place for Karr. He explored several options, including a failed plan to rescue *PM*, the radical New York newspaper, before resigning from the "Washington Merry-Go-Round" on November 1 and moving to New York. The *PM* deal, which involved Clinton McKinnon buying it and making Karr its editor, fell through when Bartley Crum, one of the planned partners, persuaded Marshall Field to sell it to him and cut Karr out, which earned him Karr's undying enmity.[45]

Jack Anderson, who went to work for Pearson as a junior reporter after Older was fired in 1947, was more conservative and anti-Communist than many of Pearson's previous legmen. He remembered Karr as a "great talker" and the "most articulate and persuasive man I ever met," someone whose "sheer eloquence" enabled him to wield influence over his boss. Karr had a way of "sucking up" to powerful people in a manner that appeared genuine; he could manipulate them without fawning.[46]

Anderson was less impressed with Karr's investigative skills as a newsman. He was an "operator," who used "any way he could to get information," but was more of a promoter than a newsman. His stories and reporting were "more glib" than investigative. Anderson said he later learned that Karr had one major source, a top correspondent who needed money, who passed material he had received "off-the-record" to Karr in return for cash. John Scali took $75 a week from Karr for information Karr then passed off to Pearson as his own work. Scali later served as a middleman between KGB officer Alexander Feklisov (a.k.a. Fomin) and the Kennedy administration to defuse the Cuban Missile Crisis, and as American Ambassador to the United Nations during the Nixon administration.[47]

Karr tried to convert Anderson politically, taking him to Harlem to show him how the poor lived. But, Anderson recalled, Karr's lifestyle belied his political sentiments. Even after relocating to New York, Karr continued to work closely with Pearson writing various columns and supervising Pearson's private bulletin that went to paid subscribers as well as obtaining the advertising for his shows. He traveled weekly to Washington, where, Anderson ruefully noted, he had to be the only newsman who moved around town in a chauffeured limousine. He enjoyed the luxury more than he cared about the jibes from his colleagues.[48]

Although he kept an office in D.C., Karr relocated to New York in 1948 as vice president in charge of public relations at the William Weintraub Company, an advertising agency, at a salary of $25,000 a year, a considerable upgrade from the $7,000 Pearson had been paying him (although Karr made additional money from some of his ancillary activities for Pearson). This was respectable money for the day and enabled him to make sizeable political contributions. In June, he sent a $1,000 check in his wife's name to his old benefactor, Clinton Anderson, who had resigned as Secretary of Agriculture to run for senator from New Mexico. Located in plush offices in Rockefeller Plaza, Weintraub was the advertising agency for Lee Hats, the chief sponsor of Pearson's radio show, and Karr spent a lot of time, not only on Pearson sponsor and advertising matters but writing for the column. One source told the FBI that as late as 1951 Pearson continued to pay Karr a $250 weekly expense account that Karr took full advantage of. The two remained close. Writing to Karr's hospitalized father in November 1949, Pearson noted that he didn't "know of many people who have more ingenuity, more energetic drive, and more loyalty than he." While he had once worried "whether his occasional impetuousness might not get him into trouble," David had grown calmer and more measured, without losing "his crusading zeal and fervor."[49]

One project Karr worked on before he left Washington continued into 1949. As a gesture of gratitude for the Friendship Train, the French government launched a "Merci Train" carrying gifts including native costumes, artwork, bottles of wine, and other souvenirs. The plan was to have forty-nine boxcars, one for each state with the last going to Washington, D.C., and Hawaii. Karr was once again thrust into the breach of organizational chaos, forced to organize welcome events, worry that the goods "would be in good taste," and there would be enough to fill forty-nine train cars: "That's a lot of boxcars." In any event, the

Train was a success, kicking off with a Broadway parade and an Air Force salute. Pearson rode on the train for much of February and exulted in the warm reception it received.[50]

Meanwhile a growing furor over Communism was enveloping Washington, D.C. James Forrestal, the first Secretary of Defense, hospitalized for depression and in the grip of paranoid fantasies, jumped to his death from his hospital room on May 22, 1949. Pearson had been pummeling Forrestal in his column and broadcast, even falsely accusing him of cowardice for fleeing his home and abandoning his wife when confronted by an armed robber. Westbrook Pegler immediately launched an attack on Pearson, blaming him for Forrestal's death. A storm of criticism followed. In addition to calls to newspapers to remove his column, Pearson also lost his radio sponsor, Lee Hats, but the Weintraub Agency quickly found a replacement, the Adam Hat Company.

Pegler wasn't through with Pearson, however. He wrote his first column mentioning Karr on July 21, 1949. In an attack on Drew Pearson, it said Karr had threatened Harry Vaughn over a passport for George Vournas. On July 29, Pegler added more detail about Vournas and about Madeline Karr's work for the *National Herald* and her access to the State Department and White House, mentioning that the *National Herald*'s new owner had let Madeline go because "she was more left than I like." Then, on August 2, Pegler retailed excerpts from Karr's Dies Committee testimony along with Adolf Berle's complaint that one of Pearson's legmen had a pipeline to Alger Hiss's office in the State Department. Pegler also included Madeline Karr's Social Security number and charged that after losing her position with the *National Herald* in 1947, she had applied for a job with Army Military Intelligence.[51]

More bad publicity came in September when Howard Rushmore testified before the Senate Judiciary Committee on the 14th. Karr had told the Dies Committee he knew Rushmore "very well" when he wrote for the *Daily Worker*. Rushmore was a reporter and movie critic at the paper before making the mistake of praising the movie version of *Gone with the Wind*. Having quit the CPUSA, Rushmore had become an anti-Communist reporter on the *New York Journal-American* in 1939. Beginning in 1947 he often testified before congressional committees investigating Communism. This time he insisted that at the *Daily Worker*, he had given Dave Katz, as Karr was then known, assignments and "he had to show me his party card to get these assignments...At the time I knew him, he was a Communist."[52]

The real fireworks didn't explode until the next year. Pearson was a constant critic of Senator Joseph McCarthy, who began his meteoric rise in February 1950 with a speech attacking the State Department for harboring dozens of Communists. Based on information he had received from Hoover, Pearson was skeptical. McCarthy had imprudently named Owen Lattimore as the top Soviet spy in the United States, but quickly backtracked, only to later trot out a Communist defector, Louis Budenz, who testified that Lattimore was a trusted Party member. This testimony was suspect because Budenz had never mentioned Lattimore in all his prior briefings with the FBI. Pearson likened McCarthyism to the Salem witch trials. He wrote dozens of columns attacking McCarthy and digging up unsavory tidbits from his past. He consulted with members of the Tydings Committee staff on how best to discredit McCarthy. On December 13, the two men were improbably seated at the same dinner table at a restaurant. After one verbal confrontation, McCarthy followed Pearson to the cloakroom where he kneed him in the groin and then slapped him.

Stewing over months of attacks, the Wisconsin senator struck again on December 15 with a tirade on the Senate floor blistering Pearson—and David Karr. He denounced the columnist as an "unprincipled liar and fake" in a compendium of vitriolic attacks on his veracity. Pearson had enraged many prominent politicians and public figures, so McCarthy was able to offer up a grab bag of insults from those who detested him: he was "a professional character assassin," the "biggest and most notorious liar in America today," a "sponge" who "gathered slime, mud and slander from all parts of the earth and let the ooze out through his radio broadcasts," "a filthy and cowardly villain, a venomous slanderer and an insinuating rogue." Representative Hamilton Fish had lamented that "horsewhipping or the old gun method" had gone out of style, since either would have been an appropriate way to deal with Pearson. Senator McKellar of Tennessee had called him "just an ignorant liar, a pusillanimous liar, a peewee liar, and he is a paid liar...This revolving, constitutional, unmitigated, infamous liar, this low-lived, double-crossing, dishonest, corrupt scoundrel." FDR had called him "a chronic liar" and Truman had advised "add[ing] another star to that fellow's crown." Senator Jenner had denied Pearson was an "SOB" because he was "only his own filthy brainchild, conceived in ruthlessness and dedicated to the proposition that Judas Iscariot was a piker." His own former mother-in-law had called him "a yellow-bellied slacker," and Senator Tydings, McCarthy's bitter foe, once explained that "I fail to find within the limits of parliamentary language words to describe this worm masquerading in the physique and clothing of a supposed man."[53]

This verbal assault was just a prelude to the heart of McCarthy's charge; that Pearson was "the ideal man" to do the work of the Communists. As an "unprincipled, greedy degenerate liar" with an enormous media audience, he was perfectly situated to destroy the reputations of anyone who challenged the Communist agenda. His most prominent victims had been Chinese leader Chiang Kai-shek, James Forrestal, and General Douglas MacArthur, but he also targeted anyone who dared expose Communists, ranging from Martin Dies to McCarthy himself. His chief collaborator, perhaps even boss, in these ventures, McCarthy argued, was David Karr. Mentioning Karr's past ties to the CPUSA and the Daily Worker, McCarthy alleged that "it is difficult to know who is the master and who is the servant" in their relationship. While conceding that Pearson had never been an actual Party member or paid Party dues, "it has not affected his willingness to follow the orders of Dave Karr, who, of course, is a most active member of the party, and who carries instructions and orders to Pearson." To counter their nefarious influence, McCarthy called on American newspapers to cancel Pearson's column and urged a grassroots campaign to pressure the Adam Hat Company to drop its sponsorship of his radio program.[54]

McCarthy renewed the attack on December 19, this time focusing exclusively on Karr, whom he called "a very active and important member of the Communist Party." After noting Pearson's derisive comment that if his legman was a Communist, "then the Washington Monument is a hole in the ground," McCarthy read the Civil Service Commission report of 1943 into the record, with its several damaging allegations and conclusion that Karr should be ineligible for federal employment. "David Karr is the connecting link between Drew Pearson and the Communist Party," he said, and the Adam Hat Company was contemptible for enabling Karr and Pearson to "pour this poison into millions of American homes." They were "the grease-monkeys of the Communist conspiracy that is trying to conquer us. Everything they touch is smeared with the filth of their hands. The blackness of their lies is mixed with the blood shed by American boys."[55]

After McCarthy's diatribe on September 15, Senator Clinton Anderson pointed out that Karr's 1943 investigation by the Kerr Committee had not found "anything in the charges which would in any way justify the assertion that David Karr was connected with any Communist-front organization, or was himself in any way a Communist," contrary to the CSC report and the FBI. In answer to McCarthy's pointed questions about whether the CSC report would change his mind about Karr, Anderson replied that FBI reports might contain unsupported allegations a full investigation would find unsupportable and that a whole file might contradict mere snippets of information, then read a letter Karr had written to thank him for his defense a few days earlier, in which he offered to contribute $10,000 to the Red Cross or another charity of McCarthy's choosing if McCarthy could prove he had been on the *Daily Worker* staff "for two minutes, let alone two years" and daring McCarthy to repeat his charges off the Senate floor where he could be sued for libel.[56]

The substance of McCarthy's charges about Karr, if not his conclusions, was borne out by the FBI files. A December 20 report sent to J. Edgar Hoover found that Karr's being a Communist Party member, having contact with high Party officials, writing for the *Party Organizer*, and being involved in several Party fronts, were all raised in FBI investigations of Karr of 1942 and 1943, but much of the information had come from informants whose reliability and accuracy could not be fully assessed, particularly as to formal Party membership. (Since much of this information remains blacked out in released FBI files, it remains murky.)[57]

David Karr's first reaction to being accused of Communism in the early 1940s had been to claim that he was an FBI informant. When the Bureau had refused to go along with the dodge, he backtracked. Now under nationwide scrutiny, he resurrected his old story that his contacts with the CPUSA had been at the government's behest. An FBI contact at the Anti-Defamation League reported that Karr was claiming to have attended Party meetings "at the direction of the FBI." The FBI heard stories circulating in New York that Karr claimed to have an FBI informant number. After McCarthy's attack, Karr told friends, according to a source of Lou Nichols's, that "he had joined the Communist Party as an undercover agent for the FBI."[58]

To double-check these claims, the FBI prepared yet another report about its Karr contacts. He had been in touch with the Bureau thirty times—twelve when Karr had come to the FBI with information. He had been interviewed seven times, of which three involved investigations of Karr himself. He approached the FBI nine times on other matters, presumably for stories he was writing, and been interviewed on non-investigative matters on a few occasions. Other than Lou Nichols, most of his interactions had been with one special agent who met him a dozen times or so, but had been wary of him, believing he was fishing for information and that his information was sometimes "incorrect or garbled." Lou Nichols and Ed Ladd agreed that the FBI should say that Karr had no official connection with the Bureau and "at no time was he directed by the FBI to join any organization or associate with anyone for the purpose of securing information."[59]

J. Edgar Hoover found Karr irksome. He ordered Lou Nichols to call him in for an interview and tell him to stop claiming to have a relationship with the Bureau. He also told Nichols to "contact Anti-Defamation outfit and set it straight." Nichols did so on January 3, telling Arnold Forster, head of the ADL, that Karr's stories "were a pack of lies." Forster said he had first heard that Karr was working for the FBI in 1943 but had been assured by another FBI official that it was "a goddamn lie." He hadn't seen Karr since, until just a few days before, when he had heard the story again. In any case, Forster allowed that Karr "was no good anyway and has been of this opinion for some time."[60]

The pressure on Karr continued to ratchet up. In late December and early January, Pegler wrote two more columns excoriating Pearson and Karr. Early in January the Adam Hat Company announced it was dropping its sponsorship of his radio program. Although Pearson soon found other sponsors, he also lost his national broadcast network and had to syndicate his show. The "Washington Merry-Go-Round" newspaper column began to lose subscribers. Pearson kept up his attacks on McCarthy as Karr tried desperately to assuage the FBI.

Karr called the FBI's New York office on January 4 and "vigorously denied ever making any statements that he was a contact of the FBI and was working at the direction of the FBI." He praised the Bureau, telling Assistant Special Agent in Charge Ed Whelan that "he has been absolutely amazed at the tenacity of the Bureau in protecting civil rights." He professed himself "flabbergasted by the allegations that he was making statements that he was working at the direction of the Bureau" and promised that if the FBI would give him the names of those who had said that, he would set them straight. He then went to Washington and met with Lou Nichols. He said the story about his being an FBI informer stemmed from the events of 1943 and that he would go to the ADL and straighten them out. He denied ever saying the FBI had given his file to McCarthy and that he "wanted to execute a signed statement, make an affidavit, or confront the individual" saying he had.[61]

Just how desperate and scared Karr was is revealed by what he next told Nichols. Unburdening himself, and retreating from the bravado and bluster with which he had previously met charges of Communist connections, he admitted to Nichols that "he had been foolish; that in his ambitions to become a newspaperman he had done things that were uncalled for and which he wouldn't do today; that the fact remained that he had given aid and comfort to Communists and Communist front groups years ago; that he had a tremendous obligation to the country to rectify this; that he would do anything, go any place, make any sacrifice to discharge his obligation to his country. He made quite an impassioned plea." Nichols impassively told Karr just to "tell the truth and be a good citizen." After years of falsely claiming to have been an FBI informant, Karr then offered the Bureau his services: "if at any time anything arose wherein we wanted something done to call on him and he would do it. I told him I did not know of anything at the moment but we would keep it in mind."[62]

Senator McCarthy kept hammering David Karr and Drew Pearson in 1951, but somewhat less venomously than in his earlier attacks. After Pearson published a decoded intelligence summary, in paraphrase, he claimed that he had Army permission to do so. The Army denied it. On January 22, McCarthy drew a parallel with the Hiss case: "Someone," he said, "is delivering secrets to David Karr, a named Communist, and Drew Pearson, who has long been doing the smear work for the Communist Party." In April, McCarthy said he had affidavits from people on Pearson's staff that Pearson knew about Karr's Communist past and that Karr was so important a Communist, someone in the American government had shown Pearson Karr's FBI file.[63]

Karr figured someone at the FBI was leaking to McCarthy. On January 27, he went back to Nichols with a copy of a report quoting from an FBI report on Karr that should not have been available to the person quoting it. Nichols defensively noted that both the OWI and the Civil Service Commission had copies of the earlier FBI reports. So, one of them must have been the source of the leak. Karr accepted this. When the FBI checked, both excerpts came from reports disseminated to the Kerr Committee, Army G-2, the Interdepartmental Committee on Employee Investigation, the OWI, and the State Department. Karr gave Nichols an affidavit from Lowell Wakefield, his old collaborator on the *Daily Worker*, in support of his benign story of his *Daily Worker* career. But it must have been obvious by then that Karr would never be able to put the Communist genie back in the bottle, unless he either admitted to having been a Communist, or publicly apologized, along the lines of what he had asserted to Nichols on January 5. He'd never be able to outrun his past. After McCarthy's dramatics, the FBI concluded that "in view of the fact no information has been received indicating that Karr has been active in connection with CP activities during the past ten years, it is not believed that we have sufficient evidence on which to consider Karr for inclusion in the Security Index... We do not have any allegation of espionage." It would be nearly two years before the FBI would again evince any interest in David Karr.[64]

3

PUBLIC RELATIONS FLACK

David Karr's government career at the Office of War Information and his work as a legman for Drew Pearson blew up over the Communist issue that was now consuming Washington, D.C. Karr had already moved back to New York when McCarthy started naming him. It was here where his flirtation with Communism had begun. Work in advertising would, he no doubt hoped, involve less public notoriety.

William Weintraub had started his advertising company in 1941. He recruited a number of men who would become legends in the industry, notably Bill Bernbach, who left to create Doyle, Dayne, Bernbach in 1949, Paul Rand, an art director and graphic designer who later created famous corporate logos for IBM, UPS, and ABC, and the improbably named Norman B. Norman, who eventually purchased Weintraub and renamed it Norman, Craig and Kummel. Karr's job was to set up a public relations arm. Among his clients were Kaiser-Frazier, Food Fair, Schenley Industries, and Anchor Hocking Glass.

It is a testimony to his charm that Karr enjoyed close relationships with Henry Kaiser, the powerful shipbuilding industrialist who established Kaiser Permanente to provide health care for his employees, and Lewis Rosenstiel, the head of Schenley Industries, one of the largest liquor companies in America, and a man with not a scintilla of sympathy for left-wing politics. Rosenstiel, born in Cincinnati, had worked in his family's small distillery in Kentucky in the 1920s. He bought another distillery in Schenley, Pennsylvania, that was licensed to make medicinal whiskey; with the end of Prohibition, Schenley was well-positioned to benefit from a surge in liquor sales, gobbling up smaller competitors and becoming one of the four major American liquor companies.[1]

As he became a tycoon, Rosenstiel faced continuing scrutiny for shady associations, an occupational hazard for men whose product was so involved with organized crime during Prohibition. He had made a fortune during that era dealing with bootleggers. Throughout his life he faced accusations that he was connected to mobsters such as Frank Costello and Meyer Lansky. To protect his interests and reputation, Rosenstiel cultivated ties with influential politicians and law enforcement officials. He contributed substantial sums to a foundation honoring J. Edgar Hoover, hired Hoover's aide, Lou Nichols, to work at Schenley in 1957, and supported the American Jewish League Against Communism, founded in 1948 by a New York rabbi, Benjamin Schultz, later a vociferous supporter of Senator McCarthy, whose chief aide, Roy Cohn, served on its board and was a close friend of Rosenstiel's.

In later years, Rosenstiel's fourth ex-wife, Susan Kaufman, sensationally charged that her husband had taken her to a party at New York's Plaza Hotel in 1958, where Cohn introduced her to Hoover who was "wearing a fluffy black dress...lace stockings and high heels, and a black curly wig." Hoover haters gleefully retailed the claim that the FBI director was a gay cross-dresser and that organized criminals kept embarrassing photographs they had used to blackmail Hoover into minimizing their presence in American life. Kaufman wasn't the most reliable of witnesses; she and Lewis had had a very nasty divorce in which Hoover had supplied damaging information about her, and she had been convicted of perjury for lying about her ex-husband's ties to organized crime. Destitute, she had been paid by the author of the book where her charges appeared.

Rosenstiel was, however, close to Cohn, whether or not they were lovers as Kaufman alleged. While Rosenstiel was dying in a Florida hospital in 1975, Cohn entered his room, placed a pen in his hand, and moved it to stimulate a signature to a codicil to his will that made Cohn a trustee and executor of his estate. The codicil was voided by a judge and the episode led to Cohn's being disbarred in 1986, shortly before his own death from AIDS.[2]

A significant part of Karr's income came from his work representing Schenley Industries, his largest account at Weintraub, and it remained his main source of fees at the firm he formed after leaving Weintraub, Market Relations Network. His personal relationship with Rosenstiel was the key to his financial well-being. Schenley paid Weintraub $36,000 a year for Karr's services and one Christmas even gave him "a small override on some oil wells," oil and gas leases that turned up in Karr's will years later, though it is impossible to tell if they generated any income. Rosenstiel enjoyed Karr's company and brought him along on cruises on his yacht and vacations in Palm Beach, San Francisco, and New Orleans. Karr fondly recalled that he "mined that gold for years."[3]

Rosenstiel couldn't have missed the fact that two of his closest confidants, Cohn and Hoover, detested Karr and considered him a Communist. Cohn's animus was enhanced by the fact that Karr was a fellow Jew who had supported Communism. Yet, despite his conservative politics and his friendship with several of Karr's most implacable enemies, Rosenstiel's confidence in Karr seemed unwavering.

As usual with David Karr, accounts of his time at Weintraub diverge wildly. As Karr would have it, the company's billings rose from $4.5 million in 1948 to $22 million by the time he left in September 1953, "principally due to [his] efforts." His salary allegedly jumped from $25,000 a year to nearly $50,000 and he held a 10 percent stock interest in the company. His resignation had been prompted by "policy differences with the principals." Others presented a far different picture. One principal interviewed for a confidential report in 1956, a high-ranking Weintraub employee, "bitterly denounced Karr in most emphatic terms," saying he "did not bring in anything near the total volume of advertising" that he claimed. In fact, he had secured only one account, whose business did increase. He had purchased only 2 to 3 percent of the company stock, which was sold back when he left the agency, at which time his salary was only $35,000 a year.[4]

Embellishing his salary or job accomplishments was nothing new for Karr. His coworkers at Weintraub, however, were scathing about his character. The anonymous principal interviewed in 1956 portrayed "Karr in a most unsavory and despicable light. It is the contention of this informant that he is absolutely untrustworthy, and that no confidence should be reposed in him." Described as someone with "a brilliant mind," Karr had managed to bamboozle his superiors for years. Eventually, his "machinations as an executive of the agency were such that when the full import" was realized, "he was summarily fired." Karr himself wrote in a book published in 1956 that during proxy fights, which bring out "the worst in men," both management and insurgents hired detectives to rummage around in the private lives of their foes and wiretap their private conversations. He presented these activities as part of the normal course of doing business, the implication being that he had often done so while doing public relations for both sides.[5]

Many years later, long after Karr's death, Norman B. Norman, one of the legendary figures in American advertising, recalled him as a loathsome and amoral scoundrel. Karr and Norman had joined the Weintraub agency about the same time. Norman might well have been the anonymous source from 1956, because he claimed in an interview in 1990 that he had personally caught Karr engaged in blackmail, confronted him, and gotten him thrown out of Weintraub. Karr, he recollected, pretended to be friendly with other account executives only to try to "glom" on to their clients—he had unsuccessfully sought to steal the Revlon account from Norman. Norman charged that Karr would offer to provide prostitutes to people, and then arrange to have detectives break into their hotel room to take pictures. With a straight face, Karr would then proceed to offer his help in getting the victim off the hook. He took payoffs and blackmailed people. Norman denounced Karr in colorful terms—"a vicious, vile scoundrel who worked both ends against the middle, an inveterate liar, a fat slob, a devil, a twisted sick mind, a loathsome worm, a hollow drum, an evil son-of-a-bitch." The only good thing about David Karr "was that he died young." What he was not, Norman recalled, was a Communist. Karr "wasn't anything. He was a Baron Munchausen who wiggled his way in and used and exploited people," a fixer and manipulator.[6]

George Biderman, a longtime public relations executive, worked with Karr in the early 1950s to promote a book published by Bantam, where he was then employed. He recalled a "wheeler-dealer of the first order, an exploiter and opportunist," someone "not honest. Very devious and shifty." He "could be charming but could also be an overbearing bully. When dealing with clients he was always charming." He "snapped a lot at his secretary" and "was very rough" with his very left-wing subordinate, Christopher Cross. Cross had lost his previous job with the United Nations after allegations of being a Communist. At Weintraub, he "did the dog-work and the writing" on Karr's accounts. Cross himself despised Karr, thought him a "twit" who lacked talent and "always seemed to be a will of the wisp."[7]

Nor could Karr entirely escape the Communism issue at Weintraub. McCarthy leveled his charges while he was working in New York. In 1952, a congressional committee investigated the Katyn Massacre, when Soviet forces shot more than fifteen thousand Polish officers. The Nazis had uncovered the bodies as they advanced into formerly Soviet-occupied areas in 1943. With both Nazis and Communists blaming each other for the massacre, the OWI was reluctant to acknowledge that an American ally could be guilty. Critics charged that the Foreign Language Division called meetings at which anti-Communists were pressured to tone down their attacks on the Soviet Union, brandishing threats of losing their broadcast licenses. Alan Cranston was present at one such meeting in Detroit, after which an anti-Communist commentator was taken off the air and a pro-Communist one retained. Cranston lamely argued that it was government policy to avoid criticism of allies and pled poor memory about the meeting. The congressmen grilled Cranston about Communist influence in his unit, repeatedly bringing up David Karr. Cranston stoutly defended his old friend, denying that he had ever been a Communist.[8]

Karr's wife's activities then provoked another attack from Westbrook Pegler. In 1953, Madeline Karr and Dale Kramer co-authored a new book on juvenile crime, *Teen-Age Gangs*, with a forward by Senator Estes Kefauver. Kramer was a onetime Communist and writer for the *New Masses*. Pegler denounced the pair—and David—and threw in a variety of made-up charges, including the claim that both Karrs had worked for the *Daily Worker* and that Madeline's Greek-American newspaper followed the Communist Party line.[9]

Karr's status at Weintraub became increasingly precarious. Perhaps it wearied of the steady drumbeat of allegations that Karr was a Communist operative, or, more likely, of the poisonous work environment he seemed to leave in his wake. Karr may have chafed at restrictions that came from working in a company he could not control. By the beginning of 1953 Karr had set up two new public relations firms, David Karr Associates and Market Relations Network. According to Karr, he had fifteen clients, five of whom were listed on the New York Stock Exchange. One was Schenley Industries. Rosenstiel continued to pay Karr the $36,000 he had been giving to Weintraub. Among Karr's other early clients were United Artists, Dreyfus & Co., Food Fair Stores, American President Lines, and Hazel Bishop Cosmetics. Among the services he boasted of providing was counsel to top management on expansion policy, evaluation of strategic market forces, developing competitive strategies, and conducting private opinion polls on new products. Between them, Karr's two firms grossed about $240,000 in 1954. In another interview Karr claimed gross sales of $100,000 in 1954, $250,000 in 1955, and anticipated revenue of $400,000 in 1956. His new ventures were largely one-man operations, operated, at least initially, out of his apartment.[10]

But his past connections to Communism continued to intrude. Early in 1954, both he and Madeline sat down for numerous interviews with attorneys for Drew Pearson, who had filed a lawsuit against Joe McCarthy, Westbrook Pegler, and nine other people, charging them with conspiracy to drive him out of business. Pearson was asking for $5.1 million in damages. The Karrs went over their respective backgrounds in great detail, including their alleged Communist ties. Once again, David threw a family member under the bus. At one of these sessions, he mentioned a "family rumor" that his sister Florence, known as Feenie, had followed the Communist line until 1952; Madeline added that Feenie had gotten into trouble at college due to her political activities. David claimed he had seen her only a few times over fifteen years—apart from several meetings after their father's death. He attributed their coldness to her "nasty left-wing attitudes."[11]

As he prepared to set up his own business, Karr knew that his past history and reputation was a public relations problem that might hurt his ability to obtain clients. His solution was to partner with someone with an impeccable record of patriotism and rectitude. His candidate was Major-General C. T. (Buck) Lanham. A West Point graduate, class of 1924, Lanham was a much-decorated WWII hero, wounded at Normandy. After the war he served as Chief of the Information and Education Division at the Pentagon and as a special assistant to General

Omar Bradley. He was Dwight Eisenhower's Chief of Public Information when Ike led NATO. In January 1953, he became commanding officer of the First Infantry Division, the "Big Red One," before returning to the United States in June 1954 as Deputy Commandant of the Armed Forces Staff College in Norfolk.

Lanham had first met Karr in 1945 while working at the Pentagon. The brash young newsman barged into his office, announced that Pearson was writing a critical column on Lanham and he had "eleven minutes to give" him to respond to allegations about the agency he was overseeing. Lanham pushed back, earning Karr's respect, but remained wary of him. Karr, he later complained, is "an unctuous, moonfaced individual...very belligerent." Despite this unpromising beginning, they became friendly. Before Lanham's departure for Europe in 1949, Karr cultivated him. Lanham wound up concluding that Karr was "honest, forthright and a goddamned good American citizen." Westbrook Pegler, who knew Lanham, warned him about Karr in 1952 and 1953, particularly in light of Lanham's close relationship with Eisenhower, but in 1954 Lanham wrote Karr that he was "well aware of the Pegler smears and have written them off."[12]

Lanham's background in handling the press, his command experience supervising large, complex organizations, his sterling reputation, and, not least, his friendly ties to the president of the United States made him a prize catch. William Weintraub, in fact, had discussed hiring him as far back as 1947. In April 1954, visiting Lanham in Germany, Weintraub dangled "a position where I would be next in line, so to speak, with a head man of a very big organization, that my duties in such a job would be to handle and coordinate the staff, and to handle the personal public relations of the head man." Although he remained friends with Weintraub, Lanham understood and supported Karr's desire to leave, and preferred to join forces with him. In one gushing note to Karr after Karr had visited him in Germany, Lanham rhapsodized that his "brilliant analytical mind cranks me up as nothing else in this sorry world ever has." After another Karr visit to Germany in 1954 and further courting of the general at his post in Norfolk, Lanham agreed to join Market Relations Network. Lanham later told Westbrook Pegler that Karr "got down on his knees" and "swore that he had never been a Communist or had Communist connections." Lanham was convinced that Karr was "as clean as that famous hound's tooth," and with an impressive roster of "devoted friends," that included "former cabinet members, presidential candidates, senators, congressmen, governors, industrialists, civic leaders."[13]

The courtship paid off. Lanham and Karr signed a contract on October 5, 1954, that Lanham would resign from the military and join Market Relations Network (MRN) in January as president and director of the company, receiving 25 percent of the gross income of all new business, once the firm's receipts went above $155,000 a year, and a bonus of 10 percent of gross profits once they went above $120,000, and favorable terms enabling him to buy 50 percent of the company for $1 if Karr died. A press release announcing the hiring was sent out on December 1.[14]

Lanham told more than a hundred friends of his new job. He wrote Karr that an unnamed friend had warned him about Karr, but he swore his loyalty: "If we fuck up we fuck up together. If we climb to glory we climb together. If you are smeared we are smeared together." Very conscious of his own reputation for integrity, Lanham was heartened when Karr turned down a contract to do public relations work for General Analine. Because it had been owned by the German conglomerate I.G. Farben (which manufactured Zyklon B gas used in Auschwitz), the U.S. government had seized the company during the war and for nearly a decade its ownership had been tied up by conflicting court claims and a decision by the Alien Property Board. Lanham told Karr that "I hope that we will always turn down anything that smacks of skullduggery... You know me well enough to know that I would damned-sight rather sell apples on a street corner than be involved in anything that even indirectly might dirty my name and my reputation for truth and honesty."[15]

It didn't take General Lanham long to realize that he had made a very big mistake in judgment. When he started working in January, MRN received a jolt of energy, opening an office in Washington and appointing Jackson Leighter as vice president for the West Coast. Leighter was a veteran newsman and copywriter who had overseen FDR's 1940 presidential campaign in Hollywood. He had partnered with Orson Welles and worked for Rita Hayworth's production company before joining Schenley Industries in 1952. He had also helped Karr organize the Friendship Train before joining MRN in 1953. Later, he followed Karr to Fairbanks Whitney where he served as international vice president. Lanham told Leighter in early February 1955 that several promising contracts were in the works. He did, however, make one disturbing reference to Karr. Always high-strung and energetic, Karr had been having trouble sleeping. He was also seeing three different doctors for unspecified issues; "he's been wound up so damned tight that he's having a hell of a time getting unwound."[16]

Early in March, Lanham announced a reorganization of the office staff—three secretaries, an accountant, switchboard operator, and three account executives. The memo hinted at tensions in the business, noting the need to "make a major effort in the future to deal with each other politely, courteously and considerately. No one likes to work in an atmosphere poisoned by personality clashes, suspicion, distrust and an array of long faces. Let's make MRN an organization of laughter, wise cracks and good will." For Lanham, however, the bloom was quickly coming off the rose. In mid-March, Major Chester Hansen, a former aide to General Bradley whom he had recruited to join MRN, backed out of his agreement, citing the stability of the company. It was too dependent on its one big contract with Schenley and that left it unable to turn down unsuitable clients—at least one of which it already represented.[17]

Lanham's relationship with Karr had also changed dramatically almost as soon as they began working together. After being courted for so long, Lanham discovered that Karr wasn't the type to collaborate with equals. He liked giving orders and having them obeyed. In late April, Lanham was sufficiently aggrieved to write a memo that at a meeting that morning Karr had "elaborated on the role I was to play henceforth." Less than two weeks later Lanham angrily wrote that "Dave laid out the following schedule for me during the week." By May, already determined to quit, Lanham said that he had begun to make contributions to MRN, citing his renegotiation of one contract, signing up another new client, and the favorable publicity the company attracted when he joined. These accomplishments, he noted, clearly outweighed his $2,000-a-month salary.[18]

Lanham wrote a formal letter of resignation on May 27. He claimed, "I have found myself in deep and vital disagreement with you in areas ranging from office management and the retention of certain personnel up to and including policy. In addition, our personal relationship has progressively deteriorated largely as a result of these differences. Quarrels between us have become increasingly frequent...our relationship that began as an association of equals has long since ceased to be that; it has degenerated into boss and hired hand." Karr responded the same day, regretting that things had not worked out.[19]

While preparing an article on Karr for *Fortune* in 1961, Spencer Klaw contacted Lanham, who by this time was once again embroiled with his former partner. Lanham adamantly refused to comment about Karr, other than to deny rumors Klaw had heard that "you just weren't cutting the mustard," or that he was angry at a burlesque spoof of him written by one of Karr's associates, or that he objected to Karr's treatment of Leopold Silberstein in the last half of the 1950s. But Lanham did tell lawyer J. Anthony Panuch, who represented both he and Karr, that the breach was "for reasons at least as grave ethically" as one could imagine and that they were serious enough that he was willing to endure considerable financial losses; it had "cost me something over half of my meager life savings." He reiterated the ethics issue to Arthur Sulzberger of the *New York Times*: "My ethical concept was repeatedly outraged and I would not accept it." He ruefully compared his relationship with Karr to a marriage; that there is a lot of courting and a belief that you know your spouse, but until the actual marriage, "do we really know the person we are married to?" And, to Westbrook Pegler, who had warned him repeatedly about Karr, he confessed that the job was "a fiasco. Within two months, I decided that I had made a hell of an error...By the end of four months, I had learned enough to realize that I could not allow my name to be associated with this particular enterprise. I have made my share of errors in the fifty-three years I have inhabited this incredible world of ours, but I truly believe that this was the worst...I suppose that I am the perfect sucker type...I was certain that the guy with whom I was so briefly associated was all that he purported to be."[20]

Karr's blow-up with Lanham was exacerbated by turmoil in his personal life, which was in shambles. He and Madeline had separated in late 1954, their marriage badly strained by his affair with one of his employees. Fighting over the disposition of his assets, seeing a psychiatrist, and struggling to establish his business, David destroyed his long-sought partnership with Lanham within just a few months.

On the surface, Karr was polite and regretful about the quick collapse of a partnership and friendship in which he had invested a great
deal of hope. After fifteen months without any contact, he sent Lanham
a copy of his new book, *Fight for Control*, and acknowledged him in its
pages. He even offered a mea culpa, admitting that "I have long owed
you an apology and a prayer for forgiveness." Karr blamed medical and
emotional problems for his behavior, admitted that he had been "a disturbed person," and vowed that in the last fifteen months there had been
"profound, deep, major and basic changes in me and my way of life."
He felt guilty for what "now in retrospect must have been one of the
cruelest personal experiences in your life." Lanham did not respond.[21]

Panuch later reproached Lanham because Karr "practically went
down on his knees to you and wrote an abject letter of apology, to which
you didn't even reply." In Karr's defense, Panuch noted that at the time
he "was desperate for dough . . . in a knock-down and drag out fight"
with his wife over terms of a divorce, and "under psychiatric treatment."
Lanham was not assuaged: "The question of head doctors, Madeline
and the alleged lack of dough had nothing to do with his activities, his
double and triple crosses, his concealment and distortion, and his pathological lies. I will never accept any of this, all of which I know in detail,
as pleas either in extenuation or mitigation." Lanham added that ever
since their break, he had heard from friends that Karr had alternated
between threats—"I will destroy him if it takes ten years"—to boasts of
control—"I can have him back with me by snapping my fingers." He
then issued his own threat: "He better Goddamned sight not try any
fancy footwork with me from here on out. And that's a plain, country,
bare-footed warning."[22]

In July 1955, shortly after his blow-up with Lanham, Karr applied
to renew his passport in preparation for a trip to France on behalf of
the Schenley liquor company. The Passport Office consulted the FBI
and then notified Karr that it was denying his request on the grounds
of his past support of the Communist movement. In accordance with
procedure, it then submitted the issue to the State Department's Office
of Security. That September, Karr's attorney, J. Anthony Panuch, the
former Deputy Assistant Secretary of State who had headed the Security
Office after World War II where he had tried to oust numerous employees suspected of Communist sympathies, intervened and obtained a

hearing for his client. Karr and Panuch met with Ashley Nichols; Karr denied ever being a Communist and pleaded that he had been stalling the Schenley company but needed the passport to conduct his business. Advised to prepare an affidavit, he mailed a forty-nine-page document to the Passport Office on September 30, along with thirty-seven exhibits.[23]

The affidavit was both conciliatory and exculpatory. Karr acknowledged the government's right to control the issuance of passports and provided an entirely benign history of his relationship with Communism, once again denying not only Party membership, but even sympathy for the Communist cause. He conceded that his association with the *Daily Worker*, "in the light of the political history of the intervening 17 years," had been "a mistake of judgment." He excused himself because of his youth, inexperience, lack of higher education, and the fact that he had "no knowledge of or experience with the Communist Party or the Communist movement, much less with its ideology and techniques of revolutionary subversion." He provided a truncated list of the articles he had written, and affidavits from Lowell Wakefield and Dixon Stewart supporting his claim that his associations with Communists had all been in the service of writing news stories about fascists and subversives. Karr repeated these claims about his work for *The Hour*. He linked his troubles with Congressman Dies solely to his connection with the *Daily Worker* and pointed to his clearance by Congressman Anderson and his resignation from the OWI to avoid embarrassment to the agency. Asked by the State Department to detail his relationships with a number of people, he explained that he knew some but not others. He had not known that Albert Kahn was a Communist when he worked for him, knew several Communist reporters, had been friendly with Harry Dexter White, whom he had no reason to suspect was a Soviet source, had used David Wahl, Philip Jaffe, Andrew Roth, Emmanuel Larsen, and John Service (the last four involved with the Amerasia case) as sources, and did not know Irving Kaplan, Duncan Lee, or Harry Magdoff, all of whom had been named by Elizabeth Bentley as Soviet sources. He said that in 1950 Lee Pressman had consulted him before he was to appear before the House Committee on Un-American Activities and confessed to having been a Communist. Karr claimed he had advised Pressman to "name names" and that he got the impression from Pressman that he could name the Hiss brothers as members of his Party cell in the 1930s.

He proudly noted that he had "reported the Pressman incident in its entirety to Lou Nichols of the FBI when I was in Washington." Karr also included a long list of people named in congressional hearings as Communists whom he denied having any knowledge of or acquaintance with. He closed with an avowal of his loyalty, emphasizing his work on the Friendship Train as an example of his willingness to work against Communism. The glittering list of politicians and industrialists whom Karr listed as willing to endorse his patriotism included future New York Senator Jacob Javits and Senator Clinton Anderson, and executives of both the Schenley and Kaiser companies.[24]

The FBI, which quickly obtained a copy of the affidavit, was not impressed. Nichols emphatically denied that Karr had ever told him the Pressman story. He belittled the statement, saying, "I have never trusted him." J. Edgar Hoover wrote Frances Knight of the Passport Office in early November that a search of FBI records failed to substantiate that Karr had mentioned Pressman in any of his meetings with the FBI. But it was too late. Knight had already told Panuch that it appeared that Karr "has covered most of the matters" in question. At an informal hearing on October 13, Karr was granted his passport.[25]

Buoyed by this sign that he might finally have put his political past to rest, Karr was also bolstered by the presence of a new woman in his life. He met Elizabeth Rappleye, known as Buffy, in the spring of 1955 on a blind date. A tall, statuesque beauty, she came from an entirely different social world than David Katz from Brooklyn. Born in 1925 in New Haven, where her father was the medical administrator of the hospital, she had grown up in luxury. Her father traced his roots to Huguenots who arrived in America in the 1600s. Her mother was a New York debutante. Buffy enjoyed a privileged upbringing, summering in Maine, attending prep school, and then graduating from Vassar. Her father served as commissioner of hospitals in New York under Fiorello LaGuardia and for decades as dean of the medical school at Columbia University, where he became good friends with Dwight Eisenhower. The family were pillars of the Episcopal Church.[26]

After a brief fling at acting, Rappleye married Alfred Clark, an heir to the Singer Sewing Machine Company in 1948. An OSS veteran, Alfred had transferred into the CIA. The marriage quickly foundered (Alfred accumulated six wives during his brief life), but her father-in-law set up a generous trust fund for her, enabling her to travel to Europe frequently over the next several years. David's divorce was not yet final when they met in 1955; he proposed after it was finalized, and they married in May of 1956. Her parents were less than pleased; her father was an anti-Semite. Many of her friends expressed reservations. But Buffy found Karr both fascinating and exotic—"I was his blond shiksa."[27]

In retrospect, Buffy saw signs that life with David Karr would not be a smooth ride. Before their marriage he insisted she see his psychiatrist to make sure she loved him. Told by the doctor that David could be dangerous if he was not under psychological monitoring, she rationalized that she would be able to make him happy. When her two new stepchildren would visit, David would "spoil them rotten" so that they would return to their mother "as spoiled and cranky children," then explain that it would be "Madeline's problem." Even David's brother, Mort, known as Skippy, asked her during their engagement, "if I was scared to marry David, at which I laughed uproariously." But, for the first several years of their marriage, such concerns did not intrude. Life as Mrs. David Karr was exciting and interesting. They lived on the top three floors of a Manhattan townhouse and bought a summer retreat on Long Island. A daughter, Lisa, was born in 1957 and a son, Frank, followed in 1959.[28]

Before having her children, Buffy worked at Market Relations Network. It was about to evolve from a small firm largely dependent on its contract with Schenley Industries into a significant player in a relatively new corner of American business life, coordinating public relations as part of proxy wars for control of public corporations. The specialty David Karr would develop held significant ramifications for his own future and, ironically, for General Buck Lanham. Despite the raw feelings left from their abortive collaboration, Karr and Lanham were destined to find themselves unfriendly allies in a corporate war in which Karr's old Communist connections were raised yet again.

While there had always been contentious battles for control of the stock of public corporations, proxy wars reached a peak in the 1950s, transfixing millions of Americans. During the Depression of the 1930s and the all-out industrial mobilization of World War II, struggles to control companies had receded. With corporate profits soaring amid the prosperity of the postwar years and more money available to finance battles for control, a series of high-profile fights broke out. None was as expensive or drew as much attention as Robert Young's war for control over the New York Central Railroad. This battle gave David Karr an idea.

Young was a wealthy Texas maverick. During the 1940s he had become chairman of the Allegheny Corporation, which controlled the Chesapeake and Ohio Railroad. In 1947, he began running a series of advertisements that slyly criticized the management of the NY Central, one of the giants of the railroad industry. Built by Commodore Vanderbilt, NY Central was the second largest railroad in the United States, with ninety thousand employees and more than $2.6 billion in assets. In addition to an extensive series of rail lines, it owned several elite New York hotels, as well as the land under the Waldorf-Astoria Hotel.

Despite its size, it had significant amounts of debt and its profits had lagged for several years. Young noted that few of the directors—many being executives of large banks—held much stock in the company. He charged that the company was being operated to benefit the banks, not the shareholders, pointing out its dismal record of paying dividends. By 1954, when he launched his public bid for control, Young and his allies held about 3 percent of the stock, making him the largest single shareholder.

Whereas most previous fights for corporate control by proxy fight had been conducted below the public radar, Young launched a media blitz. He spent more than $1.3 million, hired nearly a hundred people, many specialists in public relations, gave countless interviews, appeared on radio and television, and issued a barrage of press releases. He lobbied government regulators to issue rulings favorable to his effort, courted labor leaders, and solicited statements of support from prominent politicians. He conducted the contest for proxy votes, many of them from small stockholders, as if he were running a political campaign. One of his employees was David Karr, who later wrote that "more than ever before, businessmen and financiers now saw the vital role played by public relations in a proxy fight." Young's slate swept to victory in a May meeting.[29]

Intrigued by what he had witnessed, Karr wrote a book about proxy wars (actually, it was ghostwritten by Henry Hillman, who worked for MRN). *Fight for Control* recounted a number of the corporate proxy wars of the 1940s and 1950s, assessing the various tactics used by both raiders and management. Its theme was that success was linked to being both adaptable and ruthless. Contestants had to consider carefully the timing of their appeals, the particular allies they recruited and used, and the tactics they deployed, making sure that they fit the audience whose support they wished to attract. Proxy fighting "requires intense concentration, perpetual devotion to large and small details and the constitution of a horse." But beyond the skills and focus that were necessary, so too was a willingness to play dirty. Success often depended on getting personal, attacking the background, character, and motives of opponents. "Potent whispering campaigns" linking the other side to organized crime, financial malfeasance, or ruthless self-aggrandizement were evaluated on their efficacy rather than morality. Describing the notorious and mysterious businessman Serge Rubinstein, later found strangled to death, Karr gleefully recounted how Rubinstein had planted a bug in his girlfriend's mattress, listened in to her amorous adventures, and used his own notoriety to coerce someone into a deal by threatening to publicly claim that he and his target were collaborators.[30]

Several comments in the book eerily foreshadowed Karr's own future. He could have been describing himself when he wrote of Rubinstein: "This ambitious young man was on his way to a career which threaded its way through five continents, scores of corporations, and financial screen plays so well marked that even after he died all the pieces could not be brought into focus." Describing one battle for control of a movie studio, he noted that in Hollywood "money is discussed and paid out with an abandon that is likely to horrify practitioners of other arts." It was inevitable that "this ambitious young man" would one day make his way to such a world. And, it is no surprise that according to his wife his "Bible" was Machiavelli's *The Prince*.[31]

This next phase of Karr's life took place in boardrooms and banks. He parlayed his experience working on Robert Young's public relations team to emulate Young, albeit on a smaller scale. From working for others, Dave Karr embarked on a journey that would lead him to the top of a major American corporation. It was a heady and audacious trip for a man who had barely graduated from high school, made his reputation as a sharp-elbowed reporter, and had no experience in finance or manufacturing. But he had a genius for marketing and image making, a drive and ambition second to none, and few moral scruples about tactics.

His transition from hired gun to principal in the takeover wars required a partnership and Karr found the ideal collaborator in the fall of 1956 when he met Alfonso Landa at Drew Pearson's home. Known as Art, Landa, born in 1897 in Chicago into a prominent American Hispanic family, had dabbled in a variety of fields and schools into the 1920s, earning a reputation as "an accomplished playboy." He briefly attended Valparaiso, West Virginia, and Northwestern Universities (where his efforts to study medicine foundered on his inability to bear the sight of blood). He briefly studied under Freud in Vienna but opted not to pursue a career in psychoanalysis and abandoned the idea of becoming a playwright after a very brief stint at Yale. He finally earned a law degree at Georgetown University in 1925. While vacationing in Europe the next year, he met and became close to Joseph Davies, FDR's future ambassador to the Soviet Union, and future husband of Marjorie Merriweather Post, heiress to a cereal fortune. Davies was a prominent and successful lawyer in Washington, and he hired Landa to join his firm, Davies, Richberg, Beebe, Busick and Richardson (which years later became Davies, Richberg, Tydings and Landa).[32]

Landa quickly moved into the upper reaches of Washington politics and society, raising large amounts of cash for FDR and other Democrats, socializing with Harry Hopkins, marrying a Morgan heiress, and serving as lawyer for Louisiana demagogue Huey Long, IBM chair Tom Watson, Hollywood impresario Louis Mayer, and Wall Street heiress Barbara Hutton. He was particularly close to Maryland Senator Millard Tydings, who later became a partner in his law firm. By the early 1950s, Landa decided that he could make far more money in industry than he could working for others as a lawyer or fixer. Shortly after he agreed to take a seat on the board of Colonial Airlines, a longtime client, the Civil Aeronautics Board forced the resignation of its boss and in 1951 Art Landa assumed its presidency. The experience whetted his appetite for the corporate world.[33]

The issue of Communism in Karr's past did not put off Landa. His own mentor, Davies, had swallowed Stalin's account of the Soviet purge trials while serving as ambassador and faithfully echoed his absurd claim that the defendants had conspired with Germany and Japan to dismember the U.S.S.R. *Mission to Moscow*, his credulous account, was made into a Hollywood movie during the war to bolster American support for its Russian ally. By 1950, Davies was widely derided and denounced by anti-Communists; Landa, however, remained a close friend and shrugged off the attacks.

Landa's career had not been without its own share of controversy. Described by one journalist as "a hard man to push around," he always seemed "to gravitate toward fights and feuds, and often had several of them going at once." Married four times, he had been taken to court in 1956 by his third wife, Consuelo Morgan Landa, who was seeking $3,000 a month maintenance, amid charges that he had carried on a torrid affair with Alexandra Francesco, referred to in the newspapers as Madame X, in Europe, New York, and Florida. A congressional committee in 1952 had linked him to payoffs by four major liquor manufacturers—including Karr's employer, Schenley—to the Democratic National Committee to thwart an anti-trust prosecution. And when private investigators hired by Penn-Texas management, the prime target of the Karr-Landa alliance, looked for dirt on Landa, they found Sigmund Janas, former president of Colonial Airlines, ready and willing to spatter his former lawyer with a host of charges.[34]

According to Janas, he had installed Landa as president in name only, intending, with Landa's agreement, to return to the office as soon as his spat with the Civil Aeronautics Board was settled. Instead, Landa had conspired with the board of directors to depose him permanently. The investigators recognized that Janas had "a tremendous amount of animosity toward Landa." Janas claimed that he had given the House Committee on Un-American Activities a statement that during a visit to Bermuda, "under the influence of a few drinks," Landa had told Janas and his wife that "he had been instrumental in arranging for the murderer of Trotsky" for money. In their words, "Landa also claimed that he had assisted in the arrangement for the murder of Trotsky and that he had for some time been an intermediary for the passage of Communist funds." Janas had declined, however, to testify to the committee, and the investigation had been quashed by the influence of Joseph Davies and Millard Tydings.[35]

If this improbable story lacked any evidence, Landa's dealings with the Fruehauf Trailer Company established his reputation as an innovator in the field of proxy wars who was willing to cut corners, and thus a kindred spirit to David Karr. A lawyer for Roy Fruehauf, head of the

Fruehauf trucking firm headquartered in Detroit, Landa guided the company through a nasty proxy fight orchestrated by George Kolowich, which began in 1953. A family spat had led one of the Fruehauf brothers, Harvey, alienated from the company, to sell a large bloc of his shares to the Detroit and Cleveland Navigation Company (D&C), owned by Kolowich, which, despite its name was exclusively a trucking company, having abandoned its earlier steamship operations on the Great Lakes. Kolowich demanded a seat on the board of trustees and was refused, allegedly because of a long-ago conviction for embezzlement. This led him to begin buying more stock on the open market in preparation for a proxy raid.

Landa, a member of the Fruehauf board, hit upon a unique strategy, one destined to become his signature, for thwarting the raid. He decided to shift the terrain, by launching an attack on Kolowich's control over his own company. He contacted Robert Young, then embroiled in his own effort to take over the New York Central, to point out that federal regulators at the Interstate Commerce Committee would look askance at the Allegheny Corporation's 15 percent stake in the D&C, and persuaded him to sell that stock to Fruehauf and Landa. To forestall the possibility that Kolowich might issue more stock to dilute their shares, Landa persuaded the ICC that the D&C was in violation of rules forbidding cross-ownership of transportation companies since it owned both a trucking company and a steamship line. Kolowich promptly gave up his steamship certificate—which he was not using anyway—only to discover that Landa then persuaded the Securities and Exchange Commission that the D&C's only substantial asset was its shares in Fruehauf, meaning that it was an investment company. That meant that it was not allowed to increase the number of its shares without authorization from shareholders. And Fruehauf and Landa, who had been buying D&C stock, had enough shares to block that possibility.

Since Kolowich was still buying Fruehauf shares, Landa and Fruehauf approached Dave Beck, the scandal-plagued head of the Teamsters Union, which represented Fruehauf drivers, who agreed to lend $1.5 million from its pension fund to a charitable foundation controlled by Fruehauf to buy company stock, both to keep it away from Kolowich and shore up the stock price, making Kolowich's purchases more expensive. A later congressional investigation turned up a letter from Landa written in December 1953 offering Beck half of the profits Landa made on the deal. In response to angry charges that this was an illegal kickback, Landa denied that the offer was ever accepted and said it merely showed his "very lively sense of appreciation." Still, the Committee concluded that he had "acted in a highly questionable manner."[36]

When the D&C held its annual meeting in April 1954, Kolowich, holding a slew of proxies favorable to management, discovered to his dismay that Landa had managed to capture more. Fruehauf and Landa took control of the D&C and sold off its assets, ending the threat to the Fruehauf Company and making a substantial profit for the two partners.

Art Landa's name was conspicuously missing from *Fight for Control*. But he could recognize a talented and creative proxy warrior with skills to supplement his own. After reading the book, he got in touch with Karr and suggested an alliance. Karr was enthusiastic, and he had a perfect target in mind for the new partnership—a company, Penn-Texas, and its president, Leopold Silberstein, whom he had recently assisted, but which now employed General Buck Lanham, fresh from the worst experience of his life—his partnership with David Karr.

The saga began in 1951, when a small, struggling company, Pennsylvania Coal and Coke, was taken over by Leopold Silberstein, a flamboyant refugee from Nazi Germany. Silberstein arrived in the United States in 1948 after a harrowing escape that had taken him from Amsterdam to Australia, Shanghai, Goa, and London, and set up a brokerage house that specialized in finding companies with wide differentials between their stock price and underlying value. By the spring of 1951 he had quietly bought up one quarter of the shares of Pennsylvania Coal and Coke Corporation, launched a campaign for proxies by complaining that shareholders were not receiving high enough dividends, and stunned management by ousting them at a stockholders' meeting. Within a year, he had turned the company's fortunes around. Silberstein took control of another industrial company developing oil and gas in Texas in 1953 and renamed his merged acquisitions the Penn-Texas Corporation.

Karr had first met Silberstein when the latter made a bid for control of Niles-Bement-Pond, a machine tools company. The company's owners tried to block him by arranging a friendly stock purchase of a substantial portion of Bell Aircraft to dilute Silberstein's shares. He, in turn, obtained an injunction blocking the purchase and, with Karr's help in directing a public relations campaign, won the ensuing proxy battle in 1955, capturing Niles-Bement-Pond and changing its name to Pratt and Whitney. Silberstein would continue to pursue other companies—between 1952 and 1956 he bought fourteen of them—increasing Penn-Texas's assets from $7 million to $125 million.[37]

Silberstein had been so impressed by Buck Lanham when he met him while he was still on active duty that after their second meeting, he offered him a job with Penn-Texas. Deciding instead to go to work for Karr, Lanham just as seriously misjudged the man who had put together the Penn-Texas empire as he did David Karr, writing Silberstein in late 1954 that "the way you put this burgeoning industrial empire together with little more than your naked brain is, to my mind, a business classic and certainly one that shall be studied in the fullness of time with respect and, I imagine, a certain degree of amazement." The day after he retired from the Army, just as he joined Karr's business, MRN, Lanham became a director of Penn-Texas. Silberstein immediately increased his retainer to MRN from $6,000 a year to $18,000. After quitting MRN, Lanham had considered starting another public relations firm but in July 1955, he went to work for Penn-Texas as a vice president, at a salary of $1,500 a month, tasked with creating a Washington office. Needless to say, Penn-Texas severed its contract with Market Relations Network. But neither Silberstein nor Lanham were finished with David Karr.[38]

His acquisition of Niles-Bement-Pond in 1955 did not slake Silberstein's ambition. His next target was Fairbanks, Morse and Company, which manufactured pumps, scales, and diesel engines. With $135 million in annual sales, Fairbanks, Morse was larger than the entire Penn-Texas empire. Like the Fruehauf company, Fairbanks, Morse was vulnerable due to conflicts among its family owners. Using Penn-Texas money borrowed from Swiss banks, Silberstein bought up enough stock from one elderly, disaffected brother of CEO Robert Morse to demand the chairmanship of either the executive committee or the finance committee. Morse refused. Instead, he hired a public relations firm that organized a campaign to portray Silberstein as "having some connection with the U.S.S.R.," persuaded Senator Olin Johnston of South Carolina to demand an investigation of his entry into the United States, and solicited nasty columns by Fulton Lewis, Jr. and Leslie Gould of the

New York Journal-American. He also tried to buy a Canadian locomotive company to dilute Silberstein's percentage of Fairbanks, Morse stock. Silberstein's effort to block that sale failed, but by March 1956 he had accumulated more than 400,000 proxies, enough to gain him four of eleven seats on the board of directors.[39]

Realizing that control of his company was slipping away, Robert Morse tried to bypass the board by creating a three-man executive committee with complete authority to run Fairbanks, Morse. He also hired Art Landa in late 1956 to repel his pesky corporate raider. Landa had just recently joined forces with David Karr. His new partner had parted company with Leopold Silberstein on unfriendly terms in 1955. Karr now advised Landa that Silberstein himself had vulnerabilities that could be exploited; he and his fellow directors held little Penn-Texas stock. Landa got in touch with Morse, who agreed to finance a proxy fight against Silberstein. Landa had developed the tactic of raiding the raider; he now turned his expertise on Leopold Silberstein and inaugurated one of the messiest proxy wars of the decade.

The battles that ensued featured accusations of fraud and financial irregularities, predictably dredged up Karr's Communist past, and had enough double-dealing, secret coups, and alliance shifting to satisfy any conspiracy theorist. It even brought Buck Lanham into a temporary alliance with David Karr, the man he held responsible for the worst mistake of his life.

Landa set up the Penn-Texas Stockholders Protective Committee, with its public relations activities run by Karr, to try to take over Silberstein's own company. Just as Karr had predicted, the flamboyant raider was vulnerable. Profits were low and its stock price had dropped. Landa charged that Silberstein's personal holding company had bought many of the Fairbanks, Morse shares and then resold them to Penn-Texas at higher prices. He filed two lawsuits alleging that profits belonging to Penn-Texas had gone to Silberstein, while Robert Morse launched a separate suit charging that Penn-Texas had acquired its shares of his company illegally and should be barred from voting them. Drew Pearson helpfully wrote columns attacking Silberstein.

Silberstein struck back. General Lanham spoke with Westbrook Pegler, who wrote two columns denouncing Karr. Congressman Francis Walter, chairman of the House Committee on Un-American Activities and a representative of a western Pennsylvania district, inserted an attack on Landa and Karr in the *Congressional Record* on February 6. It targeted them for their "unscrupulous practices" that threatened "American industry and the American way of life." Along with the Morses, they had "conspired to wreck the reputation and progress" of a thriving Pennsylvania company by creating a "so-called committee representing the stockholders of the company," a "shocking fraud on the public." While tossing out nasty innuendos about Landa and Robert Morse, Walter reserved his harshest words for Karr, identified as a former writer for the *Daily Worker*, whose record "shows that when he was not working for the Communists, he was busy working for the Nazis." It was Karr who was "the moving spirit" behind this underhanded plot to destroy Leopold Silberstein, described as a "great humanitarian," who had only recently offered employment to one thousand refugees fleeing Communist repression in Hungary. Walter was particularly exercised by the efforts of Karr and Landa to use government agencies to launch investigations and cause trouble for Penn-Texas and demanded that the Securities and Exchange Commission investigate their sneak attack. He concluded by calling their tactics "un-American in the real sense of the word. Any committee for the protection of American stockholders must be straightforward and honest. It cannot masquerade and sail under false colors." Penn-Texas had to be "protected and safeguarded against Communist infiltration and brigand plots of this type." (Just a day later, Karr's faithful defender, Senator Clinton Anderson, inserted a remark in the *Congressional Record* praising Karr as "a fine, upstanding American" who had been cleared of charges of Communism.)[40]

None of the attacks had much effect. Karr was just as willing to dig up whatever dirt was available to smear Silberstein. He wrote Pearson in February 1957 advising him that Silberstein's contact with Representative Walter was Robert Duffy, a Philadelphia politician, who was living "in venal and mortal sin" with an Australian woman in the United States illegally and Walter had pulled strings to pass a private bill granting her a visa. Karr also alleged that Silberstein's immigration to the United States had been "rigged" by a lawyer who was now ready to talk since he had been "chiseled" on his fee.[41]

Under financial pressure, Silberstein, who had acquired or contract-ed to buy more than half of the outstanding shares of Fairbanks, Morse by May 1957, started to buckle. He was forced to give Penn-Texas's quarterly dividend in stock, not cash, and then suspend it in the summer of 1957. He sold a subsidiary at a loss. *Barron's* accused his company of being "less than candid" with stockholders and criticized its forecasts of earnings, adding that "by freely diluting its equity and mortgaging up to the hilt, Penn-Texas succeeded in putting together what looked like a flourishing empire. Actually it was—and remains—nothing but a loose confederation of subsidiaries, which as a group, never have earned as much as they did as separate entities. Here is a classic case of the whole being less than the sum of its parts." Moreover, Landa filed a lawsuit charging that Silberstein's personal holding company had bought much of the Fairbanks, Morse stock from Swiss banks and then sold it to Penn-Texas at inflated prices.[42]

Despite his control of more than half of Fairbanks, Morse shares, Silberstein realized that the legal challenges to voting the shares would tie up his campaign for months, so he negotiated a compromise, selling some stock back to Fairbanks, Morse, and receiving five members of the board, while Robert Morse continued to run the company. Silberstein also agreed not to mount another takeover bid for five years. In return, Morse agreed to stay out of any proxy fights involving Penn-Texas. Silberstein's surrender, however, did not save him or assuage Landa and Karr, who decided to take advantage of his increasing vulnerabilities to devour him.

"We had Silberstein on the run," Landa explained to a reporter about why he was not satisfied with merely repelling his assault on Fairbanks, Morse. "I wanted more than half a loaf." At the 1957 annual meeting of Penn-Texas, the Landa slate won two of eight seats on the board. Karr and Landa began an intense campaign to recruit additional members of the Penn-Texas board to oust Silberstein. They identified the key figure to win over as Buck Lanham.[43]

At the end of January 1957, Drew Pearson telephoned Lanham to assure him that Karr, "the young man you have been crucifying," only wanted to protect his old friend by informing him about Silberstein's dishonesty. Lanham defended his new boss and as late as April 1957 wrote Silberstein, calling him a great leader and urging him to stand strong. But, in June, J. Anthony Panuch, friendly with both Karr and Lanham, showed Lanham a plan to reorganize Penn-Texas to extricate it from its troubles. While Lanham was impressed, Silberstein, regarding it as an effort to oust him, went ballistic. This led Lanham to conclude that Silberstein was withholding key information from the board and did not understand just how dire the company's financial situation really was. Alarmed and energized, Lanham began to organize a coup against Silberstein, recruiting two other directors and sending feelers to the two Karr-Landa directors to create a majority that would take control of Penn-Texas.[44]

To Lanham's dismay, his two allies wavered and ultimately buckled under Silberstein's threats and anger. Throughout the tense negotiations, Panuch, with whom Lanham consulted regularly, kept mentioning that the Landa group regarded him "as the only thoroughly honest and forthright director" and thought him a logical choice to become the new chairman of the board. Lanham was taken aback to realize that Panuch had been in touch with Landa and Karr since January of 1957 and it "disturbed me deeply." Despite his antipathy toward Karr, Lanham kept getting pushed toward him. In one angry confrontation, Silberstein blamed all his troubles on David Karr's desire to punish him for hiring Lanham.[45]

When the Penn-Texas board met on August 26, Lanham and his last two allies, the Karr-Landa directors, were defeated. But Silberstein was not yet out of the woods. Even after he sued for peace with Robert Morse, Silberstein had continued to buy Fairbanks, Morse stock, in violation of his agreement. He was probably not looking to seize control of the company, however, but to prop up its stock price, which had risen to $65 a share at the height of the takeover frenzy but had since fallen to $40 per share. Silberstein, who held nearly half a million shares at an average purchase price of $53, had lost a lot of money. Speculation abounded that he hoped to accumulate enough shares to sell a controlling interest in Fairbanks, Morse at a premium on the market price. To compound his difficulties, much of the Fairbanks, Morse stock was pledged as collateral against $11 million in short-term loans by Penn-Texas. The 10 percent interest rate on the loans forced Penn-Texas to sell off a number of its assets; by early 1958, it had discarded almost half of its prior acquisitions, many at a loss, to raise cash. Silberstein's fire sale of assets had chopped 21 percent off of Penn-Texas's book value, reduced sales by 40 percent, and devastated future profit potential. One accounting report noted a drop in sales in 1957 from $126.1 million to $78.1, while a $7.1 million profit in 1956 had turned into a $9.4 million loss in 1957. The core of what remained in the company was in machine tools, an industry in a cyclical slump, auguring continued problems in 1958.[46]

Fairbanks, Morse itself was hurting financially as the recession led to a 25 percent drop in sales in the first quarter of 1958 and a 97 percent decrease in earnings to a paltry 2 cents a share. But its troubles, paradoxically, only ratcheted up Silberstein's woes. By May 1958, Penn-Texas had increased its stake in Fairbanks, Morse to 49.4 percent in a desperate, but futile effort to support the stock price. The price of Penn-Texas stock had collapsed by the end of 1957, falling from a high of nearly $23 a share in 1955 to under $3. Under these circumstances, Silberstein lost more support. He also had moles in his company. One report noted that "Karr was kept fully posted by, among other people, one of Silberstein's secretaries."[47]

As the shifting factions on the board of Penn-Texas maneuvered to gain control of the company, David Karr remained in the background. He and Landa did not have the financial resources to mount a proxy fight, since Robert Morse had agreed to stay out of such an effort. Moreover, Karr was actively engaged in another bruising proxy war over control of Loew's movie studio (discussed below) and was unable to devote all his efforts to Penn-Texas. During the protracted negotiations over the fate of the company, Karr floated several possibilities about his price for cooperating. At first, he expressed a desire to regain the public relations contract for the company. Later, it was to have a seat on the board of directors. Lanham continually resisted, at one point writing that disillusioned as he was by Silberstein, he would prefer him to Karr, who was "a bad actor, a very bad actor." Knowing Karr, Lanham was convinced that if he remained part of the insurgent group, it would reflect badly on all of them: "Let him stay and screw them all as he will do." Ironically, one of the few things that both Silberstein and Lanham could agree on was that neither trusted Karr nor wanted anything to do with him. When the Karr-Landa group finally raised the money for a proxy fight, Lanham reluctantly agreed to cooperate, despite the "horrible taste in my mouth and a stench in my nostrils," but still preferred not to have to attend a meeting in Karr's office. He pleaded again and again to drop Karr and Landa from the insurgent slate, fearing their old ethical issues—Landa's Teamster ties and Karr's Communist ties—would damage their cause.[48]

In February 1958, Silberstein agreed to step down as chair of Penn-Texas to avoid a proxy fight he was now sure he would lose. Karr and Landa promptly made a deal with him to remain on the board, prompting yet another round of angry recriminations from Lanham and his allies. The onetime titan, who had left a trail of enemies and a reputation for arrogance, resigned as president in June 1958 in favor of Art Landa. Two months later he left the board with a five-year consultant contract for $40,000 a year as a sop, and was replaced on that body by David Karr, praised by Landa as "a big help...a hard worker...[who] had a lot of good contacts and, most important, he knew under which rugs Silberstein had swept dirt."[49]

By the beginning of August, Karr was assistant to the president of Penn-Texas, Art Landa. The two of them quickly moved to solidify their control of the company, buying out Lanham's contract in January 1959 and pushing onetime allies off the board. Apart from consolidating their own positions, they faced another daunting task. Of $14 million in short-term loans on the company's books, $5 million was due within weeks. Few bankers were willing to provide money to a company teetering on the edge of insolvency. Karr flew to San Francisco where he parlayed old contacts with the Bank of America and Transamerica into loans of $4.5 and $2.5 million to avert disaster. Appointed vice president for finance at a salary of $36,000 a year, the onetime radical, newsman, and public relations flack was now a neophyte businessman. One of Karr's detractors reacted to his new career by visiting the FBI and advancing "the theory that Karr, through his alleged association with [redacted, but probably Alfons Landa] could possibly be attempting to get control of American industry as part of a Communist Party conspiracy."[50]

Silberstein had stripped Penn-Texas of a substantial portion of its assets to pay for his doomed takeover of Fairbanks, Morse, leaving the latter company's stock as its most significant asset. Concluding that to protect that investment, they needed to take control of a company, nearly half of whose stock they already owned, Landa and Karr pressured Robert Morse to sell his shares for $9.6 million, raising the money through a public offering of Penn-Texas and borrowing nearly $3 million. Morse had successfully fought off Silberstein, only to lose his company to the men he had hired as white knights. The duo changed the name of Penn-Texas to Fairbanks Whitney (not to be confused with Pratt & Whitney, which manufactured jet engines); in 1959, Landa became chair of the executive committee and turned the presidency over to Karr, boasting that "we have accomplished all the things we came in to do—we have resolved the financial problems [of Penn-Texas] and solved the Fairbanks, Morse situation." He praised Karr, announcing that he was well qualified to "take over a lot of the paper-shuffling that a president has to do." The somewhat dismissive comment betrayed the tensions that already had fractured their relationship. In November 1958, Buck Lanham had heard from sources that Karr was hiring "his people" "without authority or knowledge of anybody" and "Landa was really fed up." Lanham had seen the inevitable, writing to Panuch the same month that "I will make another prediction: Karr will be president of Penn-Texas within 18 months."[51]

His new coup did not go unnoticed by his old foe, Westbrook Pegler, who wrote yet another column about his bête noire, titled "Little Davey—from Red to Capitalist." He paid ironic tribute to a man "with colossal gall and indomitable impudence, a flexibility not given to most men, and a gift of ability and diligence which an enemy would be foolish to deny." Pegler confessed to "a strange awe" in beholding "'Little Davey' [who] seems to be sitting on top of a high heap in the capitalist system today."[52]

Pegler did not note that Karr had by now abandoned any sympathy for left-wing politics or government efforts to buoy the incomes of lower-paid workers. In a series of letters to President Dwight Eisenhower written between 1957 and 1959, he warned Ike of the dangers of inflation, the lack of justification for pay raises for government employees, and the need for a balanced budget. It was necessary to resist those "greedy elements" in the labor movement who pushed for higher wages and thereby threatened "the soundness of our money." He also urged Ike to veto federal aid to education bills.[53]

Karr's new position capped a meteoric rise; at the age of forty-one, he had entered the ranks of American business chief executives with what was surely one of the most unusual résumés among them. Less than twenty years after he was writing articles for Communist-aligned publications, he was president of a corporation that did contract work for the United States government.

How to Succeed in Business without Really Trying had been a bestselling book in 1952. A play adaptation written in 1955 had languished, unproduced. Two of Karr's friends, Cy Feur and Ernie Martin, told his wife that the main character, J. Pierreport Finch, a window cleaner who rises to CEO by using "every dirty trick in the book," reminded them of David; the two producers decided to make it a musical, assembled a talented team including Abe Burrows, Frank Loesser, and Bob Fosse, and developed a show that won the Tony Award. David was not amused; he refused to attend an after-performance party just before it opened in October 1961.[54]

4

CEO

After a career as a newsman and public relations flack, having never been in charge of more than a handful of employees, David Karr was now the head of a large, diversified corporation with varied challenges and financial complexities, doing business throughout the United States and several countries, in a number of markets.

Karr's new empire encompassed a dozen operating companies and subsidiaries all united under the Fairbanks Whitney name. Employing more than five thousand people, Fairbanks Whitney had a net worth as of January 1961 of more than $70 million and annual sales of almost $150 million. Its Pennsylvania Coal and Coke division mined and sold coal to utility companies, primarily in the eastern United States. Fairbanks, Morse, the largest subsidiary, manufactured and distributed pumps, scales, locomotives, diesel engines, hot water systems, and special defense products. Pratt and Whitney, once Niles-Bement-Pond, made machine tools and gauges for aircraft and automotive industries. The Chandler Evans Corporation manufactured aircraft engine accessories for private companies and the Air Force. Colt Patent Fire Arms Company, probably the most famous subsidiary, made handguns and defense weapons. Quick-Way Truck Shovel Company manufactured power shovels and cranes. The Bayway Terminal Corporation held a long-term lease on a deep-water terminal in New Jersey. And Fairbanks Whitney International, Ltd. held the rights to a process for converting seawater.

During Karr's first two years on the job, he continued to endure the fallout from his youthful brushes with Communism. Representing Karr, Louis Nizer, a well-known lawyer, wrote to the Hearst Corporation threatening a libel suit about a column by Westbrook Pegler, published after Karr's appointment as CEO, that referred to Karr's supposed Communist past and charged stock manipulation during the takeover war, which Nizer called clearly malicious and actionable. (There is no indication of what happened to the threatened suit, but Pegler did stop writing about Karr.) The FBI received a copy of the letter, presumably from a source in the Hearst Corporation, and sent the writer a memo with the public source information on Karr in its files. But the matter died.[1]

Early in 1960 the New York office of the FBI reopened its investigation of Karr, this time prompted by the Air Force Office of Special Investigations. Karr had filled out and signed a questionnaire in August 1959 for a security clearance. Since Pratt and Whitney carried out classified work for the Air Force, its directors had to obtain such approval. Karr denied membership in a host of organizations that were considered Communist fronts or Communist-controlled, including the American League Against War and Fascism and the CPUSA itself. In response to a question about whether he had ever submitted articles for publication to any of these groups, Karr appended a longer answer, noting that when he was a young man trying to break into the newspaper business, he had submitted factual articles about fascist groups to some of the organizations listed, but "they were not any part of any propaganda scheme or effort." He advised that his lawyer—at Landa's firm—could provide copies of the articles.[2]

On December 1, 1959, an Air Force investigator spoke to Annette Arons, described as a former employee and "confidante" of Karr's. An embittered Arons, who may have had an affair with Karr, said she had seen Karr's Communist Party card and it was now in the possession of his ex-wife, Madeline Karr. Based on this information, the FBI decided to investigate whether or not Karr had committed fraud in executing the affidavit he had submitted to the Air Force by denying he had been a Communist. This investigation went over much of the old ground that had already been trampled during previous probes of Karr.[3]

It proved futile. Agents contacted former writers for the *Daily Worker*, looked in vain for members of a *Daily Mirror* unit of the CPUSA, checked the files of congressional committees, sought a man in Denver who recollected knowing a "Dave Carr" in the YCL, and pored over its own files, only to conclude that there was no reliable evidence that Karr had ever had any more of a relationship with the CPUSA than he had already admitted to. Agents did interview Annette Arons (although her name is blacked out, it appears in the earlier report from the Air Force). She told the FBI that she had first met Karr when he worked at William Weintraub. When asked why Pegler was attacking Karr if he was not a Communist, she had responded: "Why of course he was, what the...do you think this is all about?" She claimed that Karr had once admitted to her that he had been associated with the *Daily Worker* and "had been a member of the Communist Party," but she "does not want to testify, does not want to furnish a signed statement, and wants the information furnished to remain in the strictest confidence." However, in subsequent interviews Arons backtracked from her earlier claims to have seen Karr's CP card. She was unable to "describe the card, the contents thereof or any particulars in connection with the card." In fact, "she was in no position to state that it was a CP membership card."[4]

Investigators did not speak to Buffy Karr, who claimed in her autobiography that before their marriage David told her he was a "card-carrying Communist" and showed her his Party card. As she recalled, he told her he still considered himself one. His Communism, she concluded in an interview, was entirely "mental; he lived like a king."[5]

It was not that those interviewed by the FBI particularly liked or admired David Karr. A report noted that "in almost all interviews conducted in this investigation, the individuals contacted always prefaced their remarks by stating how they either disliked or distrusted Karr. The reason for the distrust was usually some personal act of his towards them, and in addition, Karr's general reputation for getting what he wanted regardless of what he had to do for it or who he would hurt." As one put it, Karr was "an opportunist who cannot be trusted," someone whose "political temperament changes with the times," and whose statements "concerning Communism and the U.S.S.R. would have to be weighed very carefully and corroborated before any credence could be given to Karr's statements."[6]

Determined to run down every possible lead and aware that the Office of the Secretary of Defense had expressed interest in Karr, the FBI nevertheless came up empty. The last lead, a Denver man who reported knowing a "Dave Carr" in the YCL in the 1930s, proved futile. The witness had suffered a nervous breakdown and moved to Israel; his wife, the Bureau learned after a long search, had moved to South Africa. Hoover informed the Air Force in October 1960 that "no further investigation is contemplated" and told the SAC in NY "that there is no admissible evidence upon which prosecutive action could be based" and he could close the case.[7]

But that still did not end the matter. In February 1961, the Office of Industrial Personnel Access in the Secretary of Defense's Office notified the FBI that it was considering granting Karr an authorization for access to classified information. The Air Force furnished its file of the previous year's probe, including the reports of numerous prior investigations by the FBI, and the DOD wanted to learn more about some of the informants mentioned and whether they would be available to testify. Bureau offices in Pittsburgh, Los Angeles, San Francisco, Washington, D.C., and New York were instructed to re-interview individuals who had previously talked. One person, questioned in San Francisco, had known Karr in the American League for Peace and Democracy; he could not say that he was a Communist, but "he appeared to be a Marxist in his thinking," although he "cannot now recall why he arrived at all of these conclusions and he preferred not to testify," unless it was "absolutely necessary and for the good of the country." A person contacted by the Washington Field Office said "it would be impossible for her to testify in a personal appearance hearing."[8]

The juiciest and most perplexing information came from an informant interviewed in New York who had "furnished both reliable and unreliable information in the past." Although his name is redacted in the FBI files, he had apparently been employed to prepare a report on Karr that was published in April by *Counterattack*, an anti-Communist magazine best known for publishing *Red Channels*, a listing of entertainment figures with allegedly Communist or Communist-front associations. This individual had provided reports to the FBI back in the late 1930s and early 1940s on Communist-front meetings. (It could not have been Howard Rushmore, who had identified Karr as a Communist back in the 1940s—Rushmore killed his wife and then committed suicide in January 1958.) Whoever he was, he now recalled that he had had lunch with Karr, reporter Dorothy Kilgallen, and a now-deceased reporter from the *New York Post* during the trial of Guenther Rumrich, a Nazi agent who had confessed to espionage in October 1938 and testified against several codefendants. At the lunch Karr "stated to those present that he was a member of the CP." If his memory could be refreshed by the reports he had submitted years earlier and he was reimbursed for travel and accommodations in Washington, he was willing to testify to that. The FBI was none too impressed with this startling revelation, as his earlier reports had never mentioned it. In March 1941, he had told the FBI that Karr was a Communist, but in 1960 explained that he had no personal knowledge that Karr was, in fact, in the Party. Rather, he had based his statement on the "preferential treatment" Karr had received at the 1941 meeting of the American Peace Mobilization, a Communist-front group. When the FBI checked his report from that APM meeting, it found no mention of David Karr. The Bureau was also suspicious that this informant, who may have had ties to the Hearst Corporation or Westbrook Pegler, was trying to deflect the possibility of a lawsuit that Karr had threatened over Pegler's 1959 column. It did not even bother to interview Kilgallen.[9]

The Bureau also interviewed a former Washington-based reporter for the *Daily Worker*, who was more reliable (probably Rob Hall, who had left the CPUSA around 1959), then living in upstate New York. He had known both Dave and Madeline and described them as "standoffish." He had never seen them at left-wing meetings or functions, had never seen any signs of Communist sympathy, and emphatically denied ever saying that numerous people would testify about Karr's Communist past. The whole investigation petered out and Karr's FBI file lay dormant for a decade.[10]

Counterattack did distribute an eight-page attack on Karr in April 1961. It said, somewhat histrionically, that his "meteoric projection into high finance" rivaled the rise of Soviet cosmonaut Yuri Gagarin. It laid out Fairbanks Whitney's structure, emphasized his association with the *Daily Worker*, reprinted portions of Karr's interrogation before the Dies Committee, Robert Stripling's response, and Howard Rushmore's testimony that Karr had to have been a Communist. Noting that Fairbanks

Whitney did defense work, it demanded that he be investigated and urged the SEC to review how proxy wars were conducted, implying that "glib" public relations manipulators might be hoodwinking the American public and small stockholders. But the attack was rather mild and avoided any direct claims that Karr was a Communist. The magazine was probably chilled by the possibility of a libel suit. Karr now had the resources to cause accusers major difficulties. No one, however, seems to have paid any attention. David Karr's alleged ties with the CPUSA, which had followed him like an albatross for two decades, appeared to have become a dead issue.[11]

Karr's first year in the executive suite was a very brief honeymoon for Fairbanks Whitney. It had endured years of fierce proxy wars fending off hostile takeovers rather than focusing on running businesses. In the first half of 1959, newly appointed president Karr reported earnings of slightly more than $1 million after a loss of more than $400,000 the year before and predicted a profit of $3 million for the year. He boasted of an increase in orders of 24 percent, more than $14 million in cash on hand, and no short-term indebtedness, a remarkable turnaround from the situation a year earlier, when it had less than $1 million in cash and $14 million in debt at rates up to 20 percent. Its total assets had increased from $16 million to $93 million. Apart from the increase in orders, the only explanation Karr offered was that the new management had reduced administrative expenses at the New York home office from $5 million to $1.5 million a year.[12]

This cheery news was not reflective of David Karr's executive tenure. Neither he nor Landa had any experience running a large industrial company. Their particular talents lay in public relations and building alliances of disgruntled shareholders. Landa admitted to a reporter that "running a company is not my forte. I put a company in a sound financial position, then I turn it over to someone else who's more competent at the detail work than I am." When he had passed the presidency to Karr, Landa told one worried stockholder that his successor was well qualified "to come and take over a lot of the paper shuffling that a president has to do." Asked about his own qualifications to run a large, complicated company, Karr pointed to his extensive travel on its behalf and his previous public relations representation of executives at large firms.[13]

The contrast with what it took to successfully turn around a wounded or moribund company was starkly illustrated by yet another proxy war that Alfons Landa had waged in the late 1950s with legendary corporate raider Thomas Mellon Evans, the head of H.K. Porter Company. Evans had set his sights on the Crane Company, a Chicago-based manufacturer of valves used in hundreds of consumer and industrial products. By the summer of 1958, he had enlisted Landa—in the headlines for his take-no-prisoners attack on Penn-Texas—and sweet-talked one of the original Crane heirs into supporting his bid for control. The raiders used Landa's trademark tactic: threatening one of their rivals with a proxy war on his own company. They used Karr's contacts in the public relations business to plant stories about the upcoming raid in the financial press.

By April 1959, Landa was elected to the Crane board and Evans became chairman and chief executive, a parallel to what had just taken place at Penn-Texas. But the contrast with Penn-Texas and Fairbanks Whitney was stark. Evans, as ruthless as he was driven, quickly reduced manufacturing capacity, closed branch outlets, and cut expenses, all unpopular moves that unnerved labor unions, Chicago business leaders, and even board members. When the press wrote critical stories about his plans and decisions, and several articles appeared touting Landa as the guiding genius in the takeover, Evans, less than pleased, struck back.[14]

Evans refused to hire Karr's public relations firm, moved to reduce Landa's compensation for his assistance in the takeover, and severed his ties with both men by January 1960. Despite this contretemps, Karr insisted in his 1961 corporate report that there was "no controversy between us and Crane, Porter, or Evans." Evans quickly transformed the Crane Company and set it on the road to economic stability. David Karr, meanwhile, was struggling to do the same with his new acquisition.[15]

It wasn't easy. While Karr had managed to find loans to ease Fairbanks Whitney's crushing short-term debt problem, most of the company's divisions were struggling to make profits. For several years there had been little money for research and new products were sparse. Within three years Karr had increased R&D expenditures eight times. He negotiated agreements with Italian and English companies to sell each other's products. And, he staked a great deal of credibility on a major investment in a desalinization project in Israel.

David Karr's stint as CEO of Fairbanks Whitney was noteworthy mainly for its failures. But one corporate venture focused his attention, for the first time in his life, on Israel. Never an observant Jew, Karr developed both a business and personal relationship with the Jewish state that impacted his life and led to a host of new conspiracy theories that would dog him through the 1960s and 1970s.

Karr first visited Israel in October 1959 after learning from Drew Pearson about a new process developed by an Israeli scientist to convert seawater to freshwater. His former boss had interviewed Alexander Zarchin, a Russian immigrant to Israel, in his one-room apartment in 1957. Zarchin and his wife lived in a 12- by 14-foot residence, "cooking, eating, sleeping, experimenting" in his quest to achieve a scientific breakthrough. Two years later, Pearson put Zarchin in touch with Karr, now running Fairbanks Whitney.[16]

Zarchin, born in 1898, the son of a Hasidic Jew from Poltava in the Ukraine, had studied chemistry in Leningrad. Attending a 1931 lecture by an Arctic explorer, he became intrigued with how to develop an economic way to desalinize saltwater. Eskimos obtained freshwater from the sea by separating the minerals without heating the water. Zarchin hoped to commercialize that insight. Soviet authorities built a desalination plant in Turkestan to develop his research, but his work in the Soviet Union was interrupted by a five-year sentence to Siberia in 1934 for registering a magnesium-extracting process under the letters LZLE, the first letters of a phrase from the Book of Isaiah meaning "For Zion's sake I will not keep silent." Released to do scientific research during World War II, the deeply religious and committed Zionist worked as a chemical engineer in Tashkent before he managed to flee the Soviet Union and immigrate to Palestine in 1947. His escape was risky. He purchased the passport of a Polish inmate in his research lab, was able to get "repatriated" to Poland after World War II ended, and then made his way out of Europe.

Once in the Promised Land, however, Zarchin found that the scientific establishment regarded him as a "nudnik" and crank. He was fired from his position at the Weizmann Institute after he publicly criticized the finance minister and future prime minister, Levi Eshkol. After numerous rebuffs, he persuaded the director general of the Ministry of Development and Prime Minister David Ben-Gurion to build components for his desalinization ideas near Tel Aviv and a pilot plant in Eilat in the Negev Desert. The Israeli prime minister noted in his diary that "perhaps Zarchin's invention isn't practical, but it is also possible that it will succeed and we will have a revolution of redemptive force and with international value." Menachem Bader, head of the Ministry of Development, noted that "most inventors are crazy about one invention alone. Not Zarchin. He's crazy about thirty. The moment you give him reason to know you are ready to believe him on one invention he is ready to give you solutions to all the problems of Israel." Early returns were not promising. Machinery broke down and results were uneven. Zarchin continued to obtain a number of patents, buttressed by his faith—he prayed twice a day and studied a page of Talmud daily—and his belief that he was destined to win the Nobel Prize.[17]

Both his process and the initial Israeli experiments had been conducted in secrecy and even the location of the pilot plant had been kept confidential, largely because Zarchin was paranoid about rivals stealing his insights. He bought different parts of his apparatus from different suppliers. Even after Karr returned to Israel a second time to meet him with two top Fairbanks engineers, Zarchin refused to reveal the most important elements of his process. After arguing with Zarchin, Karr explained, he "relented. My heart stood still." The engineers were allowed to crawl underneath the machinery, "getting grease on their heads and paint on their clothes." One, with tears in his eyes, emerged and told the Russian-born inventor that "It takes a genius to make things simple." With his customary hyperbole, Karr noted "this is one of the great scientific breakthroughs mankind has been waiting for since time immemorial." He added that "it puts a new dimension into science. It goes contrary to every known principle." Zarchin's method, called vacuum freezing vapor compression, pumped seawater into a low-pressure chamber where part was turned into vapor, part was frozen, and the rest became concentrated brine. When the vapor was compressed, it turned into pure water and generated enough heat to melt the ice crystals, producing more pure water. The process was energy efficient and, potentially, economically viable.[18]

Within twenty-four hours of inspecting Zarchin's process, Karr had begun discussions with the Israeli Ministry of Development to establish a joint venture. Karr told the Israeli press that Fairbanks Whitney would build two desalinization plants near Eilat, costing about $1 million, to turn out half a million gallons of freshwater every day, establish an office, and employ Israelis to launch a new major industry. The Ministry of Development excitedly announced that Sri Lanka, Greece, India, and Fiji had all inquired about the technology. Within a short time, Fairbanks Whitney had purchased the patent rights in a partnership with the Israeli government and an announcement was made that the first commercial unit would be completed and in operation in Eilat by the end of 1961. Karr gave varying predictions of the cost, once optimistically claiming that it would be only 10 cents per thousand gallons, before settling on a more realistic 40 cents.[19]

Everything seemed to be on track; in January 1961, the two parties trumpeted the completion of the first mass production de-salter, manufactured in Beloit, Wisconsin. At the end of March, groundbreaking ceremonies were held in Eilat, with the president of Israel "and a goodly portion of the Diplomatic Corps" in attendance. Fairbanks Whitney produced a glossy ten-page public relations brochure, introduced with quotations from John Kennedy, Lyndon Johnson, and Dwight Eisenhower touting the importance of developing water resources, an interview with a company engineer, and a glowing account of the importance and significance of Zarchin's invention. Separately, Karr told the *Jerusalem Post* that "there is more know-how in that man's brain [Zarchin] than in the 127 years of knowledge accumulated during the existence of Fairbanks Whitney." A report self-published by Fairbanks Whitney, "The Well That Never Runs Dry," asserted that the de-salter would convert seawater into freshwater at a cost below $1 per 1,000 gallons, with a capacity of 1,000,000 gallons a day, well below the most economical plants already operating, which cost $1.75 per gallon. Karr sent a copy of this report to a special assistant to President Kennedy, boasting of the impact it would have on American employment, foreign trade, and alleviating world problems.[20]

Other commentators were even more effusive. A Christian evangelical newspaper quoted Karr as describing Zarchin's discovery as "a new dimension in science" and reported the confident claim by the Israeli minister of development that within three years, Israel would be supplying equipment to countries around the world. Fairbanks Whitney took out a full-page ad in the *Wall Street Journal* trumpeting its achievement. Predictably, Fairbanks Whitney's stock price soared; $7.50 when Karr became president, it rose past $14 on the news. Karr professed to be displeased, telling a reporter that the increase was premature and complaining about press leaks from the Beloit plant manufacturing the units.[21]

The enthusiasm was, indeed, premature. As early as March 1960, there were signs that Zarchin, a famously difficult man, was dissatisfied with the royalties due him under the terms of the contract. In May 1960, the new joint venture, Desalinization Facilities, was created with equity divided among Israel (36.5 percent), Fairbanks Whitney (50 percent), and Zarchin (13.5 percent), while management was divided fifty-fifty between the state and the company. Zarchin, however, was unhappy and insisted on a new lawyer to represent him in the company and Karr reassured him that if necessary, Fairbanks Whitney would provide him with an attorney gratis. The promises and deadlines were not met. In June 1961, a reporter visited the Eilat site and "found it deserted. No work had been done since the cornerstone was laid." His guide cynically commented that everyone must be waiting for a miracle—"for Moses to come back to earth and strike this stone with his rod" to produce water. By the end of 1961, Fairbanks Whitney stock had sunk from $14 a share back to $8.[22]

Changes in the design of the de-salters were still ongoing in September 1962 and they had yet to operate at full capacity. In October Karr wrote to the Minister of Development that the company planned to ship "all elements of the system by February 15th" and he believed that plant would be up and running around May 1, 1963. But the Israeli government was losing faith in both Zarchin and Fairbanks. Mekorot, Israel's national water company, unwilling to depend too heavily on the Zarchin process, received approval from the government to build a second de-salting plant in Eilat using a different technology over the objections of the Ministry of Development. In November 1962, Baldwin-Lima-Hamilton (BLH), a Philadelphia-based manufacturer, took out a full-page ad in the *Wall Street Journal* to trumpet its obtaining a contract to construct a plant in Eilat to produce one million gallons of distilled seawater a day using a different process. Karr was indignant, writing to Bader that the news gave a "black eye" to Fairbanks and he was hard-pressed to "explain why the State of Israel pays strangers to compete with itself." Karr's most innovative and hyped effort to boost the company's fortunes was now foundering. And his position as CEO of Fairbanks Whitney was in jeopardy.[23]

Not until 1964 did the Zarchin-process plant in Eilat go online. One analysis noted that "after years of planning, construction and testing, it became apparent that this process, which was supposed to be cheaper than extracting well water, was impossibly expensive." It cost more than six times as much as irrigation water produced by natural sources—which was already a significant burden on farmers. On a large scale it proved very difficult to maintain the proper temperatures in the vapor process. Zarchin blamed the problems "on the inability of others around him to understand his invention." He quit the company in 1966, the same year the BLH plant went online producing far more freshwater than its Fairbanks competitor per day.[24]

A cynical Israeli commentator—himself a veteran leader on the Israeli side of the venture—attributed the earlier buzz about the project to "the public relations advantages of a joint venture," which produced "joint press releases" from "Jerusalem and New York praising the unique technological achievements." By the time Fairbanks Whitney abandoned the project—after Karr left the company—the Israeli Ministry of Development was left "holding an unwanted baby all by itself." The only upside was that it left behind "a cadre of trained professionals, highly experienced in the pitfalls of desalination process development," which formed the core of IDE Technologies, a highly successful Israeli company operating internationally today using a seawater reverse osmosis technology to make the conversion to freshwater.[25]

When Prime Minister Levi Eshkol visited Washington in 1964, Lyndon Johnson promised Israel help in desalinization plans; Drew Pearson loyally penned a tribute to Karr for having pioneered the effort and excoriated Fairbanks Whitney for shortsightedly removing him because his vision did not produce immediate economic benefits.[26]

The Israeli venture demonstrated Karr's abilities and weaknesses. He could generate publicity and spin promising but unproven plans as world-changing events. He could orchestrate favorable stories and solicit endorsements from prominent people. His public relations acumen, however, did not enable him to disguise or patch deeper and more intractable problems or find ways to surmount them. He could not find or keep competent project managers or discover ways to keep manufacturing or engineering problems from disrupting plans.

Despite the initial hoopla after his triumph, and the brief bump provided by the Israeli venture, Fairbanks Whitney continued to struggle. In 1959, the company had made a profit of $3.2 million on sales of more than $150 million. Despite optimistic predictions that the desalinization plant would soon be operational and newly signed agreements with two European companies in early 1960, sales stagnated, and the company had a profit of a measly $138,116 for that year. In a year-end interview, Karr optimistically boasted of new products on the way. Landa blamed the national economy but took comfort that the desalinization venture was "moving forward at a pace even better than previously anticipated."[27]

That spin did not assuage angry stockholders. The annual meeting in 1960 featured disgruntled investors complaining that Karr's $90,000 annual salary with a ten-year term was excessive for a man who two years before had been earning $8,000 a year as a company publicist. The claim of one director that "your management has taken a moribund company—well-nigh dead—and made it into a living, pulsating thing" did not mollify them. Nor was 1961 any better. The company was stuck in the same rut; a disappointing first half elicited predictions of a strong second half that the numbers belied. For the year, the company lost $83,000 on sales of more than $141,000,000. The worst-performing division of the company was Fairbanks, Morse, the manufacturer of the water desalinization units intended for Israel. At the 1962 annual meeting, those defending management were greeted by cries of "stooge."[28]

As Fairbanks Whitney remained unprofitable, the tolerance for continued executive excuses diminished and dissatisfaction with its management grew. A profile of Karr in *Fortune* likened him to "a ninth grader chosen to be mayor for a day," while *Forbes* noted that he delighted to travel "around his profitless empire in a $300,000 DC-3 airplane whose purchase he had authorized." (He eventually concluded that the plane was an extravagance and a lightning rod and put it up for sale.) Executive wages and directors' fees totaled almost $600,000 in 1961, a year in which the company had only $730,000 in profits. Karr's outsized salary, guaranteed contract, and generous severance pay generated particular resentment; so did Landa's compensation of $67,000, while working only part-time for Fairbanks Whitney, and executive vice president Robert Finkelstein's $60,000 salary.[29]

Late in March 1962, Karr once again predicted a profit in the first half of the year and explained that "management had not had enough time to get things into line." But he was rapidly losing support—both in the boardroom and among stockholders. A newspaper column reported that unless he resigned, two directors, Landa and Finkelstein, both former allies, would quit in protest. More than two hundred angry stockholders who attended the company's May meeting loudly booed anyone defending the company and punctuated the four-hour meeting with cries of "mismanagement." One disgruntled shareholder bemoaned the absence of anyone with scientific experience on the board. But the greatest source of anger was the outsized perks enjoyed by those running the company. Amid demands that their salaries be cut, Landa's impolitic outburst that "this meeting illustrated how little most shareholders know about the problems of running a company" only fueled the anger.[30]

Landa and Finkelstein hoped to oust Karr at the May 1962 board meeting but were stymied by yet another director making good money out of his association with Fairbanks Whitney. Milton Weisman, originally an ally of Leopold Silberstein, was a law partner of Congressman Emanuel Celler of New York; their law firm collected more than $100,000 a year in legal fees from Fairbanks Whitney. With Weisman's support, Karr managed to repulse his former ally's attack. Landa promptly resigned all his positions with the company and soon disposed of most of his stock. He was joined by Finkelstein, the executive vice president, who had been a key member of the Karr-Landa team in its battle to take over Penn-Texas. Although both men publicly cited the press of other business, private comments emerging from the board meeting were less sugary. Landa and Finkelstein blamed Karr for the company's poor performance, citing "ineptitude"; he shot back that Landa was "a self-inflated, self-anointed authority on business management."[31]

Their departure did nothing to quell the turmoil engulfing Fairbanks Whitney; a week later a vice president, only three months on the job, quit after he learned that he would not be promoted to Finkelstein's position. Francis O'Leary said Karr "completely disavowed the previous arrangement"; Karr responded that the job "may have been promised to him by Mr. Finkelstein or Mr. Landa, but they're no longer with us. I never met him till the day before yesterday." Still another director resigned at the end of June.[32]

Karr's problems continued to mount despite a small profit—less than $500,000—for the first half of 1962. To turn around the fortunes of Fairbanks, Morse, Fairbanks Whitney's biggest and most troubled subsidiary, he had recruited Thomas Lanphier, a former vice president of the Convair division of General Dynamics, in 1960, boasting that he was his "prize acquisition" and "a real swinging guy." A genuine war hero, who had flown more than a hundred combat missions and shot down Admiral Yamamoto's plane during WWII, Lanphier confidently predicted a $3 million profit at Fairbanks, Morse in 1961. He resigned in August 1962 with Fairbanks, Morse still showing substantial losses and by mid-1962 still not having shipped any de-salting units to Israel. He was followed by a number of other Fairbanks, Morse executives unhappy with pay cuts and dissatisfaction with Karr's management.[33]

Like a skilled PR man Karr maintained his positive spin on events, telling an interviewer that he had reduced his own salary by 20 percent as part of an austerity program and company headquarters would be moved out of New York City to Yonkers to save money. He insisted that morale had improved and the board of directors was entirely supportive of his management of the company. Karr also mentioned that Landa and Finkelstein were still being paid $35,000 a year as consultants; they had "stayed in the company long enough to help put it on its feet" and "when they saw the future of the company secure they left."[34]

No amount of dissembling could disguise the dire situation facing the company. Yet another director, George Lessner, who had served on the board of Pratt & Whitney, a subsidiary of Fairbanks Whitney that made precision tools, resigned in August 1962. Citing his "frustration and being kept in the dark," Lessner charged that the board was a figurehead. Early in January, Lessner filed a lawsuit against the company and ten past and present officials, including Karr and Landa, charging them with conspiring to obtain excessive salaries and compensation for themselves. He noted that Karr had a contract running until November 1969, paying him $90,000 a year while he was running the company and a prorated share if not. The lawsuit bitingly noted that he "had no previous training, qualifications, demonstrated experience or ability to be the chief executive officer of a complex industrial company" and that he was not worth the money he had been paid and promised. Lessner also informed the SEC that he intended to mount a proxy fight against the management of Fairbanks Whitney.[35]

The board finally concluded that the hemorrhaging of personnel and money could no longer be tolerated and that it needed an experienced businessman to run the diverse and poorly managed company. In November 1962, Karr announced that George Strichman, president of the Kellogg division of International Telephone and Telegraph, had been chosen as Fairbanks Whitney's new president and CEO at a salary of $115,000 a year. Claiming credit for recruiting Strichman, Karr became chairman of the board, continuing to receive his previously reduced $72,000 salary. His days at Fairbanks Whitney, however, were clearly numbered. Strichman inherited a company that lost nearly $5 million in 1962, had to write off more than $22 million in "obsolete plant, worthless inventories and profitless products," renegotiate a bank loan after sinking below its requirements for working capital, and deal with Lessner's stockholders' revolt. After just a few months on the job, Strichman reported "this is the worst company I've ever seen."[36]

Strichman moved quickly to cut ties between Fairbanks Whitney and the reminders of the disastrous last few years. In late January 1963, his first effort to oust Karr from his new position as chairman foundered. Louis Nizer, Karr's lawyer, obtained a court order that the board meeting to remove him had been called with inadequate notice. Facing the inevitable, however, Karr resigned in early February, remaining as director of the company until the May meeting, and receiving a token honorific as American chairman of Desalination Plants, Ltd., the joint venture with Israel.[37]

Karr's ouster laid the groundwork for resolution of much of the infighting that had afflicted the company since 1957. Both Landa and Finkelstein indicated they were now amenable to buyouts of their deferred compensation contracts that had angered so many stockholders. Landa said he had retained his so he could "keep a watch on" Karr. "I wouldn't get out of there until I was sure the situation was being corrected," he told a reporter; "now that the problem has been handled, I propose to sever all my connections with the company." In July 1963, both he and Finkelstein accepted $25,000 payments and waived the remaining six years of their contracts. When Karr and another former director rejected settlement offers, Fairbanks Whitney unilaterally stopped payments. Karr explained that the issue was "in the hands of my attorney, who, of course, will file suit." By February 1964, however, the two sides compromised. Owed $877,500, Karr settled for $180,000. The stockholder lawsuit alleging overpayment was dropped. George Lessner, who had filed the original claim, had been elected to the board of directors in 1963; he now expressed his confidence in the new management of the company.[38]

During Karr's tenure at Fairbanks Whitney the company went on life support. Its stock, $7.50 when he became president, once trading as high as $14.87 a share, stood at $4.62 when he gave up control. It had suffered a net loss in 1962 and expected another bad year in 1963. Not all the bad news was due to Karr's stewardship; it had "been wrecked in twelve long years of being pawed over by three sets of financial operators and proxy-fighters." Its new boss warned that "we cannot be a sound company for at least three years and we cannot be a good company for at least five." But David Karr was undaunted. Immediately after his firing, he was scheduled to deliver a speech to B'nai B'rith, a Jewish fraternal organization. His reputation as a businessman had been badly battered. Buffy Karr recalled that everyone in the room knew he had been sacked, but Karr showed up, confident and poised, and delivered a "magnificent speech," as if he had just completed a triumphant job.[39]

5

HOLLYWOOD AND BROADWAY INTERLUDE

D avid Karr's first marriage had collapsed as he tried to establish Market Relations Network as a force in the public relations world. His second marriage imploded as his escalating troubles at Fairbanks Whitney threatened to destroy nearly a decade-long rise to wealth and influence.

Buffy Karr gradually discovered that the man she had married was more than exciting; he was also secretive, manipulative, and surrounded by an aura of danger. When a friend, former Hollywood impresario Matty Fox, who made another fortune when his American-Indonesia Corporation briefly held a monopoly on Indonesian trade with the United States, gave him a new Jaguar, and she asked why, David responded, "Don't you realize you're married to the Jewish mafia?"[1]

She began to believe him. Her first fright came early in 1957 when she had been driving to their summer home in David's Thunderbird; it felt wobbly, so she stopped at a service station and discovered the lug nuts had been removed from the tires. David refused to discuss the matter. Although his public relations business used checks, all household expenses were paid in cash; every month, he would give her ten one-hundred-dollar bills for expenses. His desk drawers were filled with stacks of bills. When she asked him for an explanation, he told her "to mind your own business." His habit of carrying large amounts of cash continued throughout his life; his son Frank recounted being asked by his father to carry a briefcase through the Paris airport. David later suggested he open it and Frank discovered $25,000 in cash, described by his father as "what it takes to run my life for a week." His Mediterranean yacht had a safe, always filled with stacks of cash.[2]

There is no hard evidence, however, that Karr was associated with organized crime. He no doubt did his best to conceal some of his income from the IRS and was certainly willing to cut ethical and legal corners if he thought he could get away with it. Some of the people with whom he did business were ruthless and neither Karr nor his associates were averse to issuing threats and playing the tough guy. His onetime British partner Ronnie Driver noted, "He knew how to make the most use of what he knew. It might be a little harsh to categorize it as blackmail, but that was undoubtedly the area in which he operated. He could destroy people overnight with the things he knew." Driver also claimed to have heard Karr offer to "get rid of" a bothersome lover of Christina Onassis. "If David said he'd get rid of somebody, that's exactly what he meant; he would get rid of them." But there is also no gainsaying the fact that by the time he died, rumors about his involvement in money laundering, bribery, gun-running, espionage, and even murder led a number of people, including family members, to give credence to grave suspicions about what he had been up to, and to make exaggerated claims about his involvement in nefarious activities.[3]

What was not in doubt was his lacerating tongue, rudeness to subordinates and staff, and self-centeredness. As his troubles at Fairbanks Whitney grew, David became more manipulative and nastier to his wife and others. When Buffy criticized his behind-the-back put-downs of his friends, he angrily retorted: "You don't know a fucking thing about business. Just stay out of it." He tried to isolate her from her friends and would not visit her parents. After David underwent a painful hemorrhoid operation, the doctor took her aside and complained that David had been "beyond rude to my nurses...demanding of the food staff, insulting to technicians and doctors alike...If he gets sick take him somewhere else." When she became active in a charity, the African Medical and Research Foundation, he complained that "you should be promoting me, not some two-bit charity run by your Park Avenue doctor."[4]

After his ouster from Fairbanks Whitney, David doubled down. Buffy was startled when "instead of laying low and licking his wounds, David with immense chutzpah…decided to rent an enormous apartment, a duplex that had once been home to Moss Hart and Kitty Carlisle," on Park Avenue. When she protested at the cost, he snarled that he had to show his enemies, who were "too many to count," that he was unbowed. He took to criticizing her as an alcoholic. Buffy broke down while speaking to Mildred Nizer, wife of David's longtime lawyer, one evening and confided her unhappiness; her friend urged her to speak to her husband, Louis, and retain him as a lawyer before David did so. Before agreeing to a divorce, David demanded she see a psychiatrist, since leaving him indicated she was disturbed. She later learned that the German au pair who worked for her was serving as a spy for her husband. Despite his anger—he could not countenance Buffy's deciding to leave him—after a six-month trial separation, she flew to Los Angeles in March 1965 and rebuffed his demand that they reconcile. The divorce quickly followed; in May, on their anniversary, he sent her one long-stemmed black rose.[5]

Armed with his severance package from Fairbanks Whitney and once again without a family, David Karr embarked on a new career, in a locale more fitted to his particular talents in public relations; he moved to Los Angeles and set his sights on show business. It was not entirely unexpected. Karr and Buffy had become acquainted with numerous people involved in the entertainment business in New York. Among their friends and neighbors on Long Island were several Broadway producers and David had been close friends with Matty Fox, who had been a high-ranking executive at Universal Pictures. Moreover, Karr had worked for several studios. In 1957, the small group of investors who had purchased the struggling United Artists from Charlie Chaplin and Mary Pickford earlier in the decade decided to take their company public. Max Youngstein, a Hollywood veteran and one of the investors, had heard about Karr from Fox, Karr's neighbor in New York, and hired him to do public relations work directed at the financial community. He had been pleased with the work, calling Karr "a cockeyed genius."[6]

That same year Karr had been retained by Loew's Incorporated, parent company of Metro-Goldwyn-Mayer, one of the major industry studios. A giant conglomerate that also owned movie theaters, music publishers, radio stations, and valuable California real estate, Loew's had 14,000 employees and earned almost $180,000,000 in receipts every year. A long-simmering feud, sparked by the removal of Louis Mayer as studio head in 1950, broke out in earnest in the mid-1950s as MGM suffered badly from changes in the industry. Plotting revenge, Mayer orchestrated a revolt against a newly installed Loew's president, Joseph Vogel, who had worked his way up the ranks. Mayer enlisted the largest single stockholder, Canadian Joseph Tomlinson, to launch a proxy fight in December 1956. Vogel eventually agreed to a compromise according to which each side obtained six seats on the board of directors, with Ogden Reid, owner of the *New York Herald Tribune*, having the decisive vote. Despite Tomlinson's assurances at the stockholders' meeting in February that harmony had been achieved, he immediately called for Vogel's removal at the first board meeting.[7]

Vogel quickly hired famed attorney Louis Nizer to plot strategy and David Karr to orchestrate public relations. The ensuing battle featured charges and counter-charges, threats of lawsuits from both sides, and carefully planned leaks as the directors, who included three former cabinet officers, distinguished businessmen, and bankers, picked at each other. All of this maneuvering was taking place even as Karr and Landa were deeply immersed in their battle with Leopold Silberstein for control of Penn-Texas and Karr was in the midst of his first divorce.

In an attempted coup in July 1957 sparked by the absence of two pro-Vogel directors from a meeting, Tomlinson tried to fire Vogel and replace Karr as publicist with Tex McCrary, the legendary master of public relations who had orchestrated the campaign to draft Dwight Eisenhower for the presidency in 1952. Nizer and Karr developed a strategy in which Vogel refused to recognize the legitimacy of the motion, issued a public rebuke and challenge, and called for a special stockholders' meeting to oust his foes. Thwarted when three of their directors resigned and the Tomlinson-Mayer group called a rump meeting to seize control of Loew's (Mayer himself showed up at the company headquarters explaining that he was "lonely for Leo the lion"), the Vogel group won a legal victory in August and, at Karr's suggestion, organized stockholder protective committees to finance the battle. After an exhausting round of injunctions, appeals, and hearings before state and federal courts, the stockholders finally met on October 15. Confronted by an organized effort to disrupt the proceedings, Nizer warned the dissidents they faced contempt charges and then saw a resolution to enlarge the board with Vogel appointees approved by a six-to-one margin.

What neither Nizer nor Vogel knew at the time was that Karr was secretly plotting with Tomlinson, even as he was being paid by Vogel and Loew's. In her memoir, Buffy Karr recalled that Tomlinson visited the Karrs' townhouse night after night during the proxy war. She asked David if Nizer knew of his meetings with their chief enemy and he responded, "Are you kidding," and laughed. Shocked, she asked how he could take money from both sides. "Nobody listens to a poor man," he replied. And, he had secretly promised to give Vogel's job to the president of a shipping company in San Francisco in exchange for his proxy votes. His response to Buffy's disdain was to tell her to "mind your own fucking business." When she confided in Mildred Nizer about her desire for a divorce, Buffy told Mildred about David's double cross; it may have played a role in Nizer's decision to represent her in the action rather than his old client and friend, David. For David Karr, as Buffy noted, "to do it straight was boring."[8]

Before committing himself to a new career in Hollywood in the mid-1960s, however, Karr was angling for other opportunities. He contracted with Simon & Schuster to write a sequel to *Fight for Control*, to be titled *Backstage in the Boardroom* (it never appeared), presumably a tell-all about the soap opera dramatics at Fairbanks Whitney. Just days after John Kennedy's assassination, he wrote to an old acquaintance, Walter Jenkins, now a special assistant to Lyndon Johnson, offering several names of "public spirited people" available for government service, including his old friends Edgar Kaiser and George Killion, chairman of the MGM board. He followed it up with a memo on the attitude of Europeans toward the new president. Immediately after writing to Jenkins, Karr got Drew Pearson to write a column praising LBJ's zeal for cutting red tape. In the column, Karr related that he had been sitting in a Fairbanks, Morse meeting in Chicago when the then–vice president called, determined to get small pumps shipped to Asia to alleviate rural poverty. Although the product was no longer produced, Karr obtained some from a warehouse and had them refurbished and shipped overseas, even as LBJ badgered Karr to fulfill his promise and checked to make sure they worked.[9]

This barely disguised effort to curry favor with LBJ by retailing stories of his deep concerns about alleviating poverty next led Karr to decide by February 1964 to write a biography of the new president. He talked to a number of old Texas friends, including Henry Wallace's former aide, Harold Young, signed a contract to produce a manuscript under the title *Come Let Us Reason Together*, and sent LBJ a telegram informing him of his venture and asking if he could have the "opportunity of discreetly and unobtrusively observing you in action this weekend in California." Karr allowed that Hubert Humphrey had relayed the president's approval, and a handwritten note on his telegram indicates that thanks to Jack Valenti, another presidential aide, Karr accompanied LBJ on at least a portion of the California trip. When a newspaper story in *Variety* noted that "among Karr's literary works, upcoming, is his reminiscences" of LBJ, "the manuscript of which is not complete," another White House aide acerbically noted on the story that "he has nothing to reminisce about." The project went nowhere.[10]

His involvement with Fairbanks Whitney had focused Karr's energies away from Hollywood for several years, but, armed with his generous severance settlement, and no doubt concluding that writing about either corporate infighting or Lyndon Johnson was unlikely to prove either lucrative or exciting enough, by early 1964 Karr had offices at Columbia Pictures. He quickly renewed his ties with Max Youngstein. After working for several Hollywood studios in the 1940s, Youngstein and a small group of partners had taken control of United Artists in 1951 and returned it to profitability, before it later became part of MGM. By 1964, he had left the company and become an independent producer. In February, Karr and Youngstein formed Diversified Films, Inc., headquartered in Manhattan, with plans to produce a series of films for Columbia after making *The Money Trap* for MGM. Coming out in 1965, starring Glenn Ford, Elke Sommer, Rita Hayworth, and Ricardo Montalbán, this first venture was a commercial success and Karr received a credit as coproducer.[11]

In later years Youngstein denigrated Karr's contributions to their projects. In an interview he suggested that Karr had appeared at his home one day, bemoaning his situation and claiming to need a job to avoid penury. Youngstein insisted that he had arranged Karr's gig as an associate producer at MGM, but that Karr did little for his salary, while enjoying the status and perks that went with the job. He was affable and "knew as many jokes as Milton Berle," but knew nothing about being a producer. In fact, contrary to this disparaging remark, Karr and Youngstein cooperated for several years on a number of projects.[12]

Youngstein remained in California and Karr soon moved back to New York. While his partner concentrated on movies, Karr set out to produce plays under Diversified's aegis. His first efforts, directed at the Broadway stage, were not auspicious. Karr raised money from a number of investors, including Drew Pearson, to finance an original play, *Xmas in Las Vegas*, written by Jack Richardson and Heywood Hale Broun. Directed by Fred Coe, whose previous credits included such hits as *A Thousand Clowns* and *The Miracle Worker*, it opened at the Ethel Barrymore Theatre on November 4, 1965 and closed two days later after only four performances. A second venture, *The Playroom*, produced by Kermit Bloomgarden "in association with Max Youngstein and David Karr," opened at the Brooks Atkinson Theatre on December 5 and closed January 1 after thirty-three shows. A third effort was more successful. *Wait Until Dark*, produced by Coe, directed by Arthur Penn, and starring Lee Remick and Robert Duvall, opened in February 1966, ran through December 31 and followed with a successful run in London.[13]

Early in 1966, Karr and Youngstein signed a contract to produce five more movies for MGM over eighteen months. Karr received coproducer's credits for Youngstein's last two pictures under contract to MGM. *The Dangerous Days of Kiowa Jones*, a pilot for a TV series, was broadcast on Christmas day 1966, and later released commercially. *Welcome to Hard Times*, based on E. L. Doctorow's western novel, starred Henry Fonda, Keenan Wynn, Warren Oates, and Aldo Ray. Released in 1967, it enjoyed a modest success. Whatever Karr's contributions to these productions, Youngstein had had enough of his partner to decide to end their business relationship. Three other planned productions, *The Playroom*, *The Fog*, and *Cry Havoc* were never made, even though Robert Vaughn, then starring in the hit show *The Man from U.N.C.L.E.*, was signed to play the lead in the latter.[14]

The break with Youngstein was made easier by a sudden change in Karr's personal life, a shift that proved life-altering. Smarting from the

Fairbanks Whitney debacle in 1964, Karr had also been beset by the collapse of his second marriage. Writing Drew Pearson in September, he bemoaned his fortunes; "having just lost a wife, home and kids is quite a jolt. In addition, moving to California constitutes a further jolt. I feel like I have had four wisdom teeth pulled simultaneously without anesthetic."[15]

David and Madeline had divorced on May 17, 1956; a week later he had married Buffy Rappleye. Neither marriage had ended without bitterness and financial obligations. One source interviewed by the FBI in 1960 during an investigation to give Karr a security clearance at Fairbanks Whitney reported that he blamed his first wife for his Communist "affiliation" and "stated that he could not obtain a security clearance at his company" because of her. His anger at his second wife was intensified because it had been her decision to leave him. He also owed child support for four children.[16]

Karr's pain over his second failed marriage did not last long. Youngstein recalled that although he was not particularly handsome, he could "charm the pants off ladies." While working on the set of *Welcome to Hard Times* in 1966, Karr got engaged to Buff Cobb, a stunning and well-connected Hollywood figure. Born in Florence, Italy, in 1927, Patrizia Cobb Chapman adopted the stage name of her grandfather, author and humorist Irvin S. Cobb. Irvin wrote for the *Saturday Evening Post*, sold his stories to Fox Film, acted in some of them, and hosted the 1935 Academy Awards. Soon after Buff's high school graduation, she began her acting career and, at the Washington home of Henry and Claire Booth Luce (a boarding school friend of her mother's), met Greg Bautzer, an up-and-coming Hollywood attorney sixteen years her senior. They had been quickly engaged and married when Buff was just seventeen. The marriage lasted only six months—both Bautzer, serving in the navy, and his bride began affairs almost immediately after the wedding. Over the next few decades Bautzer, dubbed "Hollywood Bachelor Number One," squired and had affairs with numerous leading ladies, including Joan Crawford, Lana Turner, Rosemary Clooney, Greer Garson, Marlene Dietrich, Paulette Goddard, Sonja Henie, Merle Oberon, Anne Sheridan, Dana Wyner, Ginger Rogers, Ava Gardner, Rita Hayworth, Jane Wyman, Dorothy Lamour, and Peggy Lee, as well as serving as personal lawyer for Howard Hughes.[17]

Cobb's second marriage in 1947 to an actor lasted only one year. While performing with Tallulah Bankhead in a Chicago production in 1946, she then met Mike Wallace, the future broadcast journalist (and *60 Minutes* host), just discharged from the Navy; they began a radio show that moved to television in New York in 1951, dubbed *Mike and Buff.* Done live and in color, it was the first TV talk show that featured two stars debating a different topic every day and then interviewing experts. The *New York Times* praised the show as "an object lesson in how television can be eminently educational without being self-conscious about it." They soon added a second show, *All Around the Town*, conducting live interviews from various locales around the city. It later became a prime-time series. Their professional relationship morphed into marriage in 1949; after the interview show ended, so did their marriage and they were divorced in 1957.[18]

Cobb appeared as a panelist on a TV quiz show, *Masquerade*, during the 1950s; in the first half of the 1960s, she produced two Broadway shows, at which time she probably met Karr. By 1966, they were engaged and had already planned a round-the-world cruise. But David Karr quickly jettisoned her after meeting a wealthy Frenchwoman. On a visit to Paris, Karr was introduced to Denise (Michette) Solal, a member of a prominent and well-to-do French Jewish family. Born in Algiers in 1931, she had immigrated to France with her parents and brothers and was an accomplished lawyer, employed by the Rothschild family. Her family had a very successful business; her older brother, Jean-Louis Solal, also made a fortune developing the earliest French supermarkets and malls.

Never married, Solal, described by Youngstein as having "medium good looks, bright, a lawyer in her early thirties from a very wealthy French family," accepted an invitation to visit David on the set of *Welcome to Hard Times.* Youngstein, whose animus toward his former partner no doubt colored his recollection, claimed that after meeting her, Karr had quickly pulled a Dun & Bradstreet rating on her family and began a romance. Whether it was love or calculation, within a few weeks, Karr had broken his engagement to Buff Cobb and on July 22, 1966, he and Michette were married in France. According to Karr's second ex-wife, Cobb had a nervous breakdown after their breakup; neither her future film, TV, or Broadway careers ever amounted to much.[19]

6

DEAL-MAKER

By November 1966, David Karr had moved to France with his new wife. He assured his mother that he had "never been happier in my life." Ensconced in an apartment on the Boulevard D'Inkermann bought by his in-laws for $125,000, he looked out at the Eiffel Tower, took French lessons during the mornings, and worked on screenplays in the afternoon. Michette persuaded him to have another child. Karr's sister Feenie, who nursed a lifelong resentment of her older brother, speculated that David did not want another child, but "that was the price of admission to the counting house." She presciently warned that since "he has to be the chaser, the pursuer," he might very well "desert her [Michette] when she needs him the most," just as he had done with his first two wives. In any case, his youngest son, Jean-Michel Karr, was born in late December 1967. Karr doted on him.[1]

A visiting friend reported that the Karrs lived "in the most lavish place she'd ever seen" with "five servants and two butlers." Just before leaving California, David had received a new three-year contract from MGM "for more money." One task was to produce a Leo Rosten suspense novel, *A Most Private Intrigue*, with Rosten writing the script. It never came to fruition. He also set up a new television company in Paris and planned trips to London, New York, and California. Although his efforts to produce films waned as he moved into other businesses, Karr never totally abandoned his connections to Hollywood. As late as 1977, he attempted to broker a deal for British mogul Sir Jimmy Goldsmith to buy a controlling interest in Columbia Pictures.[2]

During his early days in Paris, Karr solidified his ties to Israel first forged when Fairbanks Whitney had worked on the desalinization project. When the Arab-Israeli crisis caused by the Egyptian closure of the Suez Canal to Israeli ships and the removal of UN peacekeepers in the Sinai moved the region closer to war in the spring of 1967, Karr wrote Drew Pearson that he was preparing to fly to Israel to offer his aid. He cheered the explosion of support for Israel among the French people, in spite of de Gaulle's pro-Arab tilt, and called the large crowd that gathered outside the Israeli embassy to sing the Marseilles and Hatikvah "fantastic" and "inspiring." The upcoming conflict, he said, was a "struggle between good and evil." At the end of June, his sister mentioned that she was delighted that David and his eldest son Andy had gone to Jerusalem.[3]

Karr's connections to Israel had, of course, been made while he partnered with the government to make a success of the desalinization venture. During that failed effort, he developed a close relationship with a remarkable Israeli politician and bureaucrat who became a confidant, an employee, and, according to some sensationalistic newspaper accounts, an accomplice in some of Karr's shady business deals. His friendship with Eliezer Preminger, today a largely forgotten figure in Israeli history, also probably brought Karr into the orbit of the Israeli intelligence services.

Eliezer Preminger's life mirrored Karr's in some respects but featured far more peril and more intense ideological commitments. A onetime Communist activist who grew disillusioned with the Soviet Union, Preminger gradually transitioned into a successful businessman. He had excellent contacts in the Israeli intelligence world and his international travel, intense Zionist convictions, and connections to other disillusioned radicals may have influenced Karr's own ties to the shadow world of political intrigue.

Born in Vienna in 1920, Erich Preminger grew up in a country convulsed by both Communism and fascism. In 1934, the same year he joined a Communist youth group at the age of fourteen, the Social Democratic government of the city was dismantled after an assault by the army and private militias. Hitler marched into Austria in 1938 and proclaimed its unification with the Third Reich. Amid increasing repression Preminger was active in the Party underground until he emigrated to Palestine in February 1939. Both his parents remained in Austria and were killed in the Holocaust. He stayed politically active in the tiny Palestine Communist Party (PCP) while attending the Technion in Haifa, studying engineering, but after graduating, he became a full-time activist in the Party underground where he was known as Yossel the Tall, because of his height.[4]

To be a Communist in Palestine was to be estranged from Jewish society. A significant portion of the Israeli left was inspired by socialist ideals, but in addition to the split between Communists and socialists that divided European Marxists, in Palestine the issue of Zionism complicated political divisions and prevented Communists from gaining any significant base in the Jewish community. The Soviet Union and its Communist Party leadership had been implacably opposed to Zionism, attacking it as a bourgeois, nationalist heresy. The PCP, founded by Jews in 1923, obediently followed suit, severely limiting its appeal in a colony where most Jews strongly supported a Jewish homeland. Additionally, the Communist International frequently bemoaned the overwhelmingly Jewish composition of the PCP and pressured it to add Arab members and champion Arab interests. Many of the early PCP members, facing legal attacks by the British authorities, were either expelled, emigrated to Western Europe, or returned to the Soviet Union from which they or their parents had left years before.[5]

Jewish Communists who remained in Palestine faced different dangers and decisions. Forced by Comintern pressure to support Arab nationalism, even when it endangered the Jewish community, the PCP had little influence or presence. A party split in 1944 divided Jewish and Arab Communists. Both factions, however, opposed the creation of a Jewish state. With the end of World War II, knowledge of the mass slaughter of European Jewry, and increasing pressure for the creation of a Jewish state, such ideological rigidity sparked a revolt.

Preminger was one of the leaders of a group that broke away from the mainstream Jewish Communists in 1945 to form the Hebrew Communists, objecting to the Party's hostility to the creation of a Jewish state. The Hebrew Communists, maintaining that Jews were a nation and entitled to a national home in Palestine, attracted a number of talented people, whose future political trajectories took them in many directions. Their most prominent figure, Shmuel Ettinger, left the Communist movement in 1948 and became one of Israel's most distinguished historians.[6]

In 1948, under the impact of the Soviet Union's support for the creation of Israel, the Hebrew Communists reunited with their more orthodox brethren and the Arab Communists to form Maki; an avowedly Communist Party. Preminger was one of four Communists elected to the first Knesset, or Parliament, on the Party's list. He and an Arab Communist, Tawfik Toubi, were the only two lawmakers under the age of thirty. By the time the first Knesset took office in March 1949, however, he had already run afoul of Communist Party leadership, which supported the Soviet Union's position that Jerusalem should be internationalized. Preminger wanted the portion of Jerusalem controlled by Israel to be the state's capital. Moreover, his mentor, Ettinger, had returned from a trip to Eastern European Communist countries with disturbing reports of the horrific consequences of the Nazi-Soviet Pact and the more urgent issue of anti-Semitism in the new "people's democracies." Preminger himself visited Prague in 1948, and the reality about the Soviet Union began to sink in.

Preminger's disagreements with the orthodox Communists attracted the attention of the Zionist leadership. Preminger was expelled from the Communist Party in February 1949, at which time the Party demanded that it be allowed to replace him in the Knesset. This was rebuffed by the Zionist parties controlling that body. Following his expulsion, Preminger promptly announced the resurrection of the Hebrew Communist Party and served as its only representative in the Knesset from June until August. In March, Prime Minister Ben-Gurion received a report of a meeting of one of his aides with Preminger; the Hebrew Communists were "more cautious and intelligent than Mapam in respect of the Soviets...there are serious disagreements between them and the PCP (Palestine Communist Party). They are Zionists...they favor a [Jewish] state for its own sake, while the PCP favors it only as a tactic."[7]

Preminger disbanded his one-man Party in August and decided to join the left-wing Marxist Mapam Party. It was a strange choice for a man who objected to the pro-Soviet policies of Maki and the Israeli

Communists. Mapam was to the left of David Ben-Gurion's ruling Mapai Party, and pro-Soviet, a fact that kept it out of government coalitions until 1953, when it expelled its pro-Soviet wing and finally broke with the Soviet Communist Party. If Preminger's decision had been motivated by a desire to extend his political career, it was a failure. In elections to the second Knesset held in 1951, he lost his seat.[8]

Within Mapam, Preminger had been allied with Yaacov Hazan, an ideologue who frequently denounced Israel's pro-Western foreign policy. Whether his decision to join Mapam reflected his genuine convictions or was prompted by a covert agreement with the Israeli security forces who monitored both the Communist Party of Israel and Mapam, is not clear. The Ben-Gurion government suspected that Mapam cadres were more loyal to their ideological movement than to the state of Israel. The Shin Bet, the internal security force, recruited informers, and a onetime Communist like Preminger who had impressed Ben-Gurion with his Zionist convictions, would have been a key target.

Mapam's pro-Soviet policies were put to the test in 1952. One of its leaders, Mordechai Oren, was arrested in Czechoslovakia and convicted along with other defendants on charges of spying for America, Britain, and Zionist forces. Under torture Oren confessed and implicated his codefendants. The "Slansky" purge trials were only one of the body blows to pro-Soviet Jews in the waning years of Stalin's rule in the U.S.S.R. Purges of Yiddish writers, denunciations of "rootless cosmopolitans," and charges that Jewish doctors had conspired to poison Soviet leaders were vivid demonstrations of a pervasive anti-Semitism at the heart of the Communist project.

One faction within Mapam, however, remained loyal to the Soviet Union to the point of defending the legitimacy of the purge trials. It was led by Moshe Sneh, a former Haganah commander, and Adolf Berman, whose Marxist Zionism had led him to leave Communist Poland in 1950 and who had quickly been elected to the Knesset in 1951. Sneh, Berman, and Preminger voted against a resolution in November 1952 condemning Oren's imprisonment. In early December Preminger again sided with Sneh, accepting the accusations that Oren was a Zionist spy serving the interests of the bourgeoisie. By early January 1953, the Sneh faction had lost their jobs and positions in Mapam; soon afterward, they joined the Israeli Communist Party.[9]

Preminger did not follow Sneh and Berman into the political wilderness. He also did not defect to the Mapam majority to advance in
the Party. Meir Yaari, the leader of Mapam, offered him the position
of Secretary of the Party's Central Committee, a post that might well
have led him back to political prominence, but he declined and entered
law school, receiving his degree from Hebrew University in 1956. By
the time he graduated, Mapam, cleansed of its pro-Soviet faction, had
entered the government and he joined the Development Ministry; in
June he became its Deputy Director-General.

There is no direct evidence that Preminger worked for Israeli security organs, although his son reported that Eliezer was close friends with
a number of high-ranking Mossad officials over the years, and, he has
long suspected he cooperated with Israeli intelligence. His brief flirtation with the pro-Soviet Sneh faction may have been at the behest of
security officials. Also, an Israeli researcher with excellent contacts in
the intelligence community reported that Preminger was regarded by
retirees he spoke to as "one of the good guys."[10]

Menachem Bader, head of the Development Ministry, was one of
Mapam's less ideological figures. One of his protégés in addition to
Preminger, was Joseph Katz, a former Soviet spy. Katz had served as a
contact man for Elizabeth Bentley and numerous other Soviet spies in
America in the 1940s. Israeli intelligence questioned him extensively
when he immigrated from France, where he had broken with the KGB.
After convincing them that his break was genuine, he worked briefly
for Mapam and the Development Ministry in Europe and Africa,
before beginning yet another career as a technical advisor on lighting
for the James Bond movies. Katz and Preminger, both disillusioned ex-
Communists, were "great buddies"; their families socialized together,
and Katz later tried in vain to persuade Preminger to go to work for
Harry Saltzman, a coproducer of the Bond movies.[11]

As he transitioned from the Communist Party to the Hebrew
Communists, to Mapam's left wing, to its mainstream, Preminger
became, in the words of his son, "more and more disappointed from the
ability of Communism to cure the world and to solve the problems of
the Jews." He also gained a greater appreciation for social democracy
and "lost his belief he could change the world."[12]

Preminger worked closely with Karr as the Fairbanks Whitney

project to operationalize the Zarchin process in collaboration with the Israeli government took shape. The two quickly became friends. Apart from their common interest in the success of the desalinization plant, they shared some common experiences, though Preminger's choices had been far more fraught than Karr's. Both had grown up in middle-class Jewish families and moved to the political left in response to the rise of fascism. While Karr had been far less open and resolute in embracing Communism, Preminger leapt into underground activity when forced to live under Nazi rule. While Karr labored to hide his youthful connections to Communism in order to promote his career, Preminger became a Party apparatchik, organizing on behalf of the Palestine Communist Party and running for political office on its ticket. Both then abandoned the Communist faith of their youth. Karr had done so as he moved closer to men of influence and wealth but had never convinced counterintelligence professionals that his break was wholehearted and sincere. Preminger deliberately sacrificed his political career as he lost his political faith; his political journey to the more moderate left was accepted, in part perhaps because his old comrades denounced him as a traitor, and those in power recognized that when forced to choose between Communism and Zionism, Preminger had felt the pull of his ethnic identity and openly embraced the latter. By the early 1960s, partly due to his Israeli experiences—and Preminger's encouragement— Karr was more openly Jewish. His eldest son, Andy, was bar mitzvahed. Preminger's son recalled Karr as "very much pro-Israel" and "willing to help Israel as much as he could."[13]

Preminger spent the 1961–1962 academic year at Harvard with a Public Service Fellowship in Economic Development. In his visa application and in the biographical announcements of his speeches to American audiences, his Knesset service was mentioned, but not the political party to which he had belonged. In addition to studying, he kept up a busy schedule of talks to a variety of mainstream Jewish groups, ranging from the United Jewish Appeal to Hadassah and campus Hillels.

In early 1963, with Karr ousted as CEO—although still nominally supervising the desalinization project—Preminger, whose Mapam Party was no longer part of the governing coalition and who had lost his Development Ministry post, became commercial manager of the Chemicals and Phosphates Company, a publicly traded firm headquartered in Tel Aviv, which supplied products to both domestic and foreign sources, serving in that capacity until 1967. He was reunited with Karr in 1968 in Paris, both working for Charles Forte, the hotel magnate. Their collaboration was to spawn a series of bizarre rumors and elaborate conspiracy theories based on Preminger's "shadowy" connections that reached the tabloid press after Karr's death in 1979.

While Karr's ties to Preminger and Israel deepened in the aftermath of the Six-Day War in 1967, his activities in Paris were at first largely focused on building connections with influential men and scouting out potential business deals.

Throughout his days in Paris, Karr remained in touch with Drew Pearson, feeding him information, tips, and reflections on French politics and European views of the United States. Although both men were skeptical about the Johnson administration's Vietnam policy, they were far more positive about LBJ than any recent president; both had long-standing ties to the Texan going back to the 1930s. With the Paris peace talks getting under way in 1968, Pearson asked Karr to keep his antennae out and report any information that came his way; to facilitate his endeavors, the columnist wrote to Averell Harriman, whom Lyndon Johnson had appointed as his chief negotiator, introducing Karr. Although Harriman "ignored half a dozen phone calls," Karr did contact him before the end of the year. Harriman, however, made little progress with the talks and was about to be replaced once Richard Nixon won the presidency.[14]

Karr had more luck ingratiating himself with another American envoy to Paris, the newly appointed U.S. Ambassador Sargent Shriver. Karr met with Shriver shortly after the Kennedy brother-in-law, first director of the Peace Corps, and key architect of the War on Poverty arrived to take up his new duties and act as host of the American delegation to the Paris peace talks in July 1968. Shriver's service in the Johnson administration as his brother-in-law Robert Kennedy was launching a presidential campaign to unseat LBJ put him in the middle of American political turmoil. Meanwhile, student riots and factory takeovers were similarly precipitating chaos in France.

After RFK's assassination, Drew Pearson reminded Karr that Shriver was "at the head of the vice-presidential list," a position he eventually was offered, four years later. Karr became a frequent visitor to Shriver's

Paris office, where they smoked cigars and chatted. Karr enthralled Shriver, who called him "a wheeler dealer. You never knew exactly what the hell he was doing, or who he was with, or what nefarious or glorious thing he was doing. He was an extraordinary, exceptional, brilliant man who didn't play by any rule book."[15]

When they first met, Karr was dabbling with a variety of business opportunities. He still had his Hollywood connections, occasionally recommending scripts to MGM. He also negotiated with MGM on behalf of Electric & Musical Industries, a company with which he had dealt while at Fairbanks Whitney. EMI was trying to purchase some of MGM's London properties. Through his wife's connections, Karr met Baron Edmond de Rothschild, who admired his creativity and chutzpah, and provided him with office space, prompting Karr to boast that he worked for the most famous banking family in the world. None of these efforts, however, had yet led to any significant results.[16]

His first significant business triumph was initiated by his wife's stature in Paris. Michette's connections within the French Jewish world eased Karr's acceptance in the elite French world of high finance, whose denizens included the Rothschild family and bankers and investors associated with Lazard Frères, the very distinguished and powerful private investment firm. One of the people Karr met was Anna Dupré, widow of the hotelier and thoroughbred-racing millionaire François Dupré. Owner of three of the most famous and elegant hotels in Paris, the George V, Plaza Athénée, and La Tremoille, Mme. Dupré had resisted repeated entreaties to sell them. There were numerous obstacles to a sale; not only had President Charles de Gaulle once insisted that they were part of the French patrimony, never to be allowed to fall into foreign hands, but they faced labor troubles that had eaten into their profits.

Karr met Charles Forte in 1968. An Italian-born Englishman who had made a fortune in the catering and restaurant business, Forte opened his first milk bar in 1934 and later ran the concessions at the new Heathrow Airport. In the 1950s, he began to buy struggling hotels and turn them around financially. By the late 1960s, he was anxious to expand his operations abroad and capture more prestigious properties. Karr befriended the aging Mme. Dupré, earned her trust, and introduced her to Forte. He then helped to negotiate the deal, soothed over issues with the labor unions, and became a key executive in Forte's business in 1970. Karr also hired his old Israeli friend, Eliezer Preminger, to move to Paris to work for Forte in 1968.[17]

Always an elegant and fashionable hotel, the George V became a hub for diplomatic visitors under Karr's stewardship. Shriver suggested that he create a Paris Foreign Correspondents' Club inside. When President Nixon visited Paris in 1969, his entourage of 220 stayed at the hotel. *Variety* added that Karr's wife, a "Parisian Portia," had retired from her law practice to be a full-time mother.[18]

Karr continued to work for Forte for several more years, brokering his purchase of the Hotel Pierre in New York and, after a merger with the Trust House group formed Trust Houses Forte, explored opportunities to construct hotels in Eastern Europe and the U.S.S.R. Forte found Karr "a shrewd and usually successful negotiator." More colorfully, he told a reporter "if David Karr thought you had an interest in the Taj Mahal, he would have no hesitation about going to the Indian government and saying, 'Look, I've got this deal.'" The business relationship foundered in 1976, although Karr remained in contact with Forte. Karr's very successful brokering of the Paris hotel deal left him ebullient. His sister reported that "the old magician has conjured up still another world for himself, and I marvel at his vitality."[19]

Karr made two other business acquaintances in Paris who were later to fuel all kinds of conspiracy theories and speculation. Armand Hammer would get him involved with Russia. Although he never had a significant business relationship with Aristotle Onassis, the flamboyant Greek shipping magnate got Karr—well after both of their deaths—accused of being involved in the assassination of Robert Kennedy. Although baseless, the story, told by Peter Evans, a British journalist and biographer, used just enough factual material mixed with innuendo to enthrall the swarm of Kennedy assassination conspiracy theorists. The truth, though it was not without its share of intrigue, is more straightforward.

Karr met Aristotle Onassis in New York in 1965 while Karr was still doing public relations work. Onassis loaned him money—from $15,000 to $50,000 according to different reports—to buy the movie rights to *Welcome to Hard Times*. One source of their developing relationship was a shared dislike of Robert Kennedy. Kennedy and Aristotle Onassis had a long history of enmity, going back to Robert's involvement in a congressional investigation of Greek ships carrying goods to Communist China during the Korean War that implicated Onassis. The feud festered over Onassis's affair with Jacqueline Kennedy's sister, Lee Radziwill.

For his part, Drew Pearson enjoyed tweaking the Kennedys and heartily disliked Bobby, possibly dating to his days as a staffer for Senator Joseph McCarthy's Senate committee. Interviewed by Mike Wallace on ABC in 1957, Pearson insisted that Ted Sorenson had actually written *Profiles in Courage*, labeling Jack Kennedy the only author who had received a Pulitzer Prize for a book he did not write. Infuriated, the Kennedy clan threatened a lawsuit; Clark Clifford and Robert Kennedy extracted an apology from ABC, over Pearson's strident objections. In any case, Onassis fed Karr damaging or embarrassing material on the Kennedys, which Pearson then obligingly printed. One tidbit from 1963, alleging that Onassis's long-term affair with Maria Callas had foundered and "his ambition is to be a brother-in-law of President Kennedy," referring to his affair with Radziwill, particularly rankled. Karr, in turn, fed Onassis rumors supplied by Pearson; in January 1967, he reported that Pearson had received a tip that JFK's assassination was in reprisal for Bobby's foiled plot to kill Fidel Castro and that a right-wing scandal sheet had charged that Bobby was also implicated in Marilyn Monroe's death.[20]

Karr's associations with both Aristotle Onassis and Sargent Shriver may be connected to a lengthy and mysterious meeting he and Drew Pearson had with President Lyndon Johnson in April 1968. Karr wrote to LBJ on March 26 that he would "be making one of my rare trips back home to the States next week" and staying with the Pearsons; he asked "to drop by and pay my respects" and offer some information on the "international financial area if the President had time." Karr and Pearson met with Johnson on April 3 at 2:00 p.m., for what was originally billed as a "purely social" visit by "a great admirer of the President." Pearson had told a presidential aide that Karr had advice to offer on international banking "but understands fully that the President may not wish any extended discussion" and would be content with "a greeting and brief visit." It was a very busy day at the White House; LBJ had announced his decision not to run for reelection three days before and the North Vietnamese had just indicated their willingness to enter substantive talks in Paris; Johnson's day, which began at 8:00 A.M., ran until 12:45

the next morning, filled with meetings with senior officials. Yet, Pearson and Karr met with him for fifty minutes.[21]

Karr and Pearson clearly thought the visit was more than social or chitchat about arcane financial matters. Two days afterward Pearson referred to "your historic meeting" in a letter to Karr and Karr responded that "it was fun once again to be part of history with you"; Johnson himself wrote to Karr that "I enjoyed your letter almost as much as your visit." And, just days later, Johnson indicated to Senator Eugene McCarthy that Kennedy's presidential bid was doomed. In mid-May, Johnson asked J. Edgar Hoover for a full report on Aristotle Onassis.[22]

No notes were taken at the meeting, so it is impossible to know what was discussed. But the circumstances suggest that Karr had learned that Onassis and Jacqueline Kennedy planned to marry and he told LBJ. The relationship between the aging tycoon and the glamorous former First Lady had begun years earlier, while Onassis was still involved in an affair with her sister, Lee Radziwill. After the death of the Kennedys' prematurely born son, Patrick, in August 1963, Onassis invited Jackie to recuperate aboard his yacht. Both JFK and RFK had strenuously opposed the trip, correctly foreseeing that it would generate controversy in the United States. Congressional critics complained about influence peddling and the press blared about unseemly self-indulgence. According to Peter Evans, not always the most reliable source, Jackie, still smarting over her husband's affairs, slept with Onassis on the trip. Just a few months later, Onassis stayed at the White House as Jackie's guest during JFK's funeral, precipitating an angry outburst from Robert Kennedy.[23]

By March 1968, Onassis was determined to marry Jackie but she was ambivalent, largely because of fierce opposition from her brother-in-law. Not only did RFK despise Onassis, but he feared the impact it would have on his own presidential campaign. Evans maintained that Onassis used Karr to try to sabotage Robert by leaking information about the Onassis–Jackie affair to Kennedy's hated rival, President Lyndon Johnson. But it is also possible that Karr had learned of the affair from Shriver; the entire Kennedy clan was opposed to the relationship between the presidential widow and the wealthy Greek businessman and playboy. In any event, Robert Kennedy was assassinated in Los Angeles in June and Jackie suddenly married Onassis in October after the news of their romance leaked to the press.

Robert Kennedy's assassination by a Palestinian, Sirhan Sirhan, and the subsequent Kennedy–Onassis marriage provided the fuel for an elaborate and bizarre conspiracy theory that linked both Onassis and David Karr to Palestinian terrorism. The alleged plot was detailed by Peter Evans, a former foreign correspondent for the *London Daily Express* and author of an earlier authorized biography of Onassis.

In *Nemesis: Aristotle Onassis, Jackie O, and the Love Triangle That Brought Down the Kennedys*, published in 2004, Evans recounted how the tycoon's daughter, Christina (who had her own complicated relationship with Karr), told Evans in 1988 that her father had paid protection money to a Palestinian terrorist in 1968 to avert attacks on Olympic Airlines, money that he later learned was "used to finance the assassination of Robert Kennedy." Christina died a few weeks later, before she could fill in the details, but Yannis Georgakis, a close friend of Aristotle Onassis's and an official in his foundation, finally unveiled the "truth" several years later.[24]

According to Evans, Karr introduced Dr. Michael Hassner to Onassis in January 1968 as a consultant for the Arab Bank and someone who could solve financial problems plaguing Olympic Airlines, one of the Greek magnate's companies. Evans was unclear about whether Karr knew that Hassner was not what he pretended to be. The name was an alias; he was actually Mahmoud Hamshari, a militant member of Yasser Arafat's Fatah organization. Born near Jaffa in 1933, Hamshari had received a Ph.D. in economics from the University of Algiers. Married to a Frenchwoman, he was the PLO's chief representative in France. A suave, sophisticated figure, he also was a hard-liner within the fractious terrorist group. After the Six-Day War in 1967, he had allegedly argued at a secret meeting that Fatah, Yasser Arafat's organization that dominated the PLO, should strike at America in retaliation for its support of Israel by "kill[ing] a high-profile American on American soil" to make America "think twice about backing the Jews."[25]

When he finally met privately with Onassis in 1968, Hamshari allegedly demanded protection money to ensure that terrorists would not target Olympic Airlines planes. Onassis regarded the payoffs as a cost of doing business; instead of going to law enforcement he supposedly met several times with Hamshari and the two men developed a rapport, fueled by their common dislike of America, shared anti-Semitism, and histories of exile (Onassis's family had fled from Turkish-occupied Anatolia in the early twentieth century). According to Evans, in March 1968 the two of them agreed to kill Robert Kennedy, using a portion of the protection money provided by Onassis to finance the plot. While Hamshari's motive was allegedly straightforward—to carry out his plan to strike at an American politician—Onassis supposedly had a more personal objective: eliminating a man he perceived as the strongest obstacle to his goal of marrying Jackie Kennedy.

However much the two men might have despised Robert Kennedy, Evans's scenario implausibly conflated the threat of hijackings and the timing of RFK's assassination. While there had been a number of airplane hijackings in the 1960s, most were carried out by American radicals and malcontents anxious to reach Cuba. The only Arab plane hijacking in 1968 took place in July and was directed at El Al, the Israeli airline. Nor was the PLO involved; it was the Popular Front for the Liberation of Palestine, a rival group, that carried out the crime. Not until 1970, when the PFLP simultaneously hijacked five planes (an El Al attack failed) and flew three of them to Jordan where they were blown up (a fifth flew to Cairo), did world attention and concern spike. That a shrewd and tough businessman like Onassis would pay bribes to prevent a hijacking by a group that had not carried any out is very unlikely.

The evidence that Hamshari recruited Kennedy assassin Sirhan Sirhan is even less compelling or persuasive. A Palestinian who admitted he had killed Kennedy "for his country," Sirhan was, by the evidence of his journals, obsessed with eliminating a man he despised for his pro-Israeli policies. Some conspiracy theorists wondered if he could have been hypnotized and programmed to carry out the murder, claiming that there was a period of a few weeks about which he could remember nothing, "a blanket of white fog." Hamshari, Evans claims, had visited Los Angeles in the spring of 1968 and, supposedly at the recommendation of David Karr, had consulted with Dr. William Bryan to treat his sinus infections and headaches. Karr had used Bryan when he lived in L.A., even hiring him to wean Aldo Ray off liquor during the filming of Welcome to Hard Times. Bryan also claimed to be an expert in hypnosis who had worked with the CIA and acted as a consultant on The Manchurian Candidate, the political thriller about a programmed assassin.[26]

Investigators, however, could not find any lengthy period during which Sirhan might have been "programmed" and it would have taken a remarkable network to move from deciding in March to kill Kennedy to recruiting an assassin, programming him, and carrying out the operation a mere three months later. Evans did find old friends and relatives of Onassis who insisted that he had financed the operation. Helene Gaillet, a photographer who had a brief affair with Onassis in 1974, told Evans that a dying Onassis confessed his role to her. Christina Onassis believed that unbeknownst to Onassis, the protection money had been used to finance RFK's murder. And Yannis Georgakis, former head of Olympic Airlines, insisted that Onassis had fully known about what the money was used for. But the unsupported boasts of a dying man or the suspicions of some of those close to him are thin reeds upon which to base such serious claims.[27]

Likewise, the evidence that David Karr was at the center, or even periphery, of such a conspiracy is far from persuasive. Evans recounts an interview with Leslie Linder, a onetime agent whom Karr had known when he worked at MGM. According to Linder, Karr wanted him to sell his memoirs, in which he would reveal that Onassis had financed Kennedy's murder. Just before they were to meet for further discussions, Karr died. And Evans retells Helene Gaillet's story that immediately after learning that the dying Onassis was alone with her, and fearful of what he might reveal, several of his closest aides descended on the island of Skorpios, among them David Karr, who spooked her: "You just felt his presence, the way you feel a chill when somebody walks over your grave."[28]

Evans also claims that in 1971, Onassis had Karr inform the PLO that Hamshari had embezzled some of the protection money, hoping to remove the only concrete link between himself and the Kennedy assassination. In the summer of 1971, Karr's yacht, Asmeda Hope, mysteriously "exploded" and sank in the harbor at Cannes. A few weeks later Onassis's Learjet crashed into the sea off Cap d'Antibes, killing the pilots. According to one of Onassis's aides, Karr told him he suspected Hamshari was behind both events: "These guys have memories like flypaper for an insult," he reportedly said, without specifying the nature of the insult. (Buffy Cooke recalled that David thought that the yacht, which caught fire and did not explode, was sabotaged.)[29]

Hamshari, however, had made other enemies. In addition to serving as the PLO representative in France, he was one of the leaders of Black September, the secret terrorist group responsible for, among other actions, the Munich massacre of Israeli Olympic athletes in September 1972. Prime Minister Golda Meir had ordered the Mossad to track down and kill all those responsible for that bloody event. Hamshari was one of the targets; in December 1972 after he left his apartment in Paris, a bomb was planted on his apartment telephone. When he later answered a phone call, it was detonated, and he suffered grave injuries. A month later he died. With his usual penchant for conspiracy theories, Evans suggests that the PLO sentenced Hamshari to death for embezzlement after he was blown up and then had him medically killed while he was recuperating.[30]

There is no documentary evidence supporting the charge that Karr was involved, even if only peripherally, in Robert Kennedy's assassination, just the suppositions and recollections of several Onassis aides, who may have their own motives for lying, exaggerating, or weaving an exciting story. Moreover, Evia Karr, the last of Karr's four wives (admittedly, not the most reliable witness), has insisted that Karr never even met Onassis and that Evans fabricated what she said to him. Even if Onassis was involved in the assassination—a rather far stretch—there is no evidence that Karr himself knew at the time what was taking place.[31]

The major evidence weighing against Karr's involvement is his affection for Israel, expressed in the run-up to the Six-Day War. Would a man who wrote on June 4, 1967 that he was preparing "to fly to Israel later this week to survey the scene and see if I can do anything to help" be ready to provide aid and comfort to its most implacable and bloodthirsty enemies just a year later?[32]

Karr's detractors would point to his desire for money and suggest that he would sell his soul to the devil if he could make a profit. Years later, Armand Hammer told friends that Karr had sold Soviet weapons to the PLO: "David's Jewish, but that doesn't stop him...And he takes commissions from both sides...I wouldn't want to guess where that dishonorable bastard's going to end up." Lord Forte dismissed the idea that Karr cared about Jews as amusing and insisted the only thing he was interested in was money. Samuel Flatto-Sharon, a French businessman who fled to Israel to escape embezzlement charges and won election to the Israeli Knesset (which enabled him to avoid extradition), denounced Karr as "no friend of Israel" and insisted that the Israeli raid on Entebbe had turned up evidence that he had arranged a $10 million Soviet arms shipment to Idi Amin.[33] These are interesting allegations (although Hammer's and Flatto-Sharon's are false), but Karr had no motive for colluding to assassinate a prominent pro-Israeli American politician. Karr may have been a risk-taker, but he was not an ideological fanatic. His ties to Onassis were neither long-standing nor financially remunerative enough to justify getting involved in so deadly a plot. And, his own well-publicized involvement with the Israeli desalinization project would probably have kept a PLO representative—active in the Arab economic boycott of Israel—from confiding in him or seeking his help in a murder plot.

Ironically, the one conspiracy scenario Evans ignores completely is the possibility that Karr was feeding information to the Mossad, the Israeli intelligence service, or that Karr was actually working for the Israelis. There is some evidence for that theory. In an undated letter to his mother, written in the summer of 1969, Karr told her, "I've been on a number of secret missions for our Israeli friends which worked well." Arnold Forster, longtime head of the Anti-Defamation League, who worked closely with him from the 1930s when he worked for Drew Pearson, and cooperated with him in exposing anti-Semites, insisted that Karr was "a very intensely Jewish Jew." In 1970, Karr accompanied Shriver to Israel on behalf of Baron Edmond de Rothschild, one of his French patrons, and persuaded him to disavow his previously expressed support for the Rogers Plan, an American proposal for Arab-Israeli peace talks vehemently rejected by the Israelis as one-sided.[34]

If Karr was, in fact, working for Israeli intelligence, that might account for the fact that he had made the acquaintance of the PLO's Paris representative. Charles Forte recalled seeing Hassner in Karr's company during his negotiations for his Paris hotels in 1969. Could Karr have used his business connections in Paris and his old friendship with Eliezer Preminger to keep the Mossad informed about the PLO's man in Paris? It is a more plausible theory than the idea that overnight he morphed from a pro-Israeli Jewish businessman into a terrorist enabler.

Preminger himself, slandered after Karr's death by anonymous sources as an immoral and mysterious businessman willing to sell arms to anti-Semitic dictators pledged to Israel's destruction, is far more likely to have worked with the Mossad in defense of his country. His political trajectory had been dictated by his Zionism. While living in Paris from 1968 to 1969, he frequently met with a representative of Israeli intelligence and introduced him to Karr, who provided "intelligence gossip." And, to the end of his life, Preminger was good friends with several high-ranking Mossad officials, including Nahum Admoni, who served as a counselor at the Israeli Embassy in Paris from 1966 to 1970 and as director general of the Mossad from 1982 to 1989.[35]

For two men who had supposedly collaborated in arranging one of the most consequential assassinations of the twentieth century in 1968 and then arranged the killing of its organizer early in 1973, Karr and Onassis did not remain close. Their relationship foundered after the Yom Kippur War in 1973. Onassis's tanker business, in the midst of a major expansion, was devastated by the war's impact on oil shipping. Believing the Soviet Union knew about the plans for the Egyptian–Syrian attack, Onassis supposedly screamed at Karr: "If you're so fucking tight with the Russians, why didn't you get wind of this?"[36]

Karr's relationship with Onassis did not eventuate in any significant business deals. In the spring of 1969, Karr wrote plaintively to Pearson that "I am not getting fantastically rich, nor am I in any trouble that I am aware of," but "life in Paris is very good indeed." Nonetheless, he sounded like someone ready to give up his former life: he had realized that "something deep inside me...made me want to withdraw from the terrible competitiveness and violence of American life." Immediately after admitting that he was ready for semiretirement, Karr added "perhaps this is only in the nature of a sabbatical." It was. In July 1969, following months of illness and fatigue, worried that he was suffering from leukemia, the same disease that had killed his father, he took a lengthy vacation on his new yacht and, reinvigorated, prepared to jump back into the bear pit.[37]

After he midwifed the hotel deal for Charles Forte, Karr oversaw the operation of the George V hotel, but soon embarked on a new adventure. It came via his friendship with Sargent Shriver. After submitting his resignation as ambassador to France to Richard Nixon in early 1970, Shriver returned to the United States eager to resume his political career. He toyed with launching a primary challenge to incumbent Maryland Democratic governor Marvin Mandel as a first step in seeking the Democratic nomination for president in 1972. After that effort fizzled, he campaigned for Democratic candidates in the off-year elections. In 1971, he became a lawyer at a prominent Washington firm, soon renamed Fried, Frank, Harris, Shriver and Jacobsen, concentrating on using his international connections to bring in new business.

One of Shriver's first clients was Armand Hammer, head of Occidental Petroleum, who had long been anxious to resume doing business in the U.S.S.R. While serving as ambassador, Shriver had met with Dzhermen Gvishiani, deputy chairman of the Soviet State Committee for Science and Technology. Just as important as his position, Gvishiani was the son-in-law of Alexei Kosygin, the Soviet premier. During his work for Onassis, Karr had also established ties with Soviet officials, becoming friends with Vladimir Alkhimov, the Soviet deputy foreign trade minister, so it was natural for Shriver to bring Hammer together with Karr in 1971.[38]

Hammer quickly hired Karr as a consultant, not only for his Russian contacts, but also as a hedge against a potential hostile takeover bid for Occidental, which faced financial trouble stemming from a series of leases on oil tankers that Hammer had arranged in 1970–1971 in anticipation of a major oil shortage. Hammer, however, had guessed wrong and Occidental suffered a loss of $67 million in 1971. Karr proved useful in helping renegotiate some of these leases, no doubt because of his connections with Onassis. Their unlikely partnership, however, soon focused on the Soviet Union. Like Karr, Hammer had a long history of involvement with Communism. He had, however, been far more successful at hiding some of his more unsavory and problematic actions. And, compared to Karr's early history, Hammer's was intertwined, not only with the American Communist movement, but also with Soviet intelligence agencies.[39]

The son of a prominent founder of the Communist movement in America, Dr. Julius Hammer, Armand had first traveled to the U.S.S.R. in 1921, representing his father's company, Allied Drug and Chemical Corporation. At the time, Julius was serving time in prison for performing an illegal abortion during which the patient died, although it now appears that it was Armand himself, then a medical student, who had botched the operation; his father willingly paid the penalty.

Meeting with Lenin, Armand consummated various commercial deals and received the first American business concession in the U.S.S.R., in return for which Allied Drug and Chemical became the conduit through which Soviet intelligence funneled money to the nascent American Communist Party. In the mid-1920s the Hammer family, including paterfamilias Julius, released from prison, lived in luxury in Moscow, laundering Soviet money to pay for publication of the *Daily Worker*, the CPUSA's newspaper, and financing Comintern operations in America and Europe.[40]

Western intelligence agencies, including the FBI, suspected that the Hammers had ties to Soviet intelligence. The family patriarch, Julius, was in fact recruited by the OGPU in 1931 "to work among foreigners living in Moscow" and "signed a statement regarding voluntary cooperation with the Sov. Security organs." Given the code name "Physician," he provided little of value, but did suggest that his two sons also be recruited; the younger, Victor, agreed to work for the KGB, even establishing a password for future meetings in New York. Although Soviet intelligence tried for years to enlist Victor to assist it, using his son Armasha, a Soviet citizen, as a lure and ransom, it was never able to get him to provide help. Armand, meanwhile, sold Russian artifacts in New York, and soon branched out into other businesses that netted him considerable wealth. By the 1950s, he had taken control of Occidental Petroleum.[41]

As John Kennedy prepared to assume the presidency in 1961, Armand Hammer made plans to return to Moscow for the first time since his family was encouraged in the early 1930s to leave, when Stalin began to crack down on foreigners. In October 1960, the Soviet regime allowed his nephew Armasha to visit the United States. Armasha had gone to school and was friendly with many of the children of the Soviet elite and he told his uncle that if he returned, he would be treated as a hero by the party leadership. Hammer lobbied incessantly for a meeting with Kennedy, in order to suggest to the Russians that he had the president's imprimatur but succeeded only in getting Secretary of Commerce Luther Hodges to agree to take a report on his trip. Once in Russia, in February 1961, Hammer, to the astonishment of embassy officials, managed to arrange a meeting with Anastas Mikoyan, the deputy prime minister whom he had known in the 1920s. That private meeting quickly produced a two-hour tête-à-tête with Nikita Khrushchev himself. Upon his return to the United States, Hammer told Hodges that the Soviet leader had urged relaxation of American restrictions on U.S.–Russian trade, noting that the U.S.S.R. would be willing to buy more American goods if it was granted credits.

As part of his plan to resuscitate the moribund Soviet system of agriculture, Khrushchev needed to expand production of phosphate fertilizer. Hammer's report to Hodges made no mention of his own ambitious plans to transform Occidental Petroleum into a world power in the fertilizer business. Nonetheless, by 1963 he had purchased a number of fertilizer companies, in anticipation of a relaxing of restrictions on East-West trade. But exporting his products to the Soviet Union remained stymied by political tensions between the two countries. Hammer met again with Soviet leaders in June 1963 and hammered out a complicated deal, announced in September, that had Occidental Petroleum building ten fertilizer plants in Siberia to process concentrate shipped from the United States in newly built tankers. The ambitious plan was aimed at producing fifty million tons of fertilizer a year. Even as Hammer set out to raise money to finance this enormous project, however, it crashed and burned; Khrushchev was ousted from power two weeks after the agreement was announced and the project halted. By the time the new Soviet leadership was ready to restart it in 1965, the Vietnam War had once again chilled efforts to increase Soviet-American trade.

It was not until the late 1960s that Hammer's interest in resuming his business ties with Russia began to bear fruit. The new American policy of détente initiated by Richard Nixon and Henry Kissinger led to new optimism about American-Soviet trade. In November 1971, Commerce Secretary Maurice Stans led an American delegation to Moscow for talks. In January 1972, KGB chief Yuri Andropov personally selected Mikhail Bruk, once a classmate of Armasha Hammer at the Institute of Foreign Languages, to serve as Hammer's personal representative in Moscow. Widely assumed to work for the KGB, Bruk oversaw the arrangements for Hammer's next trip to the U.S.S.R., in July 1972, shortly after President Nixon's historic visit to Moscow that same month, the first time a sitting American president had ever visited the U.S.S.R.

One story has it that Bruk secured permission for Hammer to arrive in his Gulfstream jet, the first time a private plane had entered Soviet airspace. Another account credits Karr and Shriver with persuading Gvishiani at a Paris lunch to allow the flight, after they agreed to have it stop in Copenhagen to pick up a Soviet crew. Part of Karr's legend as a wheeler-dealer credits him with persuading Hammer to renew his ties to the Russians, telling the industrialist: "You're always talking about your old friend Lenin. Why not go to the Soviet Union and do some business?" In fact, of course, Hammer had been actively seeking to do business in Russia a full decade before he had met Karr.[42]

In Moscow the trio met with a slew of top-level bureaucrats over five days. At these meetings, Shriver recalled, Hammer would wield an original copy of a letter from Lenin to awe his hosts. Or, he would brag about the sculpture of a monkey contemplating a human head decorating Lenin's desk; Hammer had given it to him as a gift in 1921. The atmosphere was cordial and negotiations moved quickly. Hammer signed a preliminary agreement for a $20 billion fertilizer deal in April 1973. Shriver, former head of the Merchandise Mart in Chicago, suggested still another project, a hotel complex that would provide accommodations and office space for Western businessmen, which led to the construction of the World Trade Center in Moscow.[43]

Very little about Armand Hammer's business dealings was ever fully transparent, however. Even David Karr, a man often accused of cutting ethical corners and engaging in shady projects, could learn a few lessons or be startled by the personal risks that went along with his new partner. Hammer came to Russia bearing gifts, not all of them entirely legitimate. With much fanfare, he announced the donation of a Goya painting worth one million dollars to the Hermitage Museum. It later turned out that the painting was a second-rate Goya that Hammer had purchased for $60,000 through his own gallery before turning around and selling it to his foundation for $160,000. More seriously, he brought oodles of cash with him. Some of it was used to bribe the Minister of Culture, Yekaterina Furtseva. Faced with political ruin two years later after allegations that she had used state money to build an expensive dacha, Furtseva committed suicide in 1974.[44]

Finally, Hammer obtained several original Lenin letters through bribery, planning to smuggle them to the West, put them up for auction, buy them himself, then earn plaudits by donating them to Leonid Brezhnev. The plan backfired. At a meeting with two lawyers representing a company fighting off a hostile takeover bid from Occidental Petroleum in 1978, Karr told them that on one evening on this trip, he was called to Hammer's room at the National Hotel. Hammer was in his pajamas, "pleading with two K.G.B. agents not to arrest him for bribery and for smuggling Lenin treasures." A Russian account of this confrontation had the "grizzled Armand" standing "on his knees," promising to return the letters. Hammer eventually agreed to give the Soviets "a cache of Lenin memorabilia and to donate other treasures." One of Hammer's lawyers told the *New York Times* that Hammer said the story was "untrue" but admitted to being "confronted by Soviet officials upset" at his possession of the letters. Another member of the Hammer entourage, Paris lawyer Samuel Pisar, "recalled vividly the tears in the eyes of the Soviet President, Leonid Brezhnev, as he accepted the Lenin letters."[45]

Hammer's grandiose business plans were dependent on massive American government loans to the U.S.S.R., which lacked the hard currency to pay for the costs of infrastructure, or the fertilizer and phosphates. U.S. government finance, in turn, was hostage to the state of East-West relations. Battered by political instability in Washington as Watergate eroded Richard Nixon's political fortunes, Hammer's aspirations took another pounding as growing anger over Soviet restrictions on Jewish emigration led Congress to consider linking trade agreements with the U.S.S.R. to the Communists' easing pressure on Soviet dissidents and "refuseniks."

Meanwhile, by September 1973, Hammer and Karr were at loggerheads. An anonymous source told a newspaper reporter in 1978 that "Karr's a big talker and Hammer must have gotten rid of him when he could no longer stand his personality." No doubt two oversized egos found it hard to coexist, but just as likely was that Karr was trying to make his own deals in Russia. Karr had set up a Swiss holding company, Financial Engineers (FE), which he owned in partnership with Lazard Frères, to do financial consulting for corporate clients in Europe and the United States. Shriver had encouraged Karr to work with Lazard, recognizing that he needed "to be part of an entity that could also offer solid financial backing" and give heft to his "imaginative proposals." In turn, FE created a French subsidiary, Finatek S.A., to handle business in the U.S.S.R.[46]

Both entities were well stocked with prominent politicians among their principals. Augustin Hervé-Gruyer, a Lazard partner, served as chairman of Financial Engineers. Shriver was on the board although he resigned later after a dispute with Karr. Hervé Alphand, chairman of Finatek, had been France's ambassador to the United States from 1956 to 1965 and was a close confidant of Charles de Gaulle's. A veteran civil servant, his career culminated as secretary general of the Foreign Ministry, after which he went into business.

Jean Guyot was a senior partner of Lazard Frères and director of FE. A longtime civil servant, he became chief aide to Jean Monnet, who had recruited him to serve as the first financial director of the European Coal and Steel Community, the forerunner of the European Union. Recruited by Lazard Frères around 1960, he first met Karr in 1972. Guyot recalled that he was cautious and careful about getting involved with Russia because Lazard Frères had not done business there before. It partnered with Karr because of his "brilliant intelligence" and his high-level contacts in Moscow. Guyot, who met with Karr frequently and traveled with him to Russia several times, found him very reliable in his business dealings. He had no doubts about his honesty or integrity. Karr was a man with a "high degree of personal warmth" with a remarkable ability to interact with others and put deals together.[47]

And the partnership quickly yielded dividends. In 1974, Karr and Lazard signed an agreement with the Bank for Foreign Trade in Moscow that led to a $250 million private loan the next year. That deal, the first large syndicated loan to the Soviet Union by private banks, involved Lazard Frères, Morgan Guaranty, and the Banque National de Paris. Hervé-Gruyer crowed that "thanks to David, the Russians know us now." Finatek was hired by Gvishiani's State Committee for Science and Technology as consultants to judge proposed projects by Western multinational companies; the Foreign Trade Bank hired it as an advisor on large-scale foreign financing of Soviet projects. By 1979, Lazard had arranged another $250 million worth of credits for the Soviet Union.[48]

Between 1973 and his death in 1979, Karr negotiated on behalf of a wide variety of companies anxious to tap into the Russian market; Mitsubishi's bid to construct a soybean processing plant, Blue Bell's plan to set up a jeans factory, Peugeot-Citroen's plan to revamp a Russian plant used to build Moskvich cars. He represented Gulf Oil, Arthur Anderson accounting firm, Norton Simon, Volvo, Trust Houses Forte and Ferranti, a British electronics firm. By far the largest and most prominent deal FE undertook was to build four hotels in the Soviet Union. The contract, signed with Intourist in 1975, called for construction of the first luxury hotel in Moscow. The Kosmos, with 1,777 rooms, furnished entirely with French equipment, built by French and Yugoslav labor, and financed by the first Lazard-arranged loan, cost $175 million and was intended to be ready for the 1980 Olympic Games.[49]

Still another initiative launched in 1976 was a plan to partner with Novoexport, the Soviet government company involved in the export business to market semiprecious stones in Europe and the United States. Finatek conducted a professional marketing study in the United States to learn about market requirements, quality standards, pricing, and expenses. Karr wrote a memo to the minister of geology and the foreign trade department proposing a long-term agreement whereby Financial Engineers "would organize the financing and delivery" of mining equipment and diamond cutting machinery and the training of personnel in return for "an exclusive worldwide marketing contract." FE would set up marketing companies that would sell goods, not only to jewelry stores but also to department stores, creating a market that within five years "would become a large source of foreign currency income for the Soviet government." Bureaucratic delays in Moscow stalled plans to mount an exhibition of Soviet stones in Paris in the summer of 1978; the proposed deal was still in limbo when Karr died in 1979.[50]

Karr's experience with Hammer had taught him that consummating business deals with the Soviets required close and cordial personal relationships with influential Russian officials, often buttressed by add-ons that either provided some societal or personal benefits. And, like Hammer, Karr was dogged by persistent rumors that he had made payoffs to such officials, most notably Gvishiani. The Russian end required stealth in an environment where ideological platitudes precluded open influence peddling or personal enrichment. While jealous rivals complained that Karr's success in arranging business deals was fueled by bribes and sweeteners, no hard evidence ever emerged to substantiate the claims. And, Gvishiani was probably more important as a conduit to other influential Russian officials than as a deal-maker himself.

Allegations about underhanded or unethical business practices had followed Karr ever since his days as a reporter willing to use any tactic to obtain a story. And a man who had not hesitated to lie to potential sources, steal a client from a colleague, or leak misleading reports on a new industrial technique would have had few compunctions about bribing a foreign official to win a contract. Far more serious, however, were reminders about Karr's ideological past, and suspicions that his success was somehow linked to connections with Soviet intelligence.

7

SOVIET AGENT

After his death, a journalist reported that "whispers of a KGB connection followed Karr everywhere, once he started coming to Moscow in 1972. However, in his bargaining with the Russians, just as in his wheeling-dealing with everyone else, it was always difficult to be sure whose side Karr was on." His singular success in Russia stoked rumors that the Soviets valued him for more than just his ability to put together lucrative business deals. While those concerns even reached the top echelons of the White House in the 1970s, no one could be entirely sure what Karr was up to. But, with the end of the Cold War and the opening of Russian archives, documentary evidence emerged that Soviet intelligence considered David Karr to be "a competent KGB source."[1]

Sometime in the early 1970s on one of his many trips to Moscow, David Karr was recruited by the KGB. Neither the exact date nor the nature of the approach is yet known. Perhaps Soviet intelligence played upon Karr's long-ago ties to the Communist movement. More plausibly, his overweening ambition and rivalry with Armand Hammer might have made him susceptible to a quid pro quo; help us and enrich yourself. Karr fancied himself an international operator; perhaps he envisaged a role as a broker or middleman able to bridge the gaps between his own country and a nation he believed desired peace. It

is even possible that the KGB had uncovered disparaging or dangerous information on him and used it to coerce him into cooperating.
Whatever the motive, by 1974 Karr was trying, in ways both subtle
and obvious, to serve Soviet interests.

In 1992 Yevgenia Albats, a Russian journalist with excellent sources
in the former KGB, published an article in *Izvestia* angrily excoriating
Western politicians, particularly Senator Ted Kennedy of Massachusetts,
for conducting sub-rosa negotiations with the KGB in the preceding
decades. She quoted from a top-secret KGB memo to the leaders of the
U.S.S.R. (that included its archival number) reporting that Kennedy
had first approached the spy agency on behalf of a company run by his
old friend, former Senator John Tunney of California. Tunney's company, in turn, was tied to a "French-American firm, Finatek, S.A., then
chaired by a competent KGB source, noted western financier David
Karr."[2]

Albats gave no indication of when Karr had first started working
for the Soviets. A former Soviet intelligence operative, who insisted on
anonymity, reported to me that Karr had been recruited sometime in
the early to mid-1970s during one of his trips to Moscow with Armand
Hammer. He was given the code name "Fram." His handler was Colonel
Andrey Pavlov, who worked in the Second Directorate of the KGB,
which dealt with economic and industrial security. Fedor Alekseevich
Shcherbak was first deputy head of the Directorate from 1970 to 1982
and then directed it from 1982 until his retirement in 1989. Pavlov's
cover position was at the State Committee for Science and Technology,
Gvishiani's domain, where he occupied a large corner office in a building
on Gorky Street. Although this source, who read through the files years
ago, believed that Karr was recruited in part on the basis of ideology, he
also recalled that he accepted money.[3]

Albats quoted the KGB document saying "Karr provided the KGB
with technical information on conditions in the U.S. and other capitalist countries, which were regularly reported to the Central Committee."
While he was not privy to American state secrets, Karr's access to important and influential politicians, bankers, and businessmen provided him
with information about plans, proposed deals and terms, and negotiating
strategies that would undoubtedly have been of keen interest to Soviet
officials.[4]

Karr also was able to assist the U.S.S.R. in other ways. His high-level contacts made him a useful intermediary for the Soviets, providing entrée to decision-makers and passing along Russian desires in the guise of offering expert advice from a businessman with extensive experience in American-Soviet trade deals. Moreover, his friendship with Sargent Shriver, a member of the Kennedy family and a politician with a credible chance of becoming president of the United States, no doubt made him an attractive recruit for an intelligence agency.

Karr's initial trip to Moscow with Armand Hammer and Shriver in 1972 inadvertently contributed to the debacle surrounding George McGovern's presidential campaign that year. McGovern had originally wanted to select Shriver as his vice-presidential running mate, but the poorly organized campaign had done virtually no vetting of potential picks; when those tasked with questioning the contenders tried to contact Shriver during the Democratic convention, they discovered he was in Moscow and impossible to reach. Faced with a looming deadline and rejections by a number of others, McGovern hastily asked Senator Thomas Eagleton of Missouri to join his ticket. After it was revealed that Eagleton had undergone electro-shock treatments for depression, he was dropped, and McGovern turned to Shriver, but his campaign, already facing an uphill struggle, had suffered a debilitating blow. Karr traveled with Shriver during the presidential campaign that went down to a historic defeat.[5]

Although he returned to his law practice in Washington, Shriver was determined to run for president in 1976. Shortly before launching his campaign, he traveled to the Soviet Union with a large entourage in March 1975. His host was Andrey Pavlov, now head of the State Committee for Science and Technology, and David Karr's KGB controller. Karr, in fact, had introduced Pavlov to both Sargent and Eunice Shriver. Shriver suspected that Pavlov might be connected to Soviet intelligence but considered him a friend (after the collapse of the U.S.S.R., he persuaded Pavlov to join the board of Special Olympics, the athletic organization created by his wife). At the conclusion of his seventeen-day visit, Shriver announced that a consortium of banks led by Lazard Frères "would be providing the largest private loan in history ($250 million) to the Soviet Union."[6]

Shriver formally announced his presidential bid in September 1975.

But the campaign sputtered; Shriver came in fifth in the Iowa caucuses, garnering only 3 percent of the vote, and fared almost as dismally in New Hampshire, where he received only 9 percent. A sixth-place finish followed in Massachusetts, the Kennedys' stronghold, and he dropped out in March, after finishing third in his home state of Illinois.[7]

The FBI received a tip in 1985, from a defector, possibly Oleg Gordievsky, once the KGB resident in London, that there had been a KGB agent on Shriver's campaign staff in 1976. The information was considered extremely sensitive. After one investigation of a suspect then living in Mississippi had been launched, the Bureau concluded in February 1986 "a more probable suspect in this matter is the late David Karr." It found a "considerable degree of consistency between the information furnished by [redacted] and Bureau information concerning David Karr." A secret memo noted Karr's close business and political ties to Shriver, including his work on his 1976 campaign, cautiously observing that "there is no evidence to indicate that David Karr was a fully recruited agent of the KGB, [but] it is probable that he was used by Soviet officials and the KGB as a source of information." And, the report included the name of Karr's likely KGB contact; although it was redacted, he was identified as an official of the GKNT, the State Committee for Science and Technology—most likely Pavlov.[8]

While the KGB no doubt was happy to have a source at the highest levels of the Shriver campaign, Karr was not willing to put all his political eggs in one basket. During the 1976 primary season, he made sure that he remained on friendly terms with one of Shriver's rivals—and one of the Soviet Union's fiercest critics. Even before Shriver announced the formation of his presidential exploratory committee, Karr hinted in a letter to another old friend and presidential contender that he really didn't support his own lawyer and business partner. His old pal was an unlikely contact for a Soviet agent—the fiercely anti-Communist senator from Washington State and chief sponsor of the Jackson-Vanik Amendment that stood in the way of increased American-Soviet trade—Henry "Scoop" Jackson.

Karr and Jackson had once been much closer ideologically. They had first met in Washington in the early 1940s, when Jackson was a young, Democratic Congressman identified with the left wing of the New Deal coalition. They might have come into contact through the offices of Lowell Wakefield, the ex–*Daily Worker* editor who had hired Karr. Wakefield had returned to Seattle after breaking with the CPUSA over the Nazi-Soviet Pact and politically supported Jackson. In a 1943 letter to Jackson, then in the military, Karr boasted that he was about to be cleared by the Kerr Committee and had "been making all of Vice President Wallace's recent trips with him," and that he was optimistic about Wallace's renomination. Along with Karr, both Jackson and his chief aide, John Salter, "were very disappointed" that Wallace was replaced by Harry Truman. Jackson wrote Karr a letter of recommendation for his job at the *Washington Post* and fed him material for Drew Pearson's column.[9]

Karr reconnected with Jackson in 1971, bringing him up-to-date on his life in Paris. He gently tweaked him for being "prominently mentioned as a candidate of the 'right,'" recalling "when you were accused of being a man of the 'left.'" He offered to return to the States to help Jackson if he ran for president in 1972. In the early 1970s, Jackson launched a sustained attack on the Kissinger-Nixon policy of détente, excoriating the 1972 grain deal with the U.S.S.R., urging linkage of trade with human rights improvement, and demanding tougher restrictions on the export of critical technology, all policies that David Karr, a fervent proponent of better relations with the Soviet Union, would abhor.[10]

The legislation that truly enraged the Soviets, however, was the Jackson-Vanik Amendment to the Trade Act of 1974, passed unanimously by Congress and signed in January 1975, which linked easing American restrictions on trade to higher levels of emigration of Soviet Jews. In 1974, just as the fight over its enactment was reaching a climax, Karr donated $3,000 to Jackson's nascent presidential campaign. By the end of the year, the Soviets had angrily announced that the bill represented an unacceptable interference in their internal affairs and in January withdrew their acceptance of the U.S.–Soviet trade agreement. Despite the importance the Jackson-Vanik Amendment had in U.S.–U.S.S.R. negotiations, Karr never mentioned the issue in his correspondence with his old friend. Nor did it diminish Karr's support of Jackson's presidential bid. In April 1975, he suggested to Jackson that he disapproved of Shriver's plans to run for the presidency; "It has always been my feeling that everyone has the right to be President until they hold the First Primary. I still think that events will work your way." In July, Karr wired Jackson about Shriver's determination to announce his candidacy and explained that he was "sorry about this development as I had hoped for a closer liaison between both of you who are my friends." He signed it "with affectionate regards and fervent hopes for your success."[11]

Karr's friendly correspondence with and wishes for the political success of the most implacable enemy of unrestricted trade with the Soviet Union in the United States is remarkable enough. But he also suggested to Jackson that his own support for Soviet-American trade was a façade. In December 1974, Karr told Jackson that he had just returned from "Fun City East," his sarcastic name for Moscow, where he had signed another major contract. "Needless to say, you did not win the popularity award for December 1974 in the Kremlin. I suspect that there are other objectives in life beyond this, which are attainable and carry greater rewards." In an April 2 letter to Jackson, Karr linked his support for him to the changed international situation. He found it "extremely interesting that the invitation Sarge [Shriver] seized upon [to visit Russia] came from the very group in Russia that many blind people refuse to accept as existing," a clear reference to the KGB, which he was implying had succeeded in using Sargent Shriver.[12]

Was Karr's stroking of Jackson part of an elaborate KGB plot to retain a source within the camp of its most implacable Democratic enemy? It certainly would have been useful to keep abreast of Jackson's plans even if he did not get the Democratic nomination. Or, was Karr expressing his heartfelt admiration for a principled hawk and fervent supporter of Israel? Just as the KGB no doubt relished an American president with close ties to a KGB source, the Mossad would have been equally enthusiastic about an American president with close ties to one of its sources. Did Karr rue the entrée he had provided Soviet intelligence to Shriver, a leading Democratic presidential candidate? Was he hedging the bet he had placed on the Soviet Union and trying to provide himself with plausible deniability if rumors later surfaced about his ties to the Soviet Union? As with so many of Karr's motives, there are no clear answers.

What is not in doubt is that just as Karr abandoned Shriver when his prospects dimmed, he dumped Scoop Jackson as it became apparent that he, too, had no chance of capturing the Democratic nomination. Instead, Karr switched his support to Governor Jerry Brown of California, who had announced his candidacy in March 1976. Karr contributed $2,000 to Brown's presidential campaign. Karr boasted that he campaigned with Brown in eleven states in 1976; "I carried his bags for him." On a visit to Los Angeles in June 1976, Karr spent hours briefing Brown on relations with the U.S.S.R. and the SALT II negotiations. Karr and his friends claimed that he had "played a key role in developing the foreign-policy positions" of Governor Brown. Brown's staff kept a "special list" of close allies whose concerns and requests were supposed to be routed straight to Brown. Karr was one of about a hundred names on the list. In later years, he maintained his ties to the California politician. In 1977, he organized a fundraiser on Wall Street as Brown geared up for a gubernatorial reelection and gave him another $2,000 the following year. Moreover, California's finance director, Richard Silberman, introduced Karr to one of Brown's wealthy backers, a Mexican businessman named Carlos Bustamante, in 1977. Within a year, Karr and Bustamante met with Mexican President José López Portillo in Tijuana and obtained approval for three projects in Baja California, a $56 million tuna processing plant in Ensenada, bringing commercial supersonic Concorde flights to Tijuana, and building a retirement village in San Felipe financed by labor union pension funds. "And that's just the beginning" of his plans for investments in Baja, Karr told a reporter.[13]

Karr's close ties with three of California's most powerful Democratic politicians gave him remarkable entrée to the secrets of political strategy and influence. Not only was he close to Governor Brown, but his old friend and mentor from the Office of War Information, Alan Cranston, was elected to the United States Senate in 1968. And Karr had become a close business associate of John Tunney, who served one term from 1970 to 1976 as the other Democratic senator from the Golden State.

Karr's connections with Jerry Brown produced one more startling charge about his possible KGB connections. Vasili Mitrokhin, a retired KGB archivist, smuggled his hefty trove of copied documents out of Russia after the collapse of the U.S.S.R. In one subsequent book, coauthored with British intelligence historian Christopher Andrew, they mentioned a KGB agent, unnamed in the reports Mitrokhin viewed.

This person was described as "a Democratic activist in California" who had been recruited by the Second Chief Directorate on a trip to Russia in the 1970s. He was friendly with a number of leading politicians—Brown, Cranston, Senators Gene McCarthy, Ted Kennedy, Abe Ribicoff, William Fulbright, and Congressman John Conyers. During the 1976 campaign he had supplied information on the Jimmy Carter campaign. "On one occasion he spent three hours discussing the progress of the campaign at a meeting with Carter, Brown and Cranston in Carter's room at the Pacific Hotel. His report was forwarded to the Politburo." Toward the end of the race, he supposedly had direct conversations with all three men.[14]

One anonymous and enterprising right-wing blogger, posting on the Free Republic website, determined that Carter stayed at the Pacifica Hotel in Los Angeles on August 22–23, 1976 and compiled at least a partial list of those who met with him. He concluded that the Soviet mole was likely Senator John Tunney, who was present, but could only speculate about if and when Tunney had visited the U.S.S.R. prior to that date. In addition, he offered no reason why Tunney would have been amenable to recruitment or why the KGB would have risked approaching a sitting United States senator for recruitment.[15]

After leaving office, Tunney, son of the former heavyweight boxing champion of the world Gene Tunney, became associated with Image Factory Sports, a Los Angeles–based company headed by Stanford Blum, a Los Angeles producer who specialized in movie-related merchandising—he distributed the famous Bo Derek poster that mesmerized American male teenagers in the 1970s.

A subsidiary of Financial Engineers called Sports Licensing Company, jointly owned by Lazard Frères and Karr, had obtained the licensing and franchising rights to Misha the Bear, the symbol of the 1980 Moscow Olympics. It, in turn, sold the North American rights to Image Factory Sports, which sold "licenses to fifty-eight companies to market Olympic trinkets," items ranging from "tote bags, baby bibs, saltshakers and cigarette lighters to tee shirts." Until the United States decided to boycott the Olympics in protest of the Soviet invasion of Afghanistan nearly six months after Karr's death, Blum and Tunney were poised to make millions. A "glum Blum" complained that the boycott cost his company between $50 and $100 million. (Tunney was already independently wealthy; his father had made millions as a boxer and his mother was a wealthy heiress.)[16]

A far more plausible candidate for the unnamed KGB agent than Tunney is David Karr. Because Mitrokhin only saw reports in the files "based on intelligence provided by the agent," not the agent's file itself, it is possible that some of his information was garbled or misunderstood. Perhaps Tunney, "a Democratic party activist," relayed the details of the meeting to Karr, who promptly passed the information on to Moscow—but then Tunney would not have been described as an "activist," rather than as a politician and sitting senator. Like Tunney, Karr was acquainted with most of those named in Mitrokhin's summary. And, given his frequent trips to Moscow in the last half of the 1970s, he was in a far better position than Tunney to pass evaluations of the incoming administration on to the KGB.[17]

Still another reason to doubt that Tunney was a KGB agent is the memo quoted by Russian journalist Yevgenia Albats that identified Karr as "a competent KGB source." The memo, written to the Soviet government, noted that in 1978, "American Senator Edward Kennedy appealed to the KGB to assist in establishing cooperation between Soviet organizations and the California firm Agritech, headed by former Senator J. Tunney. This firm in turn was connected to a French-American company, Finatek S.A., which was run by a competent KGB source, the prominent Western financier D. Karr, through whom opinions had been confidentially exchanged for several years between the General Secretary of the Communist Party and Sen. Kennedy. D. Karr provided the KGB with technical information on conditions in the U.S. and other capitalist countries, which were regularly reported to the Central Committee." Karr, in other words, submitted information to the KGB on the technical capabilities of the U.S. and other capitalist countries, information that was regularly reported to the CPSU Central Committee.[18]

If Tunney was a KGB source, he could have appealed to the KGB for assistance himself. Instead, the plea came from his longtime friend Ted Kennedy, with whom he had partied and served in the Senate. Karr was also identified in the memo as a conduit for "confidential" messages exchanged between Kennedy and Leonid Brezhnev.

Like Image Factory Sports, Agritech was a company chartered in California, run by Joseph A. Kouba. Tunney served on its board and presumably had a financial interest in the firm. Neither Kennedy nor Tunney seem to have known for sure about Karr's connection with the KGB, only that he had excellent contacts with high-ranking Soviet officials. According to an anonymous former KGB officer, in addition to providing the KGB with assessments of American political leaders and a variety of economic issues and conditions, Karr was responsible for arranging the back-channel operation by which the Soviets communicated with Ted Kennedy.

Tunney, who told reporters several times over the years that Karr was a middleman between American government officials and the Soviet Union, himself later became a conduit between Kennedy and the KGB, after Karr's death. Tunney admitted that he had made around fifteen visits to Moscow in the early 1980s. One took place at Kennedy's behest after the U.S.S.R. occupied Afghanistan. On March 5, 1980, Tunney communicated Kennedy's belief that the Carter administration's hard line endangered détente and threatened to incite anti-Soviet hysteria. Claiming that elements in the State Department were opposed to the saber rattling, Kennedy indicated that he would push the administration to de-escalate the crisis with a speech calling for restraint, Afghan non-alignment, and the eventual withdrawal of Soviet troops, with guarantees of noninterference by both sides in the internal affairs of the country. He hoped that Brezhnev would react favorably to his proposals and emphasized the differences between his proposals and those of the Carter administration.[19]

It was hardly the first, and would not be the last, time that Russian intelligence agencies sought to influence mainstream American politicians with a variety of carrots. In the last few years, the news media and many Democratic politicians have been demanding investigations into efforts by Russia to interfere in the 2016 American presidential elections. Several American businessmen and former government officials had been hired by Russian companies or the Soviet government to consult, perform public relations work, lobby in Washington, or give well-compensated speeches in Moscow. Some, like Paul Manafort and General Michael Flynn, held positions in the Trump campaign. The latter held an intelligence post in the Obama administration, and was initially appointed national security advisor to the Trump administration, before he was forced to resign after a brief tenure.

At the time of Kennedy's earlier extraordinary effort to undercut American foreign policy, the Massachusetts senator was challenging President Carter for the Democratic nomination. Although Tunney denied he had ever discussed Kennedy's presidential ambitions (a claim contradicted by the memo discussed in the next paragraph), the Soviets could not have missed that Kennedy would be a far more Russia-friendly candidate than either Carter or his chief Republican opponent, Ronald Reagan. None of this is to say that Kennedy was a Soviet agent or asset, or even that he was insincere. His hostility to Carter and his policies may well have been heartfelt; he was certainly willing to express them publicly. However, he was also an opportunistic American politician seeking to advance his own ambitions and willing to use the contacts originally provided by David Karr to undermine the position of his own party leader and government.

Kennedy's efforts didn't end there. In May 1983, Viktor Chebrikov, head of the KGB, wrote a memorandum to Soviet leader Yuri Andropov. He explained that on May 9–10, Tunney had been back in Moscow, "charged" by Senator Kennedy to deliver a message to the Soviets. He was deeply worried by Ronald Reagan's military buildup and harsh rhetoric about the U.S.S.R. Soviet-American relations promised to become the defining issue in the 1984 election; and Kennedy, anxious to see Reagan defeated, offered to work with Andropov to carve out disarmament positions more likely to appeal to American citizens and arrange for Andropov to appear on American television. He offered to "undertake some additional steps to counter the militaristic policy of Reagan." Andropov was apparently unimpressed and did not respond.[20]

In later years, Kennedy himself met with Soviet leader Mikhail Gorbachev. Although transcripts of the meeting in March 1990 are not available, a report by Vadim Zagladin, a high-ranking official in the International Department of the CPSU, noted that during his visit Senator Kennedy complained that the results of the Geneva Summit had allowed Reagan "to slow down the process of movement to any positive results in negotiations with the U.S.S.R." He thought it "important to keep increasing pressure on the administration from different sides, both from abroad and at home." He told Zagladin that he was impressed by Gorbachev but feared that the Soviet Union was underestimating Reagan: "So far Reagan is winning."[21]

Tunney dismissed the significance of the Chebrikov document after it was published in 1992, characterizing the letter as "someone trying to sound bigger than they were." That was odd. The letter didn't read that way. And why would the head of the KGB feel any need to exaggerate or lie to the Party General Secretary—and former head of the KGB—about so delicate a matter? In the late 1980s and early 1990s, Kennedy's chief of staff, Larry Horowitz, took over the duties of meeting with the Soviets. He met frequently with Zagladin to transmit his boss's views. Thus, one of Karr's services to the KGB was to set up the process by which one of the most prominent figures in the Democratic Party regularly communicated with the Soviet Union to explore ways to undercut the foreign policy of his own country. The KGB no doubt felt Karr had earned whatever money it paid him. According to an aide, Kennedy was "shocked" when he learned of Karr's death and was convinced that he had been murdered.[22]

The original KGB file on Karr was titled "Fram," his cover name. After his death, the back-channel relationship to Ted Kennedy was labeled "Atlanticka." The relationship had begun with David Karr. Classified by the KGB as "Of Extreme Importance," a grade above "Top Secret," it went on to the very end of the Soviet Union's existence. After bits and pieces of the story dribbled out in the press upon the partial opening of Soviet-era archives, Kennedy and his aides dismissed it as insignificant or exaggerated. Apart from the conservative press, most American media outlets shied away from emphasizing the story, perhaps out of concern not to tarnish a liberal icon unfairly. Those who participated in this back-channel operation did not know all the details, or the key role played by David Karr, "a competent KGB source," in having set it in motion.

Whatever ties of friendship David Karr, Soviet source, had with Democratic presidential contenders leading up to the 1976 election, the administration in power was Republican. So, Karr sought to create a relationship with the Ford administration. The first indications that he was trying to establish a connection with the White House came in the fall of 1974. Karr used Ambassador George Feldman to build ties to the Ford administration. An old Democratic Party operative—he had been vice chairman of the Party's 1960 finance committee and lawyer for a variety of government agencies—Feldman had been named by LBJ to serve as Ambassador to Malta in 1965 and Luxembourg in 1967. Whether Karr had first met Feldman in Washington in the 1930s when he worked for Massachusetts Senator David Walsh, after World War II when he worked for both the State Department and House committees, or during his stint in Europe, Karr used Feldman's good offices to meet with John Marsh, counselor to President Ford, on October 4, 1974. Feldman was also close to Gerald Ford—in 1976 he served on the Democrats for Ford Committee.[23]

Karr inaugurated his contacts with the Ford administration at a crucial moment in American-Soviet relations. The resignation of President Richard Nixon had worried Soviet officials who had strongly supported the Nixon-Kissinger policy of détente and regarded the longtime Cold Warrior as a reliable negotiating partner. Although the U.S.S.R. was encouraged that Ford had retained Henry Kissinger, the architect of détente, as Secretary of State, Leonid Brezhnev found it hard to credit that the Watergate Affair had driven Nixon from office rather than opponents of détente. The rising tide of hostility to trade with the U.S.S.R., expressed through congressional passage of the Jackson-Vanik Amendment in 1974 and another measure imposing a $300 million ceiling on Export-Import Bank loans to the U.S.S.R., angered the Russians. By the end of 1974, despite an agreement on a framework for talks on Salt II to reduce strategic arms hammered out at Vladivostok by President Ford and Soviet leader Leonid Brezhnev, détente had taken on a decided chill.

To add to Soviet concerns, Soviet economic growth slowed in 1973. Over the next several years, just as in the West, concerns about economic stagnation grew. Declining growth rates, grain shortages, sinking productivity, shoddy goods, and a rising litany of domestic complaints and dissidence made the infusion of Western capital more urgent. People like David Karr, with access to financing that could enable Western companies to build facilities in the Soviet Union and provide much-needed consumer goods, took on greater importance.

Karr's cultivation of American officials began just months before President Ford held a Siberian summit with Leonid Brezhnev in Vladivostok in November 1974. One contact was Ron Nessen, who had worked for United Press International (UPI) as a reporter from 1956 to 1962, before joining NBC News as a television correspondent. He had covered national affairs, the White House, and Vietnam before being named Gerald Ford's press secretary on September 20, 1974. Karr had apparently met him while assisting Sargent Shriver's vice-presidential campaign in 1972. Just four days after his appointment, Karr sent him "two plush robes" bearing the George V logo. Nessen returned them in October with a regretful note that "after the era that we have just experienced" in Washington, "even the appearance of impropriety" had to be avoided. Karr also offered him accommodations at the swank hotel and Nessen responded that he looked forward to an opportunity to stay there.[24]

After meeting John Marsh, one of Ford's advisors, in October, Karr sent him a letter arguing that the time was right "for deepening, strengthening and broadening the field of international economic coop-eration as a testing ground and performing ground for détente." He sent Marsh two George V robes (Marsh did not return his gifts) and invited him to Paris for "a little bit of courtly old world hospitality which I am sure you will find is rather close to that of Charlottesville and Culpepper with a bit of Richmond thrown in." (Marsh was a former conservative Democratic congressman from Virginia who had gone to work for the Nixon administration in 1972.) Marsh thanked him and assured Karr that he had found their discussion "interesting and informative."[25]

Karr was clearly offering himself as a conduit with the Soviets. One piece of evidence comes from his correspondence with Ted Marrs, a special assistant to President Ford. A retired Air Force general with a background in intelligence, Marrs had been introduced to Karr at his October 4th meeting with Marsh. (And Karr quickly sent him a George V robe.) Marrs asked Karr for a report on what Dzhermen Gvishiani had said in private meetings during a recent visit to the United States. On October 9, Karr reported that at a dinner at Sargent Shriver's home on October 7, with Senators Ted Kennedy, Fritz Hollings, Averell Harriman, and Karr himself present, Gvishiani had said that his govern-ment was concerned by the prospects of international economic chaos and specifically pointed to problems in Britain and Italy. He had also indicated that too drastic a run-up in oil prices could lead to "serious economic disruption with the resultant political and possible alternate military implications." In response to this information Marrs noted that he was "sure you derived the same satisfaction I did from the response to your efforts. Hopefully this will proceed to fruition." He cryptically added that "documentation of the impact of anonymous individuals on history would probably be of greater interest than all existing texts and treaties," suggesting that Karr was serving as a back channel to the U.S.S.R.[26]

Just prior to the Vladivostok summit meeting, Karr sent Marsh a column written by journalist Tad Szulc warning that the United States had "dangerously misjudged Soviet intentions" in the Mideast by freezing the Russians out of its effort to negotiate the Arab-Israeli conflict. Karr noted that Szulc's concerns "parallel the point of view that is given to me in Fun City East," or Moscow. He reassured Marsh that he was not saying the Russians were right or wrong or that it was in America's interest to agree with the Soviet view on the Mideast or economic cooperation. Rather, his goal was "to make clear that we understand what they are trying to convey. It may well be that they are offering a 'poisoned apple,'" but it was crucial for the United States government to know what its options were.[27]

These cautious forays into private diplomacy continued in 1975. In early January, Karr sent Marsh a letter he had received from Gvishiani; he met Nessen for lunch in February and visited Russ Roarke, Marsh's assistant, with Feldman. When he returned to Washington again in April, he apparently brought some proposal from the Russians to try to defuse mounting tensions.[28]

The signing of the Jackson-Vanik Amendment in January 1975 had backfired. Angry Russian leaders cracked down on Jewish emigration. Blocked by congressional limits on American government loans, the U.S.S.R. turned increasingly to private companies. In early April, even as Saigon fell to the Vietnamese Communists, Brezhnev reiterated that the U.S.S.R. would not tolerate American interference into domestic affairs but still wanted to promote détente. On April 21, Russ Rourke sent Marsh a memo reporting that Karr had suggested that the Soviets would be willing to invest or build and operate plants in the United States to show their enthusiasm for détente. The obstacles to such a plan were overwhelming; there would be political, legislative, and regulatory problems and fierce opposition from both organized labor and Jewish groups. While Karr thought the idea had little traction, he volunteered, if wrong, to "quickly put together the arrangements that would be necessary to support the investment of Soviet money in the U.S." Marsh asked Rourke to sound out the National Security Council but warned him "Don't endorse."[29]

Whatever the substance of Karr's proposal or information, there is no record of any response from the NSC. Karr was back at the White House in early May and a memo dated the nineteenth of the month indicates that Rourke spoke with George Carey, who would "pursue, with noted restrictions, the David Karr matter." Nobody named Carey worked for the Ford White House, although he may be George L. Cary, who was legislative counsel of the Central Intelligence Agency in 1974. And the same day, May 19, *Business Week* included a favorable article about "David Karr's Soviet Connection," that quoted an anonymous Paris associate who explained that the Russians trusted him "and once the Russians trust you there's a snowball effect for the future of the relationship."[30]

Karr also saw Ron Nessen on his May visit to the White House. The president was planning to attend the Helsinki summit to finalize the deliberations of the Conference on Security and Co-operation in Europe at the end of July. Karr offered to let the press secretary charter his yacht, the *Ottelia*, based in Monte Carlo, following the meeting, noting that among others, John Scali had used the boat. To avoid any conflict of interest, he suggested "a charge of $50 a day," a price that obviously would hardly have covered a fraction of the cost. The yacht had a British-French crew of eight, "quite good at discreetly taking care of guests." Nessen could even travel incognito. The press secretary was intrigued and promised to respond when his summer plans were set.[31]

Even as Karr maneuvered to develop his access to some of Gerald Ford's top aides, he finally overplayed his hand. He visited Nessen yet again on May 21. This time the press secretary became suspicious. He told an NSC staffer who worked for the CIA that he had first met Karr when he had accompanied Armand Hammer to Russia. He had not heard from him again until he joined the Ford administration. When he visited, Nessen noted, Karr "frequently dropped names and more recently his names have been Russian—'when I had lunch with Kosygin,' and 'at breakfast with Brezhnev.'" Karr had been a source of information "and did not appear to be pumping him for anything." He had, however, hinted that Nessen could have a career in banking after leaving the government and offered the use of his yacht, suggestions that made Nessen uneasy.

What set off alarm bells on May 21 was that Karr had raised the stakes. He claimed to have information about the U.S.S.R. that he feared would not reach the president if passed through the people he was already dealing with—presumably Marsh and Rourke. He, "in effect, was asking for a direct channel" to Gerald Ford. Nessen thought that "if this was another international businessman trying to drop names" that was one thing, "but if there was anything else he [Nessen] thought he ought to know about it." It had finally dawned on the press secretary that Karr might have ulterior motives. His unease led Nessen to get in touch with Rob Roy Ratliff, an NSC staffer on loan from the CIA, and ask what the Agency knew about Karr. Ratliff did a preliminary search and found a 1960 entry in *Who's Who* that "might be the Karr we are interested in." He wrote a memo describing Nessen's concerns and sent it to Ben Evans, executive secretary to the Director of Central Intelligence.[32]

Three days later Stanton Ense, Deputy Director of Security, wrote a memo indicating that CIA records reflected that the FBI had investigated Karr five different times between 1941 and 1960. He briefly summarized his career and the allegations that had shadowed him, including the charges leveled by HUAC, Joe McCarthy, and the State Department's Passport Office. Evans provided this information to Ratliff on May 23 and suggested that Nessen ask the FBI to carry out any further investigation. Four pages from Karr's FBI file that likely deal with this issue are almost entirely redacted, save one reference to the "Foreign Liaison Unit." Intriguingly, Ratliff's job with the NSC at the White House was Executive Secretary of the 40 Committee that processed approvals for covert action abroad.[33]

Just one month later, Karr wrote Nessen, enclosing a letter directly addressed to President Ford, calling it "extremely delicate," thanking him for "your good offer to bring this to the attention of the President," and offering to return to the White House at any time. The letter began by reciting Karr's successful business deals with the U.S.S.R., his numerous trips to Russia, and his "extremely close ties" with the leaders of the Soviet Bank for Foreign Trade, State Committee for Science and Technology and Ministry of Foreign Trade, as well as his talks with Prime Minister Kosygin. In advance of Ford's forthcoming meeting with Brezhnev, Karr offered several new ideas that "I have strong reason to believe…would be favorably received" by the Soviet leader.[34]

None of the seven suggestions were particularly startling or even sensitive. Karr indicated that the Soviet leadership wanted a "bi-lateral declaration of intentions as to long-term prospects for future trade," discussion of the U.S.S.R. being admitted to the World Bank and IMF, making the ruble a convertible currency, cooperation in the field of energy and, particularly, such "high-energy" fields as titanium, nickel, molybdenum and ferro-chrome, further cooperation in basic cancer research, fundamental math and physics, cooperative economic development of the Northern Pacific oceans in relation to fishing and oil exploration, and discussions of cooperation in cargo vessels and tankers. He offered to meet with Ford at his convenience.[35]

There is nothing further in the Nessen papers to indicate if anything more came of this episode. Rob Roy Ratliff cannot recall the incident. Nessen himself did not respond to a request for an interview. The FBI report remains classified, as do NSC records. Nessen had apparently agreed to receive a letter from Karr conveying Soviet proposals, but what, if anything, happened to the letter is not known. Karr's open correspondence with officials in the Ford administration came to an end with this letter to the president. All that can be certain is that Karr willingly served as a conduit for the Soviet leadership and the American government was, rightfully, suspicious of his motives, unlike Sargent Shriver, Ted Kennedy, or John Tunney.

Karr certainly did nothing to refute rumors about his close ties to the Russians. Jack Anderson, the man who succeeded him as Drew Pearson's chief legman, and later inherited Pearson's column, recalled that Karr frequently offered "inside info." Other reporters, and individuals Karr wanted to impress would be regaled with stories of his exploits. Whether it was Jewish emigration from the Soviet Union, arms control, or trade agreements, Karr was constantly dropping names, boasting about his crucial interventions, or reveling in his ability to bring together rich and famous people. Karr radiated assurance and inside knowledge. One evening he had dinner with his old friend Lee Falk at the Hotel Pierre in New York; Karr "gave the impression that he owned it."[36]

There are numerous other rumors and claims about ways in which Karr served Soviet interests. After his death, newspapers reported anonymous charges that Karr and Eliezer Preminger had been involved in funneling Soviet arms to Idi Amin in Uganda and Muammar al-Qaddafi in Libya. No documentary evidence was ever provided. Even if Karr was willing to run guns to deranged and anti-Semitic dictators sworn to the destruction of Israel, it is very hard to believe that Preminger would have colluded with him in such an enterprise.

Karr did facilitate Christina Onassis's marriage to a Soviet citizen, a love affair that caused consternation and concern among Western security agencies. Even after Aristotle Onassis died, Karr remained a close friend of his daughter, Christina. A deeply troubled woman whose first two marriages had quickly ended in divorce, she inherited her father's vast fortune and business empire upon his death in March 1975. Christina met Sergei Kauzov, an official in the tanker division of Sovfracht, a Soviet agency, in November 1977 in its Paris offices. Kauzov had his own troubles; he was under investigation by the KGB for misappropriation of money. Karr boasted that he had first introduced Christina and Sergei, who quickly began an affair. During a romantic getaway to attend Carnival in Brazil, Christina proposed to him. After they returned to Paris, Kauzov was recalled to Moscow, the KGB having gotten wind of the affair, and faced arrest in Moscow.[37]

A frantic Christina turned to David Karr, who used his Russian connections to advise her how to contact her lover; she could not use a Paris operator but had to fly to London and dial his number directly. In Moscow, Kauzov met with Oleg Kalugin, chief of Soviet Foreign Counter-Intelligence, who proposed that Kauzov be allowed to wed, provided he cooperate with the KGB, and he quickly assented. After Karr wished her luck, Christina moved to Moscow in June 1978, taking a suite at the Intourist Hotel. Immediately after she left, according to an article in the Russian press, Karr informed the CIA, which was worried that her extensive fleet of oil tankers might henceforth be controlled from and by Moscow, a concern that was shared by French intelligence.[38]

Onassis and Kauzov were married on August 1. Christina received special permission to buy a Moscow apartment and import a Mercedes. The couple were later allowed to leave for France, on the condition that

Kauzov join the Communist Party and "pay $15,000 a year in dues." He ultimately paid more than $500,000 of Onassis's money to the Party. The marriage was less successful; the couple was divorced in 1980. Kauzov walked away with two oil tankers worth more than $7 million and the Soviet Communist Party received a tidy financial boost.[39]

One other issue on which Karr allegedly served as a middleman between the Soviet Union and governments in the West was the emigration of Soviet Jews. After his death, a number of unnamed friends and associates told journalists that Karr had an abiding interest in facilitating the emigration of Soviet Jews to Israel. One unsourced report claimed that "to Jewish dissidents in Russia he was a Scarlet Pimpernel—courageous and ready to spend cash to help them escape to the West." The *Daily Express* in London reported that for some time he had been making two trips a month to Moscow to assist Russian Jews in obtaining exit visas for Israel. Some of his associates, including former Senator Tunney, claimed that he had acted as a "private liaison" between the Russians and the Carter administration on emigration of Soviet Jews. Tunney told a newsman that Karr had also played a crucial role in arranging Kennedy's 1978 visit to Moscow during which they negotiated the release of several Russian dissidents. Another source confirmed that Kennedy (via Karr) was able to push for the emigration of Soviet Jewish refuseniks, especially those with relatives in Massachusetts—this channel was used by Kennedy to allow poet Joseph Brodsky's mother to leave. If Karr did, indeed, have contacts with Israeli intelligence, it is also possible that he was used as a conduit to funnel money to the U.S.S.R. to ransom specific individuals.[40]

For the Soviets, Karr's activities on behalf of Soviet dissidents did not conflict with his role as a Soviet agent. If he paid to facilitate the emigration of certain refuseniks, on his own behalf or that of others, it only put hard currency in Soviet hands. General Oleg Kalugin, a high-ranking KGB officer who later relocated to the United States, noted that the KGB "recruited agents among the hundreds of thousands of Soviet Jews who fled to Israel and America." The ultimate goal "was to place these Jewish émigrés, many of whom were scientists, into sensitive positions," but, he admits, despite numerous promises to cooperate, most "almost invariably forgot their pledges as soon as they crossed the Soviet border."[41]

For his Soviet contacts, David Karr was a well-connected business-man able to put together trade deals benefitting the Soviet Union. His ties to prominent American politicians gave them access to interesting and sometimes useful political and economic information and a way to transmit their views or slant to Washington decision-makers. If pressed while he was alive, Karr no doubt would have said that like any prudent businessman, he befriended and supported several politicians, so that regardless of which one won, he would have access. Even his covert support for Scoop Jackson and his efforts on behalf of Soviet Jews could be spun as keeping connections with anti-Soviet forces the better to pro-vide information on them. Or, alternatively, they may have represented his true feelings. Finally, an explanation endorsed by many who knew him, concluded that he was a self-interested operator and manipulator, playing every side against each other, all in an effort to enrich himself.

His Soviet friends took pains to make sure that David Karr profited handsomely from his association with them. Indeed, the Olympic coin deal that was thrown his way by the Soviets wound up earning Karr a substantial portion of the assets in his estate when he died. But, ironi-cally, the financial windfall arranged for him wound up embarrassing his friend Dzhermen Gvishiani. And, it forced Karr back into a partnership with Armand Hammer. That collaboration was not by his own choice and the arrangement was fraught with tension and animosity. Karr's split with Hammer had been over Hammer's refusal to make him a partner in his Soviet dealings. The rift was not amiable, and Karr soon had an opportunity to exact revenge.

In the summer of 1978, Occidental Petroleum launched a hostile takeover bid against the Mead Corporation. Mead mounted a fero-cious defense, hiring a law firm headed by onetime Assistant Attorney General Stanley Pottinger, which undertook a worldwide search to dig up dirt on Hammer. One of the people interviewed was David Karr, who recounted stories of their trips to the Soviet Union, Hammer's confrontation with the KGB over Lenin memorabilia, and allegations of bribery. Karr also retailed stories that Hammer had issued bribes and even paid off officials in the Nixon administration. The Securities and Exchange Commission soon launched a wide-ranging investiga-tion of the allegations. David Karr secretly testified under oath before the SEC in June 1979, just a month before his death, that Victor

Hammer had informed him that Armand had paid a $100,000 bribe to Yekaterina Furtseva. Victor Hammer later denied ever making such a statement; Armand Hammer also angrily denied the charges. Karr also testified that Armand had boasted of having the board of directors of Occidental "in his pocket" because he had forced them all to sign undated letters of resignation. The SEC confirmed that charge. Facing continued scrutiny of his business practices in Russia, Hammer withdrew his offer for Mead.[42]

What made the charges and their potential legal difficulties more complicated for Hammer was that Karr and Hammer were now partners in an actually lucrative Olympic marketing venture. The profits of the sale of commemorative coins in the United States and Europe dwarfed the licensing of Misha the Bear. Moscow planned to release thirty-nine coins, twenty-eight made of silver, six gold and five platinum, with a sales price of $3,665 for a complete set. With an estimated $300 million in worldwide sales, the coin deal promised to bring in the bulk of the non-broadcast revenue for the 1980 Olympic Games. Whoever got the contract to market the coins was assured of a hefty profit. Different parts of the Russian government, however, had promised favorable consideration to competing entities.

More than two dozen bidders were in the running. One was a consortium put together by Leo Henzel, executive vice president of United Euram, an entertainment company with a contract to bring Soviet artistic performers to the United States. Henzel was a man with a checkered past and a vast capacity for outrage. Over the years he had been involved in several businesses that had gotten him in hot water with different parts of the American government.

In 1954, he had pleaded nolo contendere to charges of adulteration and misbranding of amphetamine sulfate tablets stemming from a government seizure of pills back in 1946. In 1957, he set up the Chemoil Company to sell franchises for a synthetic floor covering—Plastiloid. Two years later the federal government indicted him for mail fraud in connection with that venture. He was able to get the case thrown out when an appeals court ruled that the evidence had been obtained illegally. Most of the company's assets and books had been seized in a lawsuit and were awaiting sale to satisfy a judgment. The court ruled that the government still needed a warrant to seize the material.[43]

The state of Florida convicted Henzel on one of five counts of grand larceny in 1965. He had agreed to be tried by a judge, but had left for New York shortly before the first day of testimony and been stranded there by an airline strike. With his apparent acquiescence, his lawyers had waived his appearance. Contending that his rights had been violated, Henzel appealed his conviction, but lost. Sentenced to five years in prison, he filed a variety of futile appeals. Even after being released on parole in 1971, he continued his quixotic crusade to obtain redress—or revenge. He filed an omnibus lawsuit against eighteen people, including the private citizens who had accused him of larceny, the judge, his prosecutors, the prosecutors who had responded to his appeals, his own defense attorneys, his probation officer, the local sheriff, and the director of the Florida prison system, accusing all of them of a conspiracy to deprive him of his rights and mistreatment. Both a state court and the United States Court of Appeals rejected his complaint. Undaunted, he unsuccessfully petitioned for a writ of error coram nobis that would have voided his conviction.[44]

After his release from prison Henzel set up United Euram. In 1976, after two years of shuttling back and forth to Moscow, he somehow won a contract and staged the Russian Festival of Music at Caesar's Palace in Las Vegas. He then sold the performance to NBC for a televised special. But despite his boasts that "the sky is the limit" for the enterprise, marketing woes beset it. To soothe him, the U.S.S.R. encouraged him to bid on the Olympic coin contract. Lacking expertise in that business, Henzel signed up Loeb, Rhoades & Company, a large New York investment bank, which put Dudley Cates onto the project as a vice president. Cates invited other large companies to join the consortium, including the *New York Times*, MCA, the Summa Corporation, and Occidental Petroleum.[45]

The Summa Corporation quickly dropped out and in late April 1978, MCA and the *Times*, represented by Sydney Gruson, decided to "walk away" from the deal, citing concerns about Armand Hammer's aggressive posture. Still, one of the *Times'* subsidiaries, Arno Press, remained interested in marketing the coins, promising in one letter "to utilize all of the services of our various companies, including the *New York Times* newspaper, our affiliated newspapers, our magazines...our radio and television stations, and the direct mail expertise of our publishing companies" to ensure "the maximum exposure and ultimate sale of these commemorative coins."[46]

The original distribution of shares in the consortium gave Occidental 70 percent and Loeb, Rhoades 22.5 percent. Occidental put up $1.625 million and Loeb, Rhoades contributed $375,000. Henzel received a 7.5 percent share in return for his "prior services and expenses in forming the consortium." During final negotiations in Moscow in June 1977, however, the Russians informed Hammer that he needed to make room for one more party. David Karr had been involved in negotiations with ABC for broadcast rights for the Olympics on behalf of Roone Arledge, a close friend. When NBC won the bidding—in a process that generated howls of anger over Moscow's pressure for favorable coverage and various payoffs to middlemen—Gvishiani moved to placate Karr by encouraging him to bid for the coin contract. Karr and Augustin Hervé-Gruyer, head of Financial Engineers, had been shuttling back and forth between Moscow and Paris all spring to sweet-talk Foreign Trade Bank officials into letting them into the deal. The Russians insisted that Karr and Hammer join forces: despite their combustible relationship, they were forced into a "shotgun marriage."[47]

Since Financial Engineers and Karr were now to receive 40 percent of the deal, to protect his share, now greatly diminished from 70 percent, Hammer determined to squeeze out Henzel. He first broached the idea in Moscow, offering Henzel $250,000 to pull out. When the offer was rebuffed, Hammer pushed him out anyway. Dudley Cates warned Hammer that Henzel would sue, but Hammer was obstinate, insisting that he was willing to pay Louis Nizer to defend a lawsuit five times what he would have to pay Henzel. Cates believed that "Henzel has been defrauded. I think it is reprehensible." He soon resigned. When the deal was finally signed in August, FE had 40 percent of the total, half of that going to Karr directly, Occidental had one-third, Loeb, Rhoades had 7 percent, and the Paramount Coin Co. was brought in for 10 percent to provide some expertise in marketing to coin buyers. Lazard Frères and the Banque Nationale de Paris got 5 percent each for financing the arrangement. The partners then set up a French company, Numinter Ltd., with an American subsidiary, Numinter B.V., to market the coins.[48]

An enraged Henzel promptly filed two lawsuits. The first, against Occidental, Loeb Rhoades, John Loeb, and Numinter B.V., alleged tortious interference with contract, and fraud against Hammer. In his defense, Hammer cited Henzel's criminal record, superciliously asserting that he would never have agreed to do business with him had he known of his background. Henzel stuck to his mantra that his conviction was a mistake and that Hammer was no paragon of virtue, having pled guilty for making illegal campaign contributions during Watergate. He demanded to know if Hammer had bribed Gvishiani. Henzel's business partner testified that Hammer's explanation for their ouster was that he "had to make room in the deal for a Mr. David Karr and his associate/friend Gvishiani" and Hammer regarded him and Henzel as "discardable baggage" once the contract was assured.[49]

Henzel also went public with his accusations, giving interviews to the press and serving as the main source for several stories in *Jewish Week* that highlighted the role played by Karr and Gvishiani. In a front-page story, the periodical repeated Henzel's claim that Gvishiani had secretly been given a 5 percent stake in the deal and "stands to make millions." Although he declined to be specific, Dudley Cates intimated that Henzel was telling the truth; he had heard rumors of their (Karr and Gvishiani's) secret partnership while in Moscow. Interviewed for the story, Karr vigorously defended Gvishiani as a respected negotiator and deal-maker and flatly denied the charges; he was "not our silent partner. We have no private arrangements with him or anybody in the Soviet Union at all and that's that.... There is no proof, because it doesn't exist." And he warned the reporter: "Now that you are on notice of it you are risking dire consequences."[50]

The publicity was highly damaging. Gvishiani was not just another high-ranking Soviet official, but the son-in-law of Alexei Kosygin, Premier of the U.S.S.R. For several years Kosygin had been fighting a losing battle for power with the head of the Communist Party, Leonid Brezhnev, and was in poor health by the late 1970s. Any scandal involving his family had the potential to weaken his position and damage Gvishiani, Karr's most significant contact in Moscow.

As if this were not enough embarrassment, Henzel also filed suit in 1978 against the Soviet Union, its Ministry of Culture, the State Concert Society, known as Gosconcert, and Madison Square Garden, accusing them of breaching a contract with United Euram to send Soviet artists to perform in America. The Soviets moved to have the suit dismissed on grounds of sovereign immunity, but a United States District Court held that it could proceed since the contract was a regular commercial arrangement not covered by diplomatic immunity.[51]

Karr hired Arnold Forster, the former head of the Anti-Defamation League with whom he had a long relationship, to represent him as the lawsuits on the coin deal proceeded, with a $50,000 retainer. Karr died before Forster had to do any work on the lawsuit. When Forster contacted Karr's family and offered to return the money, he was assured that Karr had loved him and "Pop would want you to keep it."[52]

Henzel's lawsuit was a source of anxiety for Karr, particularly as he was having to create, staff, and devise a marketing plan from scratch for Numinter. Karr called on an old friend from Hollywood, Charles Simonelli, who had worked at Universal Pictures and been executive vice president of Technicolor, assuring him that "this is going to be your biggest hit.... You'll be a superstar." But working for Karr wasn't easy. According to Simonelli, he had a vindictive streak, was prone to erupt at subordinates, and didn't take "no" for an answer. Eventually Simonelli complained to Karr's partners; the two men eventually apologized to each other and once again began to cooperate. Numinter managed to sell more than three quarters of the coins by the end of 1979, earning a profit for the partners, just in time to avoid the collapse of marketing for the Olympics as the United States and other Western nations announced a boycott of the Moscow Games. The corruption charges, however, kept Karr under considerable pressure and very stressed. Rumors of payoffs to obtain broadcasting rights to the Moscow Olympics and deals on Olympic merchandise brought calls for an investigation by the Securities and Exchange Commission or Congress, which had already implicated Lockheed in illegal payments to the premier of Japan and the president of Italy, forcing both leaders to resign.[53]

One bright spot in this onslaught of bad publicity was the completion of Karr's first major project in Russia in July 1979. The Kosmos Hotel, with 1,777 twin bedrooms and 59 suites, was the first Western hotel to be built in Moscow since the Russian Revolution. Its grand opening attracted a host of dignitaries. But, Karr was unable to enjoy the success. He became ill in Moscow and could not stay for the entire dedication on July 5. After an uncomfortable night, he recovered enough to attend some business meetings the next day and exult on the plane ride home about future investment projects in the U.S.S.R. Numinter had already been assured of hefty profits; the new hotel would be an Olympic showpiece, and his Soviet friends had reason to be pleased with his continuing high-level contacts in Washington. On the plane ride from Moscow to Paris, Karr was in a reflective mood, telling his daughter Kathy that he wasn't just chasing money, but that "money can buy credibility" and his wealth had allowed him to contribute to the search for American-Soviet peace. He was on top of the world.[54]

8

BY PERSONS
UNKNOWN?

On the surface David Karr's life could not have seemed better by the mid-1970s. The model of a successful international businessman, he regularly flew the Concorde between Europe and the United States. His frequent trips to the Soviet Union had made him one of a handful of people capable of brokering deals between East and West. Important politicians in Washington welcomed his advice and insights and were grateful for his financial support. He lived in an elegant Paris apartment in a fashionable neighborhood with servants to see to every need. Married to a wealthy and cultured woman, he spent summers cruising the Mediterranean with his family, including the children of his second marriage.

The young man who had barely graduated high school and scuffled to find a regular job had come a long way. He had survived his early flirtation with the Communist Party of the United States to become a capitalist entrepreneur. He had survived political attacks that might have devastated weaker or less determined men. He had overcome a disastrous reign at the top of a major American business to rebuild his reputation and persuade prominent corporations to cooperate with him.

Beneath the surface, however, the self-destructive traits that had always dogged David Karr were widening. His recruitment by the KGB exposed him to dangers and pressures beyond any that he had ever faced. His work on behalf of Israeli intelligence only increased the pressures and dangers. His efforts to ingratiate himself with the Ford administration had raised concerns and eyebrows within American intelligence. His activities in the Soviet Union had fractured his relationship with Armand Hammer. Striking back at Hammer, Karr testified against him in camera—testimony that, if ever made public, would anger and deeply embarrass his Soviet overseers. And, a potentially embarrassing lawsuit threatened to spotlight his close relationship with one of his Soviet patrons.

Apart from all the pressures impinging on his public and political life, Karr's personal life was also once again in turmoil. Never a faithful husband, he had managed to build relationships with three accomplished, cultured, educated, and successful women. The first two had collapsed and his third marriage began to come apart in the 1970s. The new woman in his life elicited hostility and disgust from family and friends, and their tumultuous relationship dramatically increased the strain on Karr himself.

Karr had met Evia Freiberg, a German citizen, in 1971 when she was staying at the Hotel Pierre in New York. Born in Kaiserslautern, Germany, in February 1949, she was in her early twenties, tall, slender, and sexy. Karr was in his early fifties. By her account, she was about to leave for a modeling assignment in the Caribbean and "nothing was between us at first. It took several more months and a trip to London and later to L.A. before we became involved." Once they did get "involved," Evia felt they were "married without [a marriage license] for seven years." Buffy Cooke, Karr's second wife, was less dewy-eyed: "She was a call-girl. David told me he met her that way." Her assessment: Karr's attraction to her was based purely on sex. Evia "was a pro." Whether their initial meeting was a business proposition or a romantic tryst, the relationship slowly eroded his third marriage.[1]

Most of Karr's family and friends despised Evia. Their attitude was partly due to the affection many felt for Michette Karr, his third wife. Drew Pearson's widow praised her as the nicest and best of Karr's wives: in contrast, she sniffed, Evia not only "wasn't attractive"; she was "a witch," and Karr's children "hated" her. Buffy Cooke appreciated Michette's treatment of Frank and Lisa, her children with Karr, and found her charming. Evia, on the other hand, she thought imperious, jealous, and emotionally unstable. Frank had fond memories of summer vacations on Karr's yacht, the *Ottelia*, cruising in the Mediterranean with his stepmother, but less happy recollections of his father's mistress. Michette would leave the boat to return to work in Paris and shortly afterward, Evia would arrive: "Here comes this bitch on the boat," Frank recalled. She would swoop in from the airport in a bikini bottom, stiletto heels, and a man's shirt.[2]

Karr's friends and business associates who met Evia were disdainful or appalled. Charles Simonelli, who supervised the Olympic coin marketing, thought she had "odd friends and an odd sense of fashion." Jean Guyot tactfully described her as "a very difficult person." Lee Falk, Karr's old friend from the OWI, met her at a dinner and "couldn't imagine what she modelled. Perhaps Halloween masks." Max Youngstein commented that Karr had gotten involved with "a hooker; she was the ugliest woman my wife ever saw." And "she dressed ugly too." Michette Karr would only say that the woman who destroyed her marriage was "strange."[3]

Karr's relationships with his children were also often strained. While he spoiled them with money and gifts, he was also frequently demanding and intimidating. His eldest son Andrew attended Columbia University; for months in late 1967 he did not communicate with his father. He became involved in the student protests that paralyzed the school in the spring of 1968 and was arrested. By the 1970s, he had moved to Paris and gone to work for his father at Lazard Frères, but he deeply disliked Evia, who was roughly his own age. His younger son Frank was having personal problems and seeing a therapist. Feenie Ziner complained that David tried to deal with Frank by spending money on him; "The whole direction of his life has been to try to control everyone around him through money, or superior brains, or intrigue of one kind or another. He may win all the short games, but raising children is a lifetime affair, and bribery was never an adequate substitute for understanding."[4]

During summers in the 1970s, David would bring Frank and Lisa, his teenage children, to Europe and they would cruise the Mediterranean on his yacht. Karr's affair left his children uncomfortable and complicit in his deception as he frolicked with Evia in their presence. But their affair was tempestuous. They "would fight like cats and dogs." Once some expensive glassware got broken during a quarrel and Frank and Lisa were ordered to tell Michette they had dropped it.[5]

These vacations could occasionally become rather nerve-racking. In 1971, the children were on board the *Asmeda Hope*, Karr's first yacht, docked in Cannes. The ship had recently been upgraded, including its electrical system, but a small fire broke out. As the crew worked to put it out, French firefighters arrived on a barge and ordered the passengers to disembark. The Karrs repaired to a restaurant overlooking the harbor and watched as the boat burned and then exploded. Frank Karr recalled Michette's "having a nervous breakdown" while David calmly watched. The next day he chartered another boat for the remainder of the summer.[6]

For Buffy Cooke, the unexplained destruction of the yacht only deepened her apprehensions about her ex-husband. He later told her he thought the fire had been deliberately set. (Peter Evans claimed that Karr believed it was the work of Palestinian terrorists.) The aura of menace around Karr was not her only fear. She felt he deeply resented her: David could never forget that she had left him; not the other way around. And so he found ways to torment her: her children would leave Florida in June for Europe and there would be no word from them until they arrived home around Labor Day. One year Lisa found, stuffed behind the bar on the yacht, letters she had written to her mother and given to her father to mail. Another year, he threatened to keep the children permanently in Europe and relented only after they made a scene.[7]

Life on board a boat with David Karr was also fraught with tension for the children. Frank recalled that it was very intimidating to be with him; you "never knew what to expect." He could be "sweet as candy, brutal as a snake." There were occasional quizzes about current events that could elicit scorn and anger over incorrect answers. David would taunt or emotionally abuse his children; once he had Frank call Jean-Michel, his youngest son, back in Paris and tease him about how much fun they were having on the boat without him. On another occasion, teenage Lisa arrived for a visit and he greeted her at the airport: "Christ, you've gotten fat."[8]

Karr's mercurial personality provided an additional measure of menace. One summer, Frank's best friend was allowed to accompany him. Twelve years old, he was subjected to an interrogation by David about current events that he failed. After three days, David demanded that the friend go home and delivered the traumatized youngster to a French airport with a return ticket to the United States. Another summer Lisa fell in love with a chef who worked on the *Ottelia*. According to Buffy, "David was beside himself" and had the "chef's arms broken."[9]

Inevitably, Karr's marriage collapsed under the strain of his affair and his unpredictability. By March 1976, Michette and David Karr had moved into separate residences; they legally separated in November 1977. Michette remained hopeful that they could reconcile, but, in June 1978, they signed a complex agreement in which David agreed to pay alimony and child support of $60,000 annually until 1991 when Jean-Michel reached twenty-three years of age, with a 6 percent annual increase for inflation. Michette would then receive $30,000 a year in alimony. Her payments would be reduced by half if she remarried before 1991. These funds would come from David's proceeds from Financial Engineers, the company he owned in partnership with Lazard Frères. David also promised to use "my best efforts so that you receive $1,000,000" from other sources; if that occurred her alimony payments would be reduced or eliminated. If Karr's gross income fell below $240,000 a year, she could not receive more than 25 percent of her annual alimony figure.[10]

To ensure that he lived up to the bargain, Karr agreed to furnish Michette's brother, the shopping mall magnate Jean-Louis Solal, both his American tax return and the balance sheets of Financial Engineers. He also authorized payments from his accrued cash earnings in the company if the income from Financial Engineers did not meet his obligations. Further, he designated Michette as the beneficiary on his life insurance and accident and death travel policies. The complex agreement was also signed by a principal from Lazard Frères.[11]

The divorce became final on July 11, 1978. Buffy Cooke recalled telephoning Michette with the news that David had remarried in August, just weeks afterward. Michette was shocked. David had not bothered to let her know. Karr told friends and relatives that Evia had been pressuring him to marry her. The marriage took place at the home of Max Youngstein's lawyer in southern California; the acerbic producer said in an interview that after the ceremony, having downed a few drinks, Karr confided in him: "Max, this won't last long."[12]

It didn't. Karr had immediate second thoughts about the marriage. It took place on August 1, 1978. On August 2 the two separated. And, on October 12, his lawyer filed a petition in the superior court of California in San Diego for an annulment. That same day Karr also filed for divorce but withdrew the petition on October 30. Another petition for divorce was filed in New York by Evia and later withdrawn. Their eleven-month marriage was tumultuous. On April 28, 1979, Evia signed a brief note in Paris that flatly stated: "I am leaving. I do not wish to disclose the reasons. There is nothing I want in terms of money or possession from you. If this marriage could be annulled and erased from the records I would be very grateful to you." On June 21, Karr asked his attorney to file for divorce in France.[13]

When Karr returned to Paris from Moscow on July 7, he was infuriated to learn that Evia had left for New York; he called her from their apartment and the two allegedly had an angry telephone conversation. Karr made plans to fly the Concorde to New York the next day. He finally fell asleep around 2:00 a.m. and his daughter Kathy, who had stayed with him out of concern for his health, went to her own room. Telephone records showed another call to Evia at 4:00 a.m. At 7:30 his valet found him dead.[14]

Evia Karr had a different story. They had actually spoken three times the night of his death. He had first called to tell her he had returned from Moscow. Then at 4:00 a.m. he reported that he was feeling ill and believed he had eaten something in Moscow that had precipitated it. He also speculated that perhaps he had been poisoned. Worried, she had advised him to take a Librium and, if he was still feeling poorly, to call the American Hospital in Paris. He called back a few minutes later and reported that he felt better. After a brief chat, they said good night. Although she admitted that their marriage had been a stormy one, they had recently reconciled. Her trip to New York, in fact, was to negotiate "the acquisition of an apartment on behalf of the couple." As further evidence that David had no intention of going through a divorce, Evia later produced a one-page handwritten letter allegedly signed by Karr, dated June 26, 1979, proclaiming that "out of my love for my wife" he would "unconditionally transfer to her name" all the assets of Anstalt Brigena, a Liechtenstein-based company he owned, valued in excess of $1,000,000, and to provide another $1,000,000 in shares of Financial

Engineers, from which she could draw $60,000 a year. She would be able to use these resources to buy an apartment "at a place of her choosing." He specified that the two would meet at a Geneva bank on July 11 to formally transfer the shares. And, improbably, Evia later claimed in a court filing that the purpose of the transfer was so that "I might eventually be able to take control of some of his companies and help him with their management."[15]

Whether this handwritten letter was genuine or legally binding would be contested during the probate of Karr's estate and rejected by an American court. If it actually was written by him, it is impossible to know whether he ever intended to carry out its provisions, whether it represented a financial offer in connection with a divorce, or if it was a cruel joke on a woman he was desperate to jettison. If it was a forgery, Evia had an obvious motive: to try to salvage some money from a marriage gone bad and soon to be ended.

Karr's unexpected death—he was only sixty—initially attracted little attention in the United States, but quickly became front-page fodder for the tabloid press in France. And that, in turn, stimulated a flurry of reporting from the American Embassy in Paris to the State Department. The Karr story had more than enough grist for those eager to uncover a scandal and sensationalize the news. Even without the rumors and gossip about bribery of Russian officials or ties to international pariahs like Amin and al-Qaddafi, or connections to powerful international businessmen and financial powerhouses in France, there was his tumultuous and complicated personal life, with multiple former wives, personal extravagance, and whiffs of violence or danger going back to the burning of his yacht.

All that baggage meant Karr's death would not escape notice. But it was his erratic widow who set off the fireworks after being ostracized by his family. Evia was detested by most of Karr's children and former wives. His eldest son Andrew, who worked for his father at Financial Engineers and Lazard Frères, was in no hurry to notify her of her husband's death. The body was discovered around 7:30 a.m. on July 7. Andrew did not call his stepmother in New York with the news until 5:30 p.m. (11:30 a.m. EDT). Evia promptly called Karr's longtime New York secretary who brusquely informed her that she had learned of Karr's death two and a half hours earlier and that his New York office held no personal papers. When Evia called their Paris apartment at noon, the phone was answered by one of Karr's Paris employees, who handed it to Andrew. He allegedly commented: "Forget it, you have nothing to hope for."[16]

Unable to get a late flight to Paris, Evia did not arrive until Sunday July 9 at 10:45 p.m. The delay in informing her of David's death, she was convinced, was a deliberate ploy to allow Andrew Karr and employees of Finatek to remove all of his records and papers from the apartment. His attaché case, always crammed with documents and files, was empty, his office desk had been cleaned out, and even his address book was gone. No one would tell her where any of it was. Karr's doctor, Stuart Jones, from the American Hospital, who had examined his body, would not return her calls. She was refused access to his business office, given no information about his business dealings, and not allowed to meet with his partners.[17]

Adding to her sense of grievance, Evia discovered that all of her financial resources had been shut off. David had generously provided her an allowance of $8,000 a month that was no longer being paid, and unlimited use of American Express and Bloomingdale's charge cards. The day of his father's death, Andrew had removed all his personal effects, including expensive cuff links and watches, his passport, traveler's checks, and business and personal credit cards, to a safe at another apartment. He also contacted all the credit card issuers with news that Karr had died. Evia angrily wrote that "I have totally been cut off from any monies and have had to live on my own savings. Every credit card and access to accounts has been closed."[18]

Concluding, correctly, that they were all determined to cut her out of Karr's estate, Evia also began to wonder about the official narrative of her husband's death. A police surgeon and Karr's personal physician had both set the approximate time of death at 2:30 a.m.—but Karr had been on the telephone with Evia more than two hours later. Moreover, both the valet and the police who were called to the apartment were sure that rigor mortis had not yet commenced, suggesting that his death was more recent. The second anomaly that would fuel intense speculation was the valet's claim that the lenses of his glasses had popped out of the frame but were not broken. Evia later claimed that when she had arrived at their apartment on July 9, Karr's body, still present, had "large bruises...his left cheek presenting a wide sunken furrow, his right eye covered with dried blood, his mouth swollen, and his fists clenched." She also claimed to have discovered "blood-stained pillowcases in the washing machine," either then or on a later visit.[19]

The first press reports of Karr's death had been matter-of-fact and brief, three short paragraphs in the *International Herald Tribune*. On July 9, before Evia arrived in Paris, Andrew Karr went to the American Embassy to report his father's death. He requested that a message be passed to the White House with a reminder that his father had "been asked by the White House several times to assist in various" matters related to East-West trade, and one forthcoming trip to Moscow in particular. Andrew insisted that "I am familiar with my father's activities and am willing to fulfill any commitments made by my father." That statement, with the implication that David Karr might have been working on behalf of the American government, perhaps even covertly, would lead some to speculate that he had a relationship with the CIA.[20]

David had, in fact, regularly briefed American officials about at least some of his contacts and negotiations in Moscow. In 1975, while in Moscow with Shriver to negotiate regarding Soviet equipment for the Olympic Games, he informed Ambassador Walter Stoessel that the final details of the Lazard Frères loan were complete, and the bank was in the process of arranging short-term credits to the Foreign Trade Bank. He also detailed the red-carpet treatment of Shriver, noting that he would be received by Premier Kosygin and promising to provide a complete account to a State Department official when he returned to Paris.[21]

Andrew's main task, however, was to prepare the authorities for the media explosion he was sure would soon erupt. After telling an official that a cremation had been scheduled to take place within a few days, he warned that he suspected Evia, whom Karr was in the process of divorcing, "would try to disrupt the ceremony by any means possible, including allegations that her husband's death was not natural."[22]

After her arrival in Paris, Evia made two appointments with the Embassy Deaths and Estates Officer, but she did not show up at either one. Her lawyer, who did appear, mentioned that she "had expressed suspicion" that "her husband had been murdered." On July 11, the scheduled cremation was suddenly stopped; Evia Karr's French lawyers had obtained a court order to require an autopsy. The French press was immediately energized, and a series of sensational and frequently inaccurate stories began to appear with lurid headlines: "Mysterious Death of an American Businessman," "A Most Embarrassing Corpse," and "My Husband Was Assassinated."[23]

Karr was variously described as "a former militant antifascist," who had brokered Soviet arms to Uganda, earning him a place "on the Israeli secret service blacklists," or a wheeler-dealer who had Dzhermen Gvishiani, Premier Alexei Kosygin's son-in-law, "in his pocket." One news report lionized him as a savior for Jewish dissidents in the Soviet Union. Evia told the American Embassy in mid-August that she had given several interviews to the French press about the interest of the Kennedy family in Karr's death, and asserted that she had "spoken with Senator Kennedy several times" about it. One report even had Sargent Shriver, described as David's "best friend," arriving in Paris to "study the shadowy David Karr affair more closely."[24]

Evia stoked the conspiracy theories about David's "murder" within days of his death. In late July, the autopsy report delivered to the American Embassy concluded that "cardiovascular lesions were sufficient to explain cause of death," but added that there was a "small fracture of the horn (corne) of the thyroid cartilage" that "was likely to have been caused by fall following" his heart attack. Karr's organs were sent for toxicological testing. Those results, released in late August, based on a series of tests carried out in France, Germany, and the United States, concluded that there was no trace of poisoning. The pathology report, issued in September, found no indication of foul play, but did reveal that there were "recent major lesions on his heart," suggesting a recent heart attack prior to the fatal one.[25]

Despite the autopsy and pathology and toxicology results, both the French press and Evia Karr continued to flog the charge of murder. The broken bone in his neck ignited speculation that he had been assaulted in his apartment, bringing on the fatal heart attack. L'Aurore, a conservative-leaning daily paper, cast Evia Karr as the beleaguered heroine, single-handedly fighting to uncover the truth. "A natural death," it explained, "really would have suited everyone." Reporter Jacques Lesinge demanded to know "the fractured larynx? How can this be explained? Perhaps this was also a result of the fall...this is truly bizarre." He confidently asserted that "this phenomenon has never been witnessed even among car accident victims." And, he declared: "All of the specialists agree that this is an extremely rare accident which can only occur as a result of a violent blow. Even a heavy fall generally only results in lesions in this part of the body."[26]

Christian Chapman, the embassy official reporting on the case, was convinced that "the continuing press interest in the Karr case is fueled by Mrs. Evia Karr. Stories continue to be sensational, not based entirely on fact, and often refer to Mrs. Karr." In one interview she proclaimed that "I am convinced that this was a strike by KGB. My husband knew too much about the Russians!" But she soon discounted this option "because David was worth so many billions of dollars to them in business. Why would they kill the golden goose?" Then she offered a more generic explanation, telling one reporter that "he was liquidated." She claimed to have convincing letters that said "his life was always in danger," including one that accused him of being a KGB agent, hinting that perhaps he had been killed by enemies of the Soviets or to punish him for his work for them. Chapman reported that someone close to Evia expressed to him his "certainty that the continuing investigation is Mrs. Karr's way of maintaining her publicity profile at a newsworthy level."[27]

Evia also floated other candidates for the murderer's role. In mid-August, *L'Aurore*, her favored outlet for leaks, floated the KGB and the Israelis as possible though unlikely candidates, but also included business rivals, strongly implying that Karr's decision to transfer substantial assets to his wife might not have made "everyone happy. Certain associates of David Karr will find themselves to have been wronged in this deal." Although he was not named in this article, Evia later implied in correspondence that Eliezer Preminger might have a motive for eliminating David because he held the bearer shares of Anstalt Brigena, and Karr's decision to give them to her might "have infuriated Eliezer."[28]

Evia's decision in late September to make an official charge of murder certainly upped the ante. On September 20, she filed a civil complaint in Paris "against person or persons unknown," accusing them of murdering her husband. In support of her petition she asserted that there had been a conspiracy to conceal the circumstances of her husband's death. She cited her discovery in the days afterward, of blood-stained pillows and sheets in their apartment, the purplish color of his face, and signs of injury. (The chauffeur who discovered the body had told the press that there was "a long wound starting at the top of the eye and going all the way to the middle of the cheek," but admitted he might have struck "a marble tablet hanging on the wall in his fall.") She doubted that he had "managed at the same time to hurt his face on all sides in falling, and at the same time to fall on his neck," causing the fracture in the larynx.[29]

Anticipating a dispute over property, embassy officials had placed seals on the Karrs' apartment on July 18 in accordance with regulations about the possessions of American citizens dying abroad. At Evia's request, the French police placed seals on a possible crime scene the same day, but after Andrew Karr and several employees of David's businesses had removed items from the apartment. Early in November, Evia's new American attorney arrived in Paris to goose the investigation and stir up more publicity.

Richard Ben-Veniste had achieved a level of fame and notoriety serving as a special prosecutor during the Watergate hearings. He arrived in Paris on November 5 and asked the embassy to help him get the French investigative records. The police report noted that Evia "had made no mention of [a] blood-stained pillowcase" when questioned and that the chauffeur had not suggested anything suspicious about Karr's appearance. Ben-Veniste also wanted the embassy to allow access to the Karrs' apartment; when informed that American law prohibited lifting the seal without the agreement of other family members, he bypassed the U.S. government and obtained a French court order to open the apartment on November 7 to allow Evia to remove clothing and personal effects and to "conduct investigation, making search and taking photographs." After negotiations, it was agreed that she would be allowed to take her clothing (she "was not wealthy and needed her clothes what with winter coming on"), but that no investigation would be allowed other than a police search that would take place during a second opening of the apartment a few weeks later.[30]

When the group of eight—Evia, her French lawyer, Ben-Veniste, a French lawyer for the Karr children, two American embassy officials, and two French police officers—arrived at 60 Avenue Foch at 10:30 in the morning, two reporters from *L'Aurore*, one a photographer, were waiting outside. They were not allowed to go in, but the visit still turned into a three-ring circus.

Immediately upon entering, Evia "rushed to [the] laundry room where she has alleged two blood-stained pillowcases were hidden. Police stopped her, saying they would carry out [an] investigation" and demanded that she start gathering her effects. Instead she entered David's study, "closely followed by Ben-Veniste, opened [the] desk and picked up broken spectacles Karr had been wearing when he died. Again, police ordered her to put them back and start packing." The party proceeded to the bedroom where Ben-Veniste began to question Evia about the location and position of Karr's body. Once again the police intervened and Evia finally began to pack. Ben-Veniste left the apartment, borrowed a camera from the reporter outside, and prepared to take photographs. The "police forbade him to do so." As Evia collected clothes and cosmetics, the two of them periodically flipped through an open filing container on the floor, earning repeated police warnings. After two hours Evia had jammed about 150 items of clothing into four suitcases and one garment bag, along with four framed photographs of herself and David. She took four fur coats and wore a fifth out of the apartment. The French police did not allow her to take any medication or photographic equipment.[31]

Outside, the press took pictures and interviewed Evia and her lawyer. On November 8, the front page of L'Aurore featured a picture of the pair under the headline "From Watergate to Karr Affair." Largely a rehash of previous stories, it described Ben-Veniste as the "overthrower" of Nixon's cabinet members and "heavy reinforcement" for Evia Karr. It suggested that the "blood-stained pillowcases" had been previously seen by both Evia and the chauffeur and had mysteriously vanished. Although Ben-Veniste expressed regret at the late start of the investigation, he was pleased to "have just seen the police of the criminal brigade at work, and I am somewhat reassured." Ambassador Arthur Hartman himself added a comment to the long report on Ben-Veniste's Paris excursion, noting that Evia had made no mention of "blood-stained pillowcases" in her initial statement to the police and neither had the chauffeur, calling her campaign "extremely dubious."[32]

Having for months stoked rumors of a conspiracy to murder her husband, Evia later pulled back, bemoaning "the abuse of my husband's memory, [and] the false accusations attributed to me, concerning the death of my husband." Much of the sensationalism, she suggested in a plaintive letter to the New York judge overseeing the probate of Karr's estate, had been orchestrated by the French press. It was Andrew Karr, Lazard Frères, and Christian Chapman, the Deputy Chief of Mission at the Paris Embassy, whom she labeled "a medium level and simple-minded bureaucrat...who must have daydreams in his dreary office about international espionage and 'how to catch a spy,'" who had egged it all on, she said.[33]

Written in 1980, the letter indignantly denied ever suggesting that "my husband's former business associates in the Soviet Union" were responsible for his death. She used capital letters: "THIS IS A LIE!...These people were our friends! But this was not a friendship based on bribe—no true friendship is, but a result of my husbands [sic] greatest asset: loyalty!" She also repudiated her prior claim that she had spoken to Senator Ted Kennedy: "I have never said that I spoke to Senator Kennedy or met with him personally, since the truth is that I have not." Yet she had told Chapman on August 16 that she had "spoken with Senator Kennedy several times" about her husband's death. She also mysteriously suggested that some unnamed person had falsely convinced her that Kennedy harbored "ill feeling" toward David. While she did not name anyone, one implication was that it was Roy Cohn, an old enemy of Karr's, who had been her lawyer but was no longer in her employ.[34]

Many years later Evia offered still another candidate who might have wanted Karr dead—Armand Hammer. Karr had secretly testified before the Securities and Exchange Commission in 1978, linking Hammer to the bribery of Soviet officials. The leak of these accusations forced Hammer to drop a takeover of the Mead Corporation. Locked into a forced partnership with Karr and bitterly resenting his accusations, a vengeful Hammer supposedly had a motive for eliminating Karr.[35]

Evia was hardly the only person speculating about who might want to kill David Karr. Sir Charles Forte, Karr's old employer and owner of the elegant Paris hotels where Karr had first made his mark in Europe, believed he had been killed, and thought he knew the motive, if not the perpetrator. Forte suggested that a business deal gone bad or an organized crime syndicate might have been responsible.[36]

When negotiations were under way to sell the George V, La Tremoille, and Plaza Athénée to Forte in 1968, Paul Bougenaux, a former Communist, was a concierge at the latter establishment. As leader of the union representing the staff, he had led street demonstrations opposing its sale to an Englishman. David Karr, deal-maker extraordinaire, worked out a compromise that installed Bougenaux as general manager of the Plaza Athénée in return for the union's acquiescence, along with a unique profit-sharing plan for the staff. Amid rumors in 1979 that Forte was about to sell the hotel to an Arab consortium, and that its employees faced steep cuts in their compensation, Bougenaux was fired in July 1979, just days before Karr's death. The ostensible reason for his firing was that he had provided advice to a competing hotel chain; Bougenaux had allegedly been consulting about the management of the Kosmos Hotel in Moscow that had been financed by David Karr. Upon his return from Moscow on July 6, Karr, according to one newspaper, "had a stormy meeting, to say the least," with Bougenaux. One bellhop told a reporter that "if I tell you what was said, I'll be out the door an hour later." Sir Charles Forte told the press that Bougenaux had violated the terms of his severance agreement by talking to the press. Forte also suggested that a nasty labor dispute had turned violent. He confided to a reporter that Bougenaux's intended replacement, Henri Manassero, transferred from the Plaza Hotel in New York to Paris, then got a phone call during a July 7th stopover in London and heard a voice say: "Karr is dead. Come to Paris and you're next." After consulting with Forte, Manassero went back to New York. To Forte's mind, Karr's murder was not linked to espionage or international intrigue, but run-of-the-mill workplace violence, perhaps abetted by elements of the Paris underworld.[37]

The KGB was hardly the only spy agency to be blamed—or credited—with assassinating Karr. His second wife, Buffy, became convinced that the CIA was responsible, citing Karr's work for the Russians and the fact that Ronnie Driver, a British business associate, had told her that David was a CIA double agent, a claim buttressed by Karr's supposed work on East-West trade and Jewish emigration. She also insisted that his Paris CIA contact was killed on the street within a few weeks of David's death.[38]

Given the rumors after his death reported in *Fortune*, that Karr and Eliezer Preminger had been helping some of Israel's most vitriolic enemies by supplying Russian arms to Idi Amin and Muammar al-Qaddafi, there were hints that the Mossad, convinced that the rumors were true, might have eliminated him. Samuel Flatto-Sharon, a Polish-born French Jewish financier who had been indicted in his adopted country for financial fraud, had shopped these rumors after he fled to Israel. To avoid deportation, he ran for the Knesset and won a seat. His legislative immunity enabled him to avoid French justice.[39]

When a rebellion broke out against Amin in 1979, Flatto-Sharon financed a band of mercenaries to travel to Uganda to locate the remains of Dora Bloch. An Israeli citizen, Bloch had been in a Ugandan hospital during the raid to free Jewish hostages at the Entebbe Airport in 1976, and had been murdered in retaliation, allegedly at the hands of Amin himself. Daniel Waltener, the mercenary group's leader, hyped the role his small band of fifty men played in the fighting, spinning tall tales about nonexistent Arab forces and Russian weapons deployed on behalf of the dictator. After Karr's death, Flatto-Sharon said his men had located documentary evidence of Karr's role as a middleman in the arms sales to Amin—but his credibility was dubious, for shortly afterward, he was indicted and convicted in Israel for having bribed several thousand people to vote for him in 1977. Several of those to whom he promised money or apartments, in exchange for their votes, denounced him after he stiffed them. Flatto-Sharon was also tried in absentia in France and convicted of fraud, forgery, and tax evasion. Sentenced to perform community service in Israel, he never returned to France. Instead, he launched another career, becoming a well-known radio personality, a pastime he still practiced in 2016.[40]

In death as in life David Karr was divisive, even within his own family, whose members all entertained different theories about his demise. Some were convinced he was murdered; others were sure he had succumbed to a heart attack. His daughter Kathy, who was the first family member to see his body, believed it was a natural death. He had been ill in Moscow and on the plane returning had looked gaunt; in his apartment he told her he thought he might be having a heart attack. His third wife, Michette, shared that belief, based on a previous heart attack that had sent him to the hospital during their marriage. Evia, of course, inflamed the press and frustrated American and French officials with her charges of murder and her suggestion that the CIA, KGB, Mossad, or Mafia might have been responsible. Buffy, his second wife, thought the CIA had killed him. His second son, Frank, nominated the KGB. The

French press, happy for a scandalous story, retailed all the possibilities, and various friends, enemies, and business associates freely speculated without any evidence.

Karr's death also embroiled the French Minister of Foreign Affairs in a purported scandal involving Finatek, which Karr co-owned with Lazard Frères for deal-making in Eastern Europe and the Soviet Union. Finatek had commissioned the Kosmos Hotel deal through Financial Engineers, and held shares in Mostec, which was negotiating with a Soviet government entity to build a technology center in Moscow.

In 1976, French President Giscard d'Estaing appointed Jean-André François-Poncet, a Finatek board member since November 1974, secretary general in the office of the president. In 1978, he became minister of foreign affairs, holding the position until 1981. In August 1979, an accusatory article in *Minute* was published that alleged that several Finatek executives, including Poncet, had received gifts from the Soviets, compromising his independence. Poncet indignantly denied the charges, insisting that he had resigned from the board in November 1975 and had received no compensation, dividends, or gifts during his year of service. Lazard Frères primly explained that Finatek's executives had not received any gifts from the Russians, but had made them to the Russians, "a common practice in international business" and a barely disguised admission that to do business with the Soviet Union required payoffs to Soviet officials.[41]

While the specter of Karr and his companies paying off Soviet officials seemed to be a motive for the KGB to eliminate a potentially embarrassing scandal—particularly if the publicity would involve Gvishiani—another rumor offered a more direct motive. Evia told reporters that Eliezer Preminger was Karr's secret partner on the Olympic coin deal, had hid some of the income, and inflated expenses. Unnamed Israeli sources suggested that the two men had also skimmed money on arms deals they had brokered with Uganda, Libya, and, for good measure, the PLO. Cheating any of these parties would have provided a motive for them to kill Karr.[42]

Was David Karr murdered? The only answer that can be given with any certainty is...maybe. Even the official finding that Karr had died of a heart attack does not preclude the possibility that he was attacked in his apartment and in the resultant struggle went into cardiac arrest.

Nor is it impossible that the broken bone in his larynx was the result of Karr's falling after suffering a heart attack and his neck hitting a sink or a piece of furniture in his apartment. The bruise on his face could be accounted for in a similar manner. But none of the findings precluded murder. There is no evidence that there were any bloodstained items in the apartment; that story was most likely concocted by Evia Karr and retailed by a gullible press. What is certain is that no one ever claimed responsibility for killing Karr, and no paper trail has ever turned up implicating any spy agency. Nor has any rogue agent or defector ever surfaced with an account of hearing about an operation to eliminate him. That does not mean he was not murdered; the absence of evidence is not proof of anything, but it does mean that the case for murder remains unproven.

Some of the candidates for murderer make less sense than others. Eliezer Preminger, labeled as Karr's mysterious and shadowy associate by the press, was accused of running Soviet weapons to Idi Amin, Muammar al-Qaddafi and the PLO, and bilking the Russians, not only on these transactions, but on the coin deal as well. Evia speculated that he might have killed Karr out of fear of losing control of a Liechtenstein-based company whose assets were about to be conveyed to her.

But at least on the surface, Preminger was a respectable businessman. After concluding his work for Charles Forte in the late 1960s, he returned to Israel where he worked for ARAD, an industrial company, then went to work for the Johananoff Group, a large Israeli chemical company, in 1970, later named Gadot and then GBI. Between 1970 and 1973, he worked in its Amsterdam headquarters, where the company operated special tankers to transport chemicals around the world. Although he returned to Israel in 1973, he spent considerable time abroad on business and eventually rose to become its general director. Friends with many high-ranking Mossad officials, he remained a fervent Zionist and died in 2001.[43]

There is one piece of evidence that Preminger was entangled with Karr's web of European-based businesses. On November 8, 1977, just one week before obtaining a legal separation from Michette, Karr handwrote and signed a one-page letter addressed to "My Dear Evia Freiberg" to note their "understanding" that on the following day he would transfer $70,000 to her German bank account plus four "California Real Estate interests that are held in my name," which would be held by a new hold-ing company named David Freiberg and Co., Ltd. on the Isle of Jersey to be jointly owned by the two of them. Karr and Eliezer Preminger would transfer to that same holding company "all their shares" in several corporations owned by Karr. There is no evidence that this agreement was ever carried out. At the time of Karr's death, the Isle of Jersey com-pany does not seem to have been formed, nor shares transferred. The document was attached to an affidavit filed by Evia on July 31, 1979, but never became an issue in subsequent pleadings or testimony now in the records. While she sought to have the one-page letter handwritten just before David's death enforced as an obligation of the estate or a final will, neither she nor her lawyers ever mentioned any Isle of Jersey Company co-owned by the two of them.[44]

Whether or not Preminger had control of any of the assets of any of Karr's businesses, he was not involved in the Olympic coin deal and had no motive to want Karr dead. Moreover, had he and Karr been in cahoots, why had the KGB spared him and killed his partner-in-crime, who was of far more use to them?

By the same token, the Mossad would not have killed Karr if he had been assisting the Jewish state for years, most recently by helping Soviet Jews get out of the U.S.S.R. There is no evidence to suggest that Karr and Preminger were engaged in the activities inimical to Israeli interests that were mentioned in the press. Even if they were, why would the Mossad kill Karr but spare Preminger? Preminger remained friendly with top Mossad agents for years afterward.

Armand Hammer no doubt hated and resented Karr, who had cost him a significant portion of the Olympic coin proceeds. Karr's charges of bribery before the SEC had also exposed Hammer to legal problems in the United States and may have damaged Hammer's relationship with the Soviet Union. As ruthless a businessman as Hammer was, however, there is no evidence that he ever put out contracts on his enemies.

The union troubles at the Forte hotels in Paris had generated a good deal of anger and threats. Lord Forte hinted to reporters of underworld figures, murder, and a Byzantine struggle for control over lucrative deals. However, Karr had little to do with operating the prestigious and profit-able hostelries. At the time of his death, he had no operating control of the hotels, so why would the underworld or a corrupt union figure want him murdered?

And why would the CIA kill him? If he was a double agent for the Agency, why eliminate him? Even if he was a Soviet agent, or asset, the CIA would be unlikely to murder an American citizen for that. It would rather try to use him or ultimately, prosecute him. Contrary to urban legends about the ruthlessness and long arm of the CIA, it did not routinely assassinate American citizens, much less prominent businessmen.

The one organization with a motive and the means to kill Karr was the KGB. Whether or not he was cheating the Soviets in his business deals, Karr was a potential major embarrassment to the U.S.S.R. True or not, the leaks that had appeared in the press about his relationship with Gvishiani implicated a close relative of a Soviet leader in bribery. Karr had already testified against Hammer secretly; perhaps, the Soviets might have worried, he had also done so or might do so about Gvishiani. And his very success at arranging financing for Soviet development projects through several French banks meant that his death would not unduly inconvenience Soviet interests.

The KGB had a long track record of "wet jobs," or targeted killings of troublesome or dissident figures. Anti-Soviet activists had been killed across Europe in the 1930s by trained assassins. And the KGB continued that tradition after World War II. In 1978, less than a year before Karr's death, Georgi Markov, a Bulgarian dissident, was killed by a ricin pellet injected into his leg from an umbrella. KGB defectors reported that the agency had arranged the murder. If David Karr was killed, the most likely perpetrator was the KGB.

John Grombach, a secretive retired Army officer who for many years ran a shadowy American intelligence organization, soon after Karr's death speculated that the Soviets might have assassinated him because his profit motives for Image Factory Sports clashed with his activities "as [an] agent of the U.S.S.R." With thirty-plus years in intelligence, Grombach's was certainly an informed opinion. A West Point graduate and Olympic boxer, he had been working for General William Donovan when the Joint Chiefs of Staff, hostile to the OSS, set up a small secret intelligence service of its own in 1942 and put Grombach in charge. Known under a variety of names, including the Secret Intelligence Branch, but generally referred to as "The Pond," it operated under commercial cover. Its activities were unknown to all but a handful of government officials, one of whom was President Roosevelt. Hired by the CIA as a separate unit in 1951, Grombach's operation was a constant source of problems for it. Starting in the early 1940s, Grombach, obsessed with Communist infiltration of the government, developed dossiers on federal employees suspected of radicalism. By 1953, he was leaking material to George Sokolsky, a conservative columnist and confidant of Senator McCarthy and Roy Cohn. After learning of these contacts, the CIA ended its association with Grombach and the Pond went out of existence in 1955.[45]

Whether or not Grombach provided McCarthy with information on Karr is unknown. But Grombach certainly would have known who Karr was. Not only had he likely developed a dossier on Karr going back to 1943 when he was forced out of the Office of War Information, but Grombach worked for and had provided information to Lewis Rosenstiel, Karr's old friend at Schenley Industries, from 1955 until the mid-1970s.[46]

Grombach stayed active on the United States Olympic Committee for many years after his athletic career ended. He found it irksome that American money financed most of the costs of the approaching Moscow Olympics—particularly that Image Factory Sports, the Karr-Tunney partnership, was paying only a small part of its revenues to the U.S. Olympic Committee. By congressional statute, the U.S. Olympic Committee controlled the use of the Olympic logo in America. He published an article in the then anti-Semitic *American Mercury*, once owned by H. L. Mencken, that described Karr as a shady character with a long history of Communist ties who had seemingly been converted to capitalism. It lent some credibility to Evia Karr's claim that he had been murdered. Implying that the Russians had good reason to liquidate Karr, he compared the manner of his death to the techniques used by a French Communist doctor who, during World War II, killed dozens of people by injecting an air bubble into their veins.[47]

Even if David Karr had died a natural death, many people no doubt breathed a sigh of relief upon hearing the news. While he was a valuable resource for the Soviets, the possible embarrassment and scandal of his ties to top officials had to have been of concern. If he was working for the Israelis, his ties to sketchy international figures and possible double-dealing with the Russians might have been worrisome. American intelligence agencies were no doubt concerned about his frequent trips to Moscow and connections to leading politicians in the United States. His business associates, both present and past, made money from their dealings with him, but could not be sure that they might not become ensnared in his complicated and opaque deals and maneuvers.

While all these players sorted out the implications of his death for their interests, his large and unwieldy family had more immediate interests and concerns. Karr's business interests were scattered across several continents and hidden in a maze of corporations, holding companies, blind trusts, and partnerships. Where were his assets? And who would inherit them? With three ex-wives and one current spouse whom he was in the process of divorcing, and five children, one a minor, an American citizen who had lived for years in France, he was a poster child for a nasty, contentious, and long-running battle over his estate. And that is exactly what ensued.

9

THE WILL

Davidd Karr was only sixty years old when he unexpectedly died. Although wealthy people usually make elaborate preparations for the distribution of their assets, both to minimize taxes and to ensure that their wishes about who gets what are carried out, he had neglected to do so. The only will ever located had been executed in September 1966, a few months after he had married Michette. He had added a codicil in 1975 to make a specific bequest to his youngest son. Neither his divorce nor his remarriage nor the marital turmoil that ensued had prompted him to alter the terms of the will or change the distribution of his estate.

Dying had clearly not been on his mind the last year of his life during his tumultuous marriage to Evia; they had spent most of that time threatening each other with divorce. But it certainly was on her mind. She was a much younger woman married to a much older wealthy man. She had few resources of her own. By 1979 she was entirely dependent on him for her income and lifestyle, her modeling career having reached its expiration date. For eight years he had supported her. In the months before his death, she had to have been thinking about her future.

Although she insisted that their marital problems had been resolved before his untimely death, Evia Karr had clearly been preparing for the end of her marriage. In less than a year of marriage there had already been two divorce actions instituted. Another reconciliation was unlikely to be more than a brief hiatus to the inevitable conclusion.

One of her French lawyers, visiting the American Embassy after Karr's death, told a consular official that the couple were in the process of divorcing. Though far from impartial witnesses, his children believed he was preparing to end the marriage and told French reporters that their tumultuous relationship was over. In May 1979, Evia Karr had consulted a New York lawyer named Jeffrey Shuman. Shuman was a member of the Saxe, Bacon & Bolan law firm, whose most prominent member was Roy Cohn, Joe McCarthy's former chief aide. Although he had represented a variety of prominent figures, including mobster Carmine Galante, the New York Catholic Archdiocese and, later, Donald Trump, one of Cohn's specialties was high-profile divorce cases. Saxe, Bacon & Bolan had represented Evia when she had filed for divorce in New York before withdrawing her suit.[1]

Evia gave Shuman a limited power of attorney on June 28, 1979, ostensibly to represent her on a real estate matter, presumably the purchase of the apartment Karr had promised her in his June 26th letter, offering her $2 million. If she and her husband were still on good terms, it was a puzzling choice. Hiring Cohn's law firm was one of the last things David Karr would have done. She, however, already had a relationship with them.

Roy Cohn, after all, was one of the most flamboyant and notorious figures in the New York bar, and a man whose political escapades had made him the bête noire of American liberals and radicals and a sworn enemy of David Karr and everything he symbolized. Cohn and Louis Nizer, Karr's longtime attorney, despised each other and had faced off several times in nasty and contentious courtroom duels.

Cohn had been a boy wonder in right-wing circles ever since he had played a key role as an assistant prosecutor convicting Julius and Ethel Rosenberg of conspiracy to commit espionage and helping to send them to the electric chair. He had gone on to serve as chief aide to Senator Joseph McCarthy in his investigation of Communist infiltration of the government. With Karr's background as an accused Communist, his ties to Drew Pearson—one of McCarthy's major targets over the years—and the constant attacks over decades by such anti-Communist columnists as

Westbrook Pegler, Evia Karr couldn't have picked a lawyer more likely to enrage and infuriate Karr, if and when their divorce moved forward, or to embarrass his family in a contentious fight over his estate.

When Evia received belated word from her stepson that David was dead, she immediately booked a seat on the Concorde to fly to Paris the next day. Confronted there by her hostile stepson, within a few days she telephoned Shuman back in New York on July 11. He advised her to "immediately petition the surrogate's court in New York County for letters of administration since David Karr was a United States citizen." He also recommended she hire French attorneys and she quickly employed Jacques Elis and his assistant Danielle Gouriou.[2]

Evia also had to decide what to do about the handwritten letter that David Karr had signed just a week before his death, signifying his intention to transfer more than two million dollars' worth of shares in two of his companies to her. The transfer was to have taken place at a Swiss bank on July 11, just days after he died. The letter made no mention of a divorce—it began with his proclaiming his love for his wife—but it could have been interpreted as an offer of a divorce settlement. In fact, it had been shown to an American Embassy official by Evia's lawyer as evidence of a pending divorce settlement.

Before July's end it was obvious that the fight over Karr's estate would be nasty. When Andrew first visited the embassy, he brought a copy of Karr's 1966 will naming Michette as the principal beneficiary. When Danielle Gouriou, Evia's lawyer, visited the embassy on July 27 with the news that the Karrs had intended to divorce, she left a xeroxed copy of David's handwritten agreement to transfer more than $2 million to her and told the official monitoring the case that "she would bring him on July 30 a certified copy of [the] new will." She called that day and canceled those plans because Evia was leaving for New York and believed that courts there would settle the case. Gouriou also offered the "opinion that the agreement signed on June 26 by Mr. and Mrs. Karr could be considered as [a] will."[3]

According to Evia's later testimony, immediately after writing that one-page letter at the Hotel Pierre in New York, David had called Shuman and "related the substance of the agreement to him," telling the lawyer what he was planning to do. During their July conversation while she was in Paris, Shuman asked her to send him the original document. She arranged to have her friend who was keeping it do so. Shuman stamped his notary seal on the agreement. In his own hand-writing Shuman certified that the letter had been "sworn to before me this 16th day of August 1979," a patent falsehood, since Karr had been dead for more than a month and Evia was in Paris.[4]

Back in New York, Evia was worried that "I was the sole witness to my husband's drafting and executing the June 26, 1979 agreement, [so] I requested Jeffrey Shuman to set forth in affidavit form his recol-lection of his telephone conversation" with David. Shuman prepared an affidavit and sent it to her in Paris sometime in September. After acknowledging the substance of his telephone conversation with Karr, Shuman purportedly noted that "David Karr executed the agreement before me and signed his name thereto." Evia was stunned. Shuman had lied. She made a copy and gave his original affidavit to her French lawyer and it vanished, either lost or destroyed. Evia retained only the copy. She swore that she had not discussed the false statement with anyone but her French attorney and the lawyer she hired to replace Shuman. She specifically denied ever discussing the false affidavit with Roy Cohn.[5]

Both Karr's handwritten letter promising Evia $2 million and Shuman's affidavit attesting to his conversation with Karr about the promise were now tainted. The clear implication of this bizarre incident was that determined to use the letter to make a multimillion-dollar claim on the Karr estate, either Evia, or more likely her New York lawyers, had attempted to authenticate the handwritten letter as a legally bind-ing document. Roy Cohn had a long-standing reputation as a lawyer willing to cut ethical corners; in fact, he was disbarred shortly before his death from AIDS in 1986. One of the complaints against him was that in December 1975 he had entered the hospital room of his long-time friend and client, Lewis Rosenstiel—also Karr's old client—and grasped the nearly comatose man's hand to squiggle a signature to a codicil naming Cohn as trustee of his estate. Saxe, Bacon & Bolan did not have a sterling reputation for efficiency and precision. If Cohn's plan had been to give greater credence to Karr's handwritten letter, it failed. Evia's French lawyer had her own plan. She advised her that the letter would remain valid under French law even without the affidavit, which was never used.[6]

In the end the only valid will of David Karr's was made in September 1966, just two months after he had married Michette. He left approximately half his estate to her in trust, and the other half equally to his children, with provisions for any of their future children to be held in trust until they reached twenty-five years of age. Michette's share of the estate would revert, in full, to her estate after her death. He appointed Sam Harris, a lawyer in Sargent Shriver's firm, as executor and named his sister, Florence Ziner, and the First National City Bank of New York as substitute executors. In August 1975, seven months before he and Michette separated, he signed a codicil, granting $250,000 to his youngest son, Jean-Michel, prior to any disposition of the remainder of his estate. Both the will and the codicil were executed in New York; in the former, Karr described himself as a resident of New York City; in the latter, he declared himself an American citizen "domiciled in Monte Carlo." Both were filed in New York Surrogate's Court by Karr's executors on August 7, 1979, a month after his death.[7]

The complications with the will and Karr's estate began immediately. Drafted in 1966, it of course excluded his fourth wife, Evia. Their brief marriage left him no time or inclination for a new will, but under New York law Evia stood to receive one-third of the estate as Karr's surviving spouse anyway. Sam Harris, named as executor, declined the position. Florence Ziner stepped in, but quickly concluded that given her five children and inability to travel to Europe, and the complexity of the estate, she could not serve. An attorney for the estate added that she "found that following in her late brother's footsteps was a disastrous emotional experience for her, and I don't think her lawyers were optimistic about ever being paid." Evia also filed a petition in New York objecting to her as executrix. The bank also declined to act.[8]

Evia's petition objecting to Florence Ziner as executrix alleged a conspiracy involving Ziner, Andrew Karr, and Gertrude Kramer, Karr's New York secretary, to deprive Evia of her rightful inheritance, with accounts of missing files and papers, lies about the cause of death, complaints about the sealing of the Karrs' Paris apartment, and her inability to get reimbursement for more than $10,000 in funeral expenses. She also complained that they were spreading rumors she was not legally married to David.[9]

The litany also included language that Evia Karr later admitted was false. The petition, prepared by Jeffrey Shuman, accepted the New York Surrogate's Court's jurisdiction over the estate and made statements agreeing that David Karr had been based in New York, that he "maintained his domicile at the Pierre Hotel" in New York, voted in New York elections, kept an office and apartment on Park Avenue, and paid U.S. income taxes. Evia added that she and her husband "maintained an apartment" in Paris that they used while he was there on business. Those admissions complicated her later efforts to have the estate distributed according to French law, under which she would have been entitled to a significantly larger share than one-third of the estate.[10]

According to Evia, when she phoned Shuman from Paris on July 11, he had advised her to file a petition for Letters of Administration in New York, as it did not matter where David had lived and worked since he was an American citizen. He asked her whether David had ever written a will. She replied that she thought he had, but Shuman advised her to say in her petition that she had no information. Claiming she was distraught and in ignorance of New York law and the distinction between a residence and a domicile, Evia agreed that Shuman would airmail her the petition that she would sign in the presence of an embassy official and send back to him for filing. She later contended that she was too upset and confused to understand what she was signing, and that "material changes" were "made without my knowledge and consent between the time I executed said Petition and the time it was filed" in court on July 24. She attributed the mistakes to "how careless and misinformed" Shuman was. She claimed she did not become aware of the changes he had made until January 11, 1982, more than two and a half years later.[11]

Most of the errors—listing Evia as an American citizen in one place and a German in another, incorrect addresses, sloppy wording about the potential size of the estate, etc.—bespoke simple carelessness. The claim that David Karr's domicile was in New York, however, was more serious. If his domicile was in France, as Evia would later contend, then the New York Surrogate's Court should recognize that French law pertaining to a surviving spouse should control the disposition of the estate. In short, she was claiming that an error by her attorney had mistakenly allowed New York law, under which she would receive one-third of the estate, to trump French law, under which she would receive more than half the estate.[12]

Consequently, in October 1979, Evia filed a copy of David's hand-written letter promising to transfer substantial assets to her with a French notary, along with her insistence that Paris was David's last domicile. The hope was that the French legal system would recognize that the letter was a valid gift from David to Evia, meaning that the promised $2 million would become a legal obligation of the estate prior to any distribution to beneficiaries. The notary, however, went much further, presumably at Gouriou's urging. Back in July, when she had visited the embassy, the French lawyer had suggested that the handwritten letter might be considered a will. Not only did the notary now agree that it was a legally enforceable gift, but he went further, accepting the letter as a last will and testament, even though nothing in the letter said a word about its being a will. To Evia and Gouriou, that nullified Karr's 1966 will and its codicil that had been filed in New York. While Shuman tried to block the appointment of an executor from Karr's family in New York but recognized the jurisdiction of the New York Surrogate's Court to supervise probate, Gouriou embarked on a new and complicated legal strategy that ultimately proved disastrous for her client. Under French law, the next step was for the Paris notary to locate the assets of the estate, a task made inestimably more difficult by Andrew Karr's control of David's papers and files.[13]

Evia's path of self-destruction had begun with her choice of lawyers. She had already dismissed Shuman because he had falsely asserted that David had signed his letter of gift in his presence. She also fired her first French attorney, Jacques Elis. He later admitted to some sympathy for Evia, since she was very upset and under the shock of an older husband's death. But he also found her neurotic and an extraordinarily difficult client. She "was on our backs every day for two months." He thought she had fantasies and enveloped everything in a cloud of mystery. Elis did not believe her tales of murder and conspiracy—although he agreed that Lazard Frères was anxious to suppress information on Karr's business dealings—but he still filed her complaint in the French courts against an unknown person responsible for his death. In addition to everything else, Evia had no money to pay him for his time. And, when he finally had had enough of this difficult client, Evia persuaded his assistant Danielle Gouriou, to leave his firm and represent her.[14]

The next casualty was Evia's celebrity lawyer, Richard Ben-Veniste.

In February 1980, she wrote to Judge Millard Midonick of the New York Surrogate's Court. She denounced Ben-Veniste because he "had clearly acted against my interest." According to Evia, she had revoked his power of attorney because he had failed to stop the sale of Karr's yacht, the *Ottelia*, in December, or to establish her rights in Karr's estate as the surviving spouse.[15]

Judge Midonick responded to her letter a month later, "distressed that you seem to know practically nothing about your situation in this court." Since she was subject to the jurisdiction of the Surrogate's Court, it was important that she be represented by competent counsel. Her dismissal of Ben-Veniste and his associate Henry Lowet had put her in a precarious legal situation. While he was prepared to allow her French attorney to represent her, it would be "very unusual and inefficient" to have someone protecting her interests "across the Atlantic Ocean" and he suggested that Gouriou advise her on a New York co-counsel. Just because she had discharged Ben-Veniste and Lowet, he was "not obliged to permit counsel to withdraw from the case" and he ordered Lowet to remain so as to "keep you informed as to what others are doing." Since she had "stopped your lawyers from protecting your interests here," Karr's four children from his first two marriages had been named to administer the estate following Florence Ziner's withdrawal as executrix. He admonished Evia that "private letters from litigants to the judge are inappropriate" and that the estate and the disputes over it would be handled by lawyers from contending sides. He also sent a copy of his letter to Danielle Gouriou.[16]

Henry Lowet, Evia's dismissed attorney, also responded to her letter. He vigorously denied that either he or Ben-Veniste had failed to protect her interests. They had advised her of her options and sought to ensure her rights under New York law. He repeated the necessity of her obtaining legal counsel, adding that "we ourselves have no desire to resume such representation and have undertaken to reply to your inquiries only because Judge Midonick has instructed us to do so as part of our withdrawal from the case. You are also aware that all of our efforts at this firm to date have been without any compensation."[17]

The biggest mistake Evia made was ordering Lowet and Ben-Veniste not to make a claim on the estate in New York, but to challenge the jurisdiction of the New York Court to distribute the assets. Under New

York law, widows had a "right of election." This was a provision that protected them from a vengeful spouse disinheriting them or handing over the bulk of an estate's assets to other people. The surviving spouse could claim a share of the estate that would take precedence over other beneficiaries. When there were children, as in Karr's case, the widow would be entitled to one-third of the assets. Such a claim had to be filed within a specified period of time. Other beneficiaries wishing to contest the widow's demand would have to establish either that the marriage was invalid or that the widow had abandoned her spouse.

Henry Lowet had appeared before Judge Midonick at the end of January 1980; he told the court that Evia was well aware of her election rights but preferred to proceed abroad; he also told the judge that "she may feel that whatever she would gain from" filing such a claim in New York "may not be as significant," his language indicating that he was not entirely sure of her motives or supportive of them. Evia presumably believed that armed with the decision of the French notary, they could locate assets in Europe, where the bulk of Karr's estate would be found, and Evia would receive far more than one-third. Her decision to follow that course proved a major mistake.[18]

Evia had also complained to Judge Midonick that despite his September 1979 order that she be provided a monthly allowance of $2,500 from the estate, she had not received anything. She also sent him funeral bills she had paid but for which she had not been reimbursed. Admitting that her story sounded like a "third-rate movie," she lamented being left "virtually penniless and homeless," barred from entering the apartment she had shared with her husband, reduced to living first in hotels and then with her grandmother in Germany, who was forced to "be the banker and financier of the caprices of Andrew Karr." She demanded a check for $25,000.[19]

While Judge Midonick's letter responding to Evia had been limited to the question of her attorneys, Lowet patiently went through her litany of complaints and answered them. He pointed out that granting her a monthly allowance had been contingent on her posting a bond as security, since other outstanding claims on the estate, including those by the Internal Revenue Service, "would have a priority over paying you the temporary allowance." Since she had never obtained such a bond, no allowance had been forthcoming. Additionally, following informal discussions about the allowance, some of Karr's children "raised a question as to the status of your marriage to David at the time of his death," complicating her rights as the surviving spouse. Likewise, payment of funeral expenses was in abeyance since "David's body has—to this day—still not received its final interment." All of his property would eventually be turned over to the administrators of his estate; the apartment had to be sealed until those administrators were appointed. Rather than squabbling over domicile, her lawyers suggested "that it might be beneficial to work with the other parties in locating your husband's assets and then to work for an agreement as to the division of the assets without reaching final conclusions on domicile at this time." The sale of the *Ottelia* had been carried out by a shadowy corporation that David Karr had organized, headquartered in Gibraltar, that none of the other parties could control. The receipts on the sale of the yacht were probably far less than what David had paid or owed for it.[20]

Her lawyer churning had proved disastrous for Evia Karr—and it wasn't over. She had issued a limited power of attorney dealing with real estate matters to Jeffrey Shuman on June 28, 1979, before David's death. On October 22, 1979, she had given Richard Ben-Veniste a power of attorney and, in a November 1979 retention agreement, stated that she "has not previously executed any power of attorney relating to her interest…at any time heretofore." On January 8, 1980, she fired Ben-Veniste and Henry Lowet and asked that all papers and correspondence henceforth be sent to Gouriou.[21]

But suddenly, in April 1980, spurred by the realization that the American administrators had located substantial assets, while the French notary had not, Evia developed second thoughts. She decided to rehire Jeffrey Shuman despite her earlier claim that he had falsely notarized David's letter to her, lied in his affidavit, and mishandled her affairs. Shuman appeared in Surrogate's Court three times between the end of April and June 1980, asking for an extension of the deadline for filing a notice of election. He succeeded, and the extension was granted on June 17, giving Evia until September 19 to assert her claim as a surviving spouse, but then she failed to sign the form. Shuman submitted the notice of election on the deadline, signed by him as attorney for Evia Karr, to the administrators of the estate, but did not submit it to the court itself. This opened the argument that Shuman had no authority to act for Evia Karr after having been dismissed and never formally rehired. Evia later, in an affidavit to the court, filed the power of attorney of June 1979 stating that it was in force and that it gave Shuman the authority to act for her and that she had sent a new supplementary power of attorney that reaffirmed his status. But the judge ruled that Evia had clearly signaled her intention "to proceed in France and to abandon proceedings in this court," that Shuman had no authority to act on Evia Karr's behalf, that the power of attorney she had signed in June was limited to real estate matters, not inheritance, and that despite being in contact with her, Shuman had not obtained a power of attorney subsequently. Hence, the notice of election that Shuman filed in September was not only improperly filed, but invalid.[22]

Evia's fortunes thus ran aground on the shoals of attorney shopping. By 1981, nine different law firms had appeared on her behalf in both France and New York, frustrating everyone involved, not least Judge Midonick. He complained in 1981 that "I can't seem to get any continuity here.... I have been waiting for the fourth Mrs. Karr for—it must be more than a year now—to do something, and I am not going to spend any more time waiting for her.... We have given her every courtesy.... She has a French lawyer. We have been notifying her about everything and nothing ever happens. If she ever does get a lawyer that she is content with here, that lawyer is just going to have to do whatever it is that he or she thinks they ought to do in this jurisdiction. But I am not going to wait one more minute for this lady. We have been waiting month after month after month. She has fired lawyer after lawyer after lawyer. I just don't care what she does at this point, because I can't wait anymore. [Any papers her lawyers file] may have no effect whatsoever because of her default after default after default after default." After requesting through a New York lawyer for papers to be served on her through her Paris attorney, lawyers for the estate found that material sent via registered mail was refused, forwarded to an address in Germany, and then returned unopened. The exasperated judge responded to that news with the comment: "I am just going ahead as though she didn't exist... [s]he does nothing except impede this proceeding."[23]

In response to the judge's diatribe, Evia's brother Ralph Freiberg, a Connecticut resident present at the session, tried to defend his sister, claiming that she had only wanted her American lawyers to establish that David was a French resident, but had been unable to find any law-yer able to do that, so, she had not been well served. Midonick angrily told him: "I don't care if Mr. Karr, the decedent, was a resident of the moon. Do you understand me? Our statute says that he does not have to be domiciled in New York for me to take jurisdiction, as long as he has property here and in my discretion I want to do it."[24]

Lawyers for the Karr children forcefully rebutted Shuman's plea for a rehearing on the surviving spouse election issue. When Shuman blamed her French lawyer for a flawed legal strategy, they noted that "Evia Freiberg Karr is responsible for her lawyer (or lawyers), not this court and certainly not the administrators." If that meant she lost, well, she had only herself to blame. Lastly, they asserted that the Karrs' brief marriage had been marked by two divorce proceedings, so she scarcely deserved significant assets.[25]

While neither Florence Ziner nor the French notary, who, under French law, were responsible for locating assets of the estate, had been able to unearth much, attorneys for the estate hired by Andrew Karr and the other children had, by early 1981, taken control of the stock of two companies owned by David Karr: Financial Engineers and Pamir S.A., registered in Panama. Under their plan, Pamir would be dissolved, and its 50 percent share of Nomisma Eastern Corporation stock would be held by the estate, after Nomisma paid Pamir 50 percent of its liquid assets (estimated to be approximately $8 million in cash plus its hold-ings of the Olympic coin firm Numinter, which was estimated to be 20 percent of the stock). More assets were unearthed in early 1982 when Lazard Frères disclosed that Karr's interest in Numinter would yield more than $5,000,000 in dividends. And so, having abandoned her efforts in New York in 1980, Evia tried to reassert them. In 1981, she failed to overturn Judge Midonick's decision that she had forfeited her right of election with her recycled lawyer, Jeffrey Shuman. She launched a new effort in 1982.[26]

What had seemed a quite modest estate now promised to provide its beneficiaries with very generous payouts. Desperate to salvage some-thing, Evia Karr hired a new lawyer, Richard Pikna, and abandoned hope of probating the will in a French court. Instead, she focused her efforts on New York's Surrogate's Court. During one of Pikna's first appearances on her behalf, Judge Midonick closely questioned him: "She hasn't discharged you yet, Mr. Pikna?" He responded: "Oh no, Your Honor, no." The judge sarcastically answered, "Good for you." Pikna worked in close coordination with Danielle Gouriou. In January 1982, he filed a new motion in New York to have the handwritten "holographic will" authenticated, to provide an annual $60,000 annuity for Evia, and to recognize her marital rights under French law to half the estate and a further one-eighth of the remainder. In her filing Evia blamed Jeffrey Shuman for misleading her about her situation and her rights, for altering her answers in prior filings, and for providing false information to the court about the holographic will. She also requested a monthly allowance and reimbursement of the funeral costs she had paid.[27]

Lawyers for the estate agreed to reimburse Evia $10,000 for funeral expenses, and to pay for her to travel to Germany to locate documents, as an administrative expense, not as a part of her share of the estate. Judge Midonick signed off, warning that "if she doesn't bring the papers or if she doesn't answer the questions [about them] then she won't get paid for the trip. . . She is very hard to pin down. She just changes her mind all the time." But, he was willing to approve the expense as "a drop in the bucket" of total estate assets that might move the dispute forward.[28]

The opportunity to put Evia Karr under oath was a godsend for her stepchildren given her proclivity to zigzag and contradict herself. She, herself, claimed her documents had been corrupted by her prior attorneys. The lawyers for the estate questioned her for five days in January and once in early February 1982. Although the transcripts of the January sessions are missing from the Karr records in Surrogate's Court, the guardian ad litem, John Vaneria, who represented Karr's youngest minor son, indicated that Evia was extensively and exhaustively grilled about the divorce actions during their marriage, the agreements that allegedly gave her a share of the estate, and the Karrs' living and travel arrangements. The estate lawyers investigated "whether or not acts of perjury and forgery had been committed" with the holographic will, "whether documents had been tampered with where there appeared to have been alterations after the time said documents were allegedly executed," whether "affidavits sworn to and on file before this court contained factual misrepresentations," and whether Evia had abandoned her husband.[29]

Although the transcripts are not in the Surrogate's Court file, a forgery issue might have been raised over the 1977 and 1979 handwritten letters granting Evia substantial assets. Some of the same assets were described in both letters. Could the 1977 letter, if genuine, have been used as a crib to produce the 1979 letter? There is no way to know.

Although she and her lawyer resisted providing many of the documents, enough were produced and challenged to convince Evia that she held a losing hand. The size of the estate had by now persuaded the Karr children that it was in their interest to compromise with her to avoid still more litigation. Consequently, the administrators reached a settlement with Evia, granting her a one-sixth share of the assets, equal to that of each of the children and ensuring payment of reasonable travel and living expenses in relation to the estate and her funeral bills. In return, she agreed to settle.[30]

Evia had made a number of claims. In April 1980, she sued several of Karr's businesses, including Financial Engineers and Finatek. Two months later, she sued to be appointed executor of the estate in Paris, filed a plea in Surrogate's Court for an elective share of the estate under New York law, which was denied, then, in 1981, appealed the denial. In 1981, she brought claims against the estate based on her rights under French law with the handwritten letter as the chief piece of evidence. In January 1982, she demanded reimbursement from the estate for funeral expenses and a monthly allowance. Finally, in settlement, Evia agreed to cooperate in settling the estate and refrain from making statements or providing documents that might result "in the publication of information concerning the Decedent or the circumstances surrounding his death."[31]

The saga of Evia Karr and her rotating band of lawyers was, however, not over. After all her hiring and firing, her last lawyer, Richard Pikna, was suspended from practicing law in May 1984 due to his failure to cooperate with the disciplinary committee of the New York bar after it had received several complaints alleging misconduct in the handling of client funds. In the course of that investigation, information surfaced that his admission to the New York bar in 1973 was tainted because he had concealed the fact that he had been disbarred as an attorney in Canada. After his suspension, Pikna had continued to practice law, and to steal from clients. In the words of a judge on the Second Circuit Court of Appeals, he had "practiced law, though not lawfully, in New York." Pikna pled guilty to six counts of grand larceny in September 1984. He failed to appear for sentencing and was a fugitive for two months before he was sentenced to two to six years in prison in January 1985.[32]

His troubles—and Evia's—didn't end there. Probate of the Karr estate went on. After learning Pikna was ineligible to practice law, Evia hired yet another law firm, LeBoeuf, Lamb. Pikna had been hired on a contingency basis. In July 1985, Evia's new legal team began proceedings in Surrogate's Court to rescind that agreement, which granted him 23 percent of her final settlement—which promised to approach a million dollars. Meanwhile, two of Pikna's former clients had sued him for embezzling more than $305,000 during a real estate transaction. When they discovered that his only asset was his retainer fee in the Karr case, they filed a motion to oppose its rescission. Pikna was already in prison, so the court appointed a guardian ad litem to protect his interest. Finally, in December 1987 the dispute was settled; Evia agreed to pay Pikna $77,500 from her share of the estate and his guardian $7,500. The larger sum was placed in escrow until the question of who should get the money could be resolved. That triggered a fight between Pikna's creditors and the United States government. In addition to all his other sins, for some years he had failed to pay federal withholding and income taxes and the IRS had filed tax liens against him that exceeded the amount of money in the escrow account. The government rejected a proposed compromise to split the escrowed money with those he had defrauded and sought to foreclose on its liens. That in turn led to litigation over whether the Surrogate's Court retained jurisdiction to decide how to distribute the money or whether the case should be removed to federal court. After the U.S. Court of Appeals sent the case back to the U.S. District Court, that body decided in April 1990 that the federal government's claims had precedence.[33]

As if dealing with Evia Karr and her numerous legitimate and not-so-legitimate lawyers wasn't enough, Karr's four children by his first two wives and Michette Karr and her son also had their difficulties and disagreements. In March 1981 in Paris, Michette sued the estate to enforce claims based on her divorce decree, and the Surrogate's Court appointed an attorney, John Vaneria, as guardian ad litem to represent the interests of Jean-Michel Karr, who was still a minor.

The divorce decree had prescribed child support and alimony to Michette. For the first two years after David's death, while the child support was forthcoming, it seemed possible that there would not be enough assets to fulfill all of his other commitments. Moreover, there was some question of whether the divorce settlement had negated Michette's rights under the will. So, in June 1981, Michette settled with the estate, waiving her claims to half the estate (as provided for in the will) in return for a payment of $420,000 ($250,000 of it immediately upon the sale of stock in two of Karr's corporations). The agreement also included complex stipulations about the timing of her payments, child support payments, the placing of monies due Jean-Michel in escrow ($1,000,000), French taxes, and unblocking the release of assets held in Swiss banks.[34]

That settlement, however, led to further squabbling between the estate, the guardian ad litem, and Michette and her brother over assets one or the other party held in Switzerland and whether they ought to be considered advances on amounts due under Karr's will, or on child support under the divorce agreement. Jean-Michel had an interest both as beneficiary of the will—one-sixth of the residual estate—and in regard to what he was entitled to under the divorce settlement, which was a prior obligation of the estate, due before the remaining assets of the estate could be distributed to the beneficiaries. Finally, in December 1985, an agreement was signed giving Michette fixed payments from blocked funds starting at $3,500 a month in 1985 and escalating to $4,700 a month in 1990. The total amount she would receive—when added to the $180,000 already received—would not exceed $450,000. Jean-Michel, who had also already received $180,000 in payments, would receive up to an aggregate of $340,000 ($212,000 would be counted as child support and the rest as part of his share of the estate).[35]

When the final accounting of David Karr's estate was accepted by the court in 1990, its total value, before taxes and administrative fees, was recorded at just over $15 million. Most came from liquidating David Karr & Co. and its subsidiaries, Chesterfield Ltd., and Brigena A.G., European corporations wholly owned by Karr, yielding $11 million. These corporations had been the recipients of the proceeds from Karr's partnerships with Lazard Frères, Numinter, and Image Sports Factory.

The largest single liability on his balance sheet was a debt of $350,000 owed to the State Bank of the U.S.S.R.[36]

When all the fallout from the various familial disputes, complicated negotiations about alimony, child support, and codicils, and compromises over spousal rights finally concluded in early 1990, estate and income taxes had taken almost $3 million of the estate, lawyers and accountants had eaten up another $3 million, and administrative fees to Karr's four oldest children (and a payment in lieu of executor's fees to the youngest) had cost nearly another million. Each of his five children received roughly $1 million with Jean-Louis getting a bit more, and Evia received approximately $800,000. Michette received just over $400,000.

It was an impressive financial legacy for a man who had started life in a middle-class Jewish home and never attended college. David Karr had clawed his way to wealth after years as a government employee, reporter, and public relations flack. His audacious strategy of corporate raiding had catapulted him to the helm of a major American company, despite his lack of skills to run it successfully. Having made a modestly impressive stake, he jumped into another league after his third marriage connected him to international bankers. He had used considerable charm, native shrewdness, and amoral tactics to play for high stakes, at the highest levels of international business and politics. And some unknown amount of money had come courtesy of his grateful Soviet intelligence employers who had ensured that he profited nicely from his business dealings in the Soviet Union.

CONCLUSION

D avid Karr enjoyed the luxuries and perquisites his wealth and connections brought. He reveled in the attention and deference that came from his globe-hopping lifestyle and access to some of the world's most powerful people. Supremely confident of his own intelligence and abilities, he was capable of flattering those whose favors he needed and intimidating those beneath him. Although his earliest political instincts were radical, he was prepared to abandon them when they were an impediment to his own career, and for years tried desperately to appease the FBI. In his climb up the greasy ladder of business, he befriended and defriended men of every political variety; those who could be useful to him, whether arch-conservatives like Lewis Rosenstiel or die-hard liberals like Drew Pearson, remained part of his circle. Business partners like Al Landa or Buck Lanham remained partners only so long as they acquiesced to his whims. He courted and abandoned politicians ranging from Henry Wallace to Sargent Shriver. He cooperated with and fought nasty battles with tycoons like Armand Hammer and did favors—some probably illegal—for capitalists and Communists alike.

By any measure his life was remarkable. He made a mark in several different fields—journalism, public relations, industry, and international trade. A government job with some responsibility led to his being denounced on the floor of Congress as a subversive and cost him his position. He brushed off the disaster and became a successful reporter, working for one of the most powerful columnists in the nation. After several years he was once again attacked on the Senate floor as a KGB agent and soon decamped to New York. He reinvented himself as a public relations expert, set up his own firm, and attracted major clients based on his ability to orchestrate successful proxy fights, eventually seizing control of a major American corporation. His limitations as a CEO led to a stockholder revolt that shoved him out the door. He dabbled in show business before moving to France and successfully ingratiating himself with powerful tycoons who found his deal-making skills useful, ultimately becoming one of a handful of Westerners capable of cutting deals with the Soviet Union. No one without formidable intelligence, enormous self-confidence, iron determination, and a ruthless desire to succeed could have managed such a journey.

David Karr cooperated with Soviet intelligence agencies, tried to act as a middleman between the U.S.S.R. and the U.S. on several issues, and attempted to get close to American officials and politicians at the behest of the KGB. With his outsized ego, he no doubt thought that he was manipulating all of them. Although direct evidence is lacking, it is quite probable that he was also working on behalf of Israeli intelligence. One of his few close friends, Eliezer Preminger, was probably the conduit through whom he assisted Israel both in its war with Black September and in arranging the emigration of some Soviet Jews. But it would be a mistake to make too much of any of David Karr's political allegiances; his primary loyalty was to himself and his own interests. He was driven to win, whether the game was getting a news scoop, stealing a client for his public relations firm, gaining control of proxies in a battle for control of a business, putting together a business deal so complicated or unlikely that others thought it hopeless, or receiving accolades as the Kremlin's favorite capitalist. That overwhelming drive produced considerable wealth and notoriety, as well as the stress on his heart that killed him at the age of sixty.

The same personality that drove his public career and made him a business success left his private life in shambles. Three failed marriages were about to become four when he died. His relationships with his children alternated between affection and resentment, leaning heavily toward the latter. His desire to control their lives led to worries by their mothers about his influence.

His sister shrewdly analyzed his obsessive need to demonstrate his superiority and brilliance and resigned as executrix of his estate rather than deal with the emotional turmoil of his legacy. Feenie Ziner, David's sister, married a talented artist, Zeke, and lived in Chicago before giving birth to triplets, bringing her family to five children. She became a very successful children's book author, writing *Dark Pilgrim*, *The Story of Squanto*, *Counting Carnival*, and *The True Book of Time*, the last of which sold half a million copies. In the mid-1970s, she began to teach at the University of Connecticut and retired as a professor in 1994. Her tortured relationship with her brother held her back from cooperating with this project; she died in 2012. Mortimer Katz, David's quiet and reserved brother, became an accountant. He died in Olmito, Texas, in 2008.[1]

Karr's first wife, Madeline, went to work for CBS news after their divorce and later became one of the first female producers in television after moving to WABC. She was the first female producer for *60 Minutes* and earned three Daytime Emmy Awards for a spin-off, *30 Minutes*, directed at children. She also remarried. Madeline Karr Amgott, who refused to talk about her first husband, died in 2014.[2]

Karr's second wife, Buffy, married Bob Cooke, a former reporter, after their divorce and lived in Miami. Following Cooke's death, she moved to rural New York. She now lives in Atlanta, Georgia, near her son, Frank Karr, his wife, and their children. She has published an autobiography and a novelistic account of David Karr's death and spoke openly and candidly about her ex-husband.[3]

Denise Solal (Michette) continued to live in Paris after their divorce and worked as a lawyer. She talked—guardedly—about their life together in 1990, but efforts to contact her in recent years have failed. Evia Karr returned to Europe after agreeing to a compromise about the will. A few years ago, she exchanged a series of informative emails about her life with David Karr. When last contacted, she lived in Cyprus.

Karr's children found it hard to come to grips with their demanding, difficult father. Andrew, the oldest, had worked for him at Lazard Frères, and continued that job for a few years after his death. He eventually settled in Halifax, Nova Scotia, after studying with two revered Tibetan

Buddhist teachers. He teaches and has written several books on Buddhist themes. Despite repeated letters over several years, he has politely turned aside requests to discuss his father, offering several explanations—he had moved past that period in his life, he was too busy, and his father had been dead for a long time. When his son, Doug, began work on a short dramatization of his grandfather's life, Andrew was reluctant to cooperate. Doug attributed his father's reticence to his painful relationship with David. Kathy Karr married and divorced, as did Lisa Karr. In 1989, Lisa raged at her mother, Buffy, denouncing her for causing her estrangement from her father. The two have not spoken since. Frank lives in Atlanta with his second wife and three children and owns a successful business. Jean-Michel was deeply affected by his father's death and the lurid publicity about it in the French press. He currently lives in a small town in Switzerland where he serves as a municipal councilor and mayor. He politely declined to discuss his father, citing old wounds and requesting that he not be mentioned in any way in any book about David Karr.[4]

David Karr's family and friends continued to grapple with his legacy for years after his death. He was such an outsized personality and man of mystery that even those close to him remained puzzled about his motives and his legacy.

In 2009, his grandson Doug, son of Andrew Karr, wrote and directed a short film, *Ten for Grandpa*, that was shown at a number of international film festivals, including Sundance, and received several awards. It asked ten questions about David Karr, some whimsical and others that reflected the tortured legacy he left. Some of the questions provide an appropriate coda to this book.

"Why did he change his name from Katz to Karr? Was he embarrassed about being a Jew?" Unlikely. Like many Jews in the 1930s, David Katz found a Jewish-sounding last name a burden. He never hid his origins or his religion, although he certainly was not religious or observant in any way. His emotional attachment to Israel was an important part of his life.

"Why four wives? We're Jews, not Mormons," his first wife, Madeline, intones in the movie. Living with David Karr was not easy. Madeline was part of the world in which he had grown up, Jewish New York, and, like David, had been in the Communist Party's orbit. His second wife, Buffy, called herself his "blond shiksa," a wealthy WASP from an old

American family. His third wife, Michette, was from a wealthy French Jewish family. Evia, his fourth spouse, was neither wealthy nor politically active. Karr was serially unfaithful to all his wives. Life with him was exciting, adventurous and stressful. He was never satisfied.

"Why did FDR call you a chronic liar?" Whether Roosevelt ever did so, there is no doubt that David Karr was a chronic liar. He lied about his political activities and beliefs throughout his life, he lied to obtain scoops as a reporter, he lied to convince people to join his business, he lied to bolster his shaky position at Fairbanks Whitney, and he lied to put together business deals. To Karr, lying was simply using whatever means were at his disposal to achieve his ends.

"Why were you such a jerk to my father?" Like many egoists, David Karr wanted to control his family, including his children, and lashed out at them when they defied him or did not meet his expectations.

"Did you consider the effect of your actions on your family?" Obviously not. Karr's thoughts were rarely focused on anything or anyone but himself.

"Why did McCarthy finger you? Were you a Commie?" Whether or not he ever formally joined the Communist Party, David Karr was ideologically attached to Communism as a young man. Even after he put some distance between himself and the CPUSA, he remained a sympathizer. At some point in the late 1940s, probably concluding that the fellow-traveling Left had no future in American life, he abandoned his old politics and presented himself as a typical liberal. Despite his friendship with several people associated with Soviet intelligence, he was not a spy when McCarthy accused him of being one. Ironically, his career as a Soviet source began more than twenty years after McCarthy accused him of being one.

"Did you tell that crazy story to the Securities and Exchange Commission about Armand Hammer?" Whatever he told the SEC was closed for many years by a Hammer lawsuit and has now been "lost" by the agency. There is little doubt that Karr did turn on Hammer. Their toxic relationship might have provided grist for a major scandal if Karr had not died suddenly.

"Why did you steal wristwatches from the George V hotel?" If he did shoplift, Karr no doubt regarded the hotel's goods as belonging to him. When he owned a private business or when he ran a public corporation, he treated the company's assets as his own. He charged personal purchases to company accounts. For years he dealt largely in cash, eschewing personal checking accounts. Whether or not he was ever audited by the Internal Revenue Service, Karr no doubt did his best to hide income and assets from the tax man.

"Why were four autopsies performed on you? Were you poisoned?" Karr was such a controversial figure and his death so convenient for so many people and governments that speculation and conspiracy theories were inevitable, even without his widow's lurid charges. However tempting the theories, there is no hard evidence that David Karr was murdered. If he was, it was most likely at the hand of the KGB.

"Who were you?"

This last question is the subject of this book. The narrator in Douglas Karr's short film says, "Maybe you should let Grandpa be a colorful story you tell at cocktail parties."

David Karr's life, however, has more significance than as party gossip. It offers an uncomfortable window on a world where unscrupulous and driven men navigate through the spheres of politics, business, and information, using their connections to enrich themselves no matter what the cost or who gets in the way. In Karr's case, it also meant that he was willing to provide information to the Soviet Union in return for being allowed to consummate business deals that enriched him. He was not the last American enticed to cooperate with a foreign power hostile to American interests.

NOTES

INTRODUCTION

1 Telephone interview with Feenie Ziner, August 8, 1992.

2 Westbrook Pegler, untitled column, 1959, box 49, Drew Pearson—David and Madeline Karr folder, Westbrook Pegler papers, Herbert Hoover Library.

3 Interview with Jack Anderson, Washington, D.C., March 23, 1990,

4 Interview with Hervé Alphand, Paris, France, June 4, 1990; interview with Arnold Forster, New York, June 26, 1989; Elizabeth Cooke, *Life Savors* (New York: Troy Book Makers, 2011), 164; telephone interview with George Biderman, May 15, 1990; Peter Evans, *Nemesis* (New York: Harper, 2004), 131–32; telephone interview with Daniel Bell, June 11, 1990.

5 *Congressional Record*, Senate, vol. 96, part 12, December 19, 1950, 16744; "Feenie Ziner to Mom," September 28, 1967, Feenie Ziner papers, University of Connecticut.

6 Cooke, *Life Savors*, 124–25, 208.

CHAPTER 1: YOUNG RADICAL ON THE MAKE

1 "Morris Katz," 1920 United States Federal Census; "Morris Katz," "Sophie Katz," 1930 United States Federal Census; "Morris Katz," 1925 New York State Census.

2 DK Conference, January 21, 1954, DP v. WP (two cases) folder, Drew Pearson papers, LBJ Library.

3 Spencer Klaw, "Dave Karr in the President's Chair," *Fortune*, LXIII (June 1961), 156. Although Karr claimed to have had an IQ of 187, an FBI report noted that it was 118, above average, but hardly in the genius range.

4 "Report Made at New York City," June 25, 1942, FBI file 65-32550-15; DK Conference, January 21, 1954, DP v. WP (two cases) folder, Drew Pearson papers.

5 "Morris Katz to Drew Pearson," December 4, 1949 in David Karr 1949, Drew Pearson papers.

6 DK Conference, January 21, 1954, DP v. WP (two cases) folder, Drew Pearson papers.

7 United States Department of State Passport Office; "In the Matter of the Application of David Karr," September 30, 1955.

8 "Report Made at New York City," June 25, 1942, FBI file 65-32550-15; DK Conference, January 21, 1954, DP v. WP (two cases) folder, Drew Pearson papers.

9 Department of State Passport Office; "In the Matter of the Application of David Karr," September 30, 1955; DK Conference Home, February 18, 1954, DK Conference, January 21, 1954, DP v. WP (two cases) David Karr folder, Drew Pearson papers, LBJ Library.

10 Department of State Passport Office; "In the Matter of the Application of David Karr," September 30, 1955.

11 Ibid. Phillip Musica was a fraudster whose criminal record went back to 1909. He had managed to take over two legitimate companies, Adelphia Pharmaceutical and McKesson & Robbins, under two different assumed names and then loot them for personal gain. He committed suicide before his trial. The scandal led to SEC-mandated reforms of the way audits were conducted. *Daily Worker*, December 14, 1938.

12 Department of State Passport Office; "In the Matter of the Application of David Karr," September 30, 1955.

13 Ibid.

14 *Daily Worker*, December 27, 1938; Department of State Passport Office; "In the Matter of the Application of David Karr," September 30, 1955.

15 Department of State Passport Office; "In the Matter of the Application of David Karr," September 30, 1955.

16 In fact, Vonsiatsky had been the subject of numerous articles and his indictment came several years after Karr's piece appeared. Karr did appear as a witness at his trial.

17 Telephone interview with Daniel Bell, June 11, 1990; telephone interview with Arthur Derounian, June 26, 1989; telephone interview with Leo Bogart, May 10, 1990.

18 Telephone interview with Oscar Brand, June 13, 1990.

19 Conference. Madeline Karr. Friday, February 26, 1954 in DP v. WP (two cases) David Karr folder, Drew Pearson papers.

20 "Hearings Before Subcommittee on Investigations of Committee on Judiciary," 81st Congress, 1st Session, 1949, 798–99; "Leaks to Press Regarding Hopkins-Stalin Conversations in Moscow," July 31, 1945, Harry Truman Library, President's Secretary's Files, 49; Department of State Passport Office; "In the Matter of the Application of David Karr," September 30, 1955; B. L. Brynko, "Lowell Wakefield," *Alaska Business Monthly*, January 1, 1990.

21 Elizabeth Bentley, Golos's courier and lover, later told the FBI that Kahn had been one of his sources, particularly for information on Ukrainians. Bentley Deposition. Kahn is identifiable in the Venona decryptions under the code name "Fighter," although he was not formally recruited until 1942. Harvey Klehr and John Earl Haynes, *Venona: Decoding Soviet Espionage in America* (New Haven, CT: Yale University Press, 1999), 254–55. Julia Older was fired from the Office of the Coordinator of Information in 1942 for trying

to gain access to a file on a Ukrainian-American who had sued Kahn for libel. Older, a Communist, was the sister of Andrew Older, who was Karr's colleague on Drew Pearson's staff. See FBI FOIA Silvermaster file 65-56402, vol. 1. Serial 1938, memo 23, December 1946, D.C. field office. A garbled version of the story told by a man interviewed by the FBI during the Judith Coplon investigation had Karr learning from the Justice Department that there was no evidence against the Ukrainian, Nicholas Grigorieff, and encouraging Kahn to settle the libel suit out of court. See Judith Coplon FBI file 165-58365-246.

22 *Investigation of Un-American Propaganda Activities in the United States*, 78th C, 1st Session, vol. 7 Executive Hearings, GPO, Washington, 1943, 3,388–90; George Britt, *The Fifth Column is Here* (New York: Wilfred Funk, 1940); Department of State Passport Office; "In the Matter of the Application of David Karr," September 30, 1955; "Report Made at New York City," April 13, 1943, FBI file 65-3255039.

23 *Investigation of Un-American Propaganda Activities in the United States*, 78th C, 1st Session, vol. 7 Executive Hearings, GPO, Washington, 1943, 3,391; Ann Kimmage, *An Un-American Childhood* (Athens, GA: University of Georgia Press, 1996); *Investigation of Un-American Propaganda Activities in the United States*, Appendix, xi, 1944, 695, 698.

24 "Karr to John Spivak," February 6, 1940, John Spivak papers, box 9, Special Collections Research Center, Syracuse University.

25 DK Conference Home, February 18, 1954, in DP v. WP (two cases) folder, Drew Pearson papers.

26 For Jackson, see Murray Kempton, *Part of Our Time: Some Monuments and Ruins of the Thirties* (New York: Simon & Schuster, 1955), 41–81.

27 "Jackson to Karr," December 7, 1940; "Karr to Jackson," undated, Gardner Jackson papers, box 40, FDR Library, Hyde Park; DK Conference, February 18, 1954, DP v. WP (two cases) folder, Drew Pearson papers.

28 "Karr to Jackson," undated, Gardner Jackson papers, box 40, FDR Library.

29 DK Conference Home, February 18, 1954, DP v. WP (two cases) folder, Drew Pearson papers.

30 FBI file 65-32550-1, "Hoover to Special Agent in Charge," New York, December 18, 1940. This is the first entry in Karr's FBI file. While names are blacked out, it appears that it was Walter Winchell who first called Hoover's attention to Karr; "Report Made at Washington, D.C.," February, 28, 1941, FBI file 65-32550-4; "Report Made at Washington, D.C.," January 18, 1951, FBI file 65-32550-69; DK Conference Home, February 18, 1954, DP v. WP (two cases) folder, Drew Pearson papers.

31 http://globetrotter.berkeley.edu/people/Cranston/cranston-con2.html; interview with Alan Cranston, Washington, D.C., July 20, 1989.

32 Department of State Passport Office; "In the Matter of the Application of David Karr," September 30, 1955; Karr gave different figures for his salary, ranging from $4,100 to $4,600 a year. In a conference with a lawyer in 1954, Karr claimed that Cranston had called him on the evening of Pearl Harbor to offer him the job. Since Cranston had not yet been hired, that could not have happened. DK Conference Home, February 18, 1954, DP v. WP (two

cases) folder, Drew Pearson papers. Cranston testimony in *The Katyn Forest Massacre, Hearings before the Select Committee to Conduct an Investigation of the Facts, Evidence, and Circumstances of the Katyn Forest Massacre*, 82d Congress, 2d Session, part 7, 2,175–76, Washington, D.C., government printing office, 1952.

33 Karr's employment records were obtained via an FOIA request to the Office of Personnel management.

34 "To FBI," February 18, 1942, FBI file 65-32550-9; "Report Made at New York City," June 25, 1942, FBI file 65-32550-15; "Report Made in Washington, D.C.," June 26, 1942, FBI file 65-32550-18.

35 On Spivak see John Earl Haynes, Harvey Klehr, and Alexander Vassiliev, *Spies: The Rise and Fall of the KGB in America* (New Haven, CT: Yale University Press, 2009), 160–64.

36 "Statement Made by Mr. David Karr in the Investigations Office," Office for Emergency Management, on July 14, 1942, FBI file 65-32550-16.

37 "Karr to Jackson," February 12, 1942; Karr letter of February 21, 1942, Gardner Jackson papers.

38 "Karr to Jackson," March 17, 1942; "Jackson to Karr," April 22, 1942 in Gardner Jackson papers; "To Mr. Ben Maidenberg from David Karr," April 1, 1942, OWI Files, RG208NC-148 box 1075, National Archives; Report of Efficiency Rating February 3, 1942–March 31, 1942 in David Karr OPM file.

39 Interview with Alan Cranston, July 20, 1989; telephone interview with Lee Falk, July 9, 1990; "Karr to Cranston," June 16, 1942, OWI Files, RG208NC-148 box 1075, National Archives; *Chicago Sun*, June 21, 1942; *PM*, July 14, 1942.

40 Telephone interview with Lee Falk, July 9, 1990; DK Conference Home, February 18, 1954, DP v. WP (two cases) folder, Drew Pearson papers.

41 *Communist Activities among Aliens and National Groups*, U.S. Senate, Special Subcommittee to Investigate Immigration and Naturalization of the Committee of the Judiciary, September 29, 1939, 887.

42 Allen Weinstein and Alexander Vassiliev, *The Haunted Wood: Soviet Espionage in America—The Stalin Era* (New York: Random House, 1999), 140–150.

43 August Ogden, *The Dies Committee* (Washington, D.C.: Catholic University Press, 1945), 250–73.

44 Stripling's testimony is in *Un-American Propaganda Activities*, 3,398. Nichols' memos are in FBI files 65-32550-20 and 21.

45 "Memorandum for Tolsen," February 2, 1943; Memorandum for Mr. Tolsen, February 24, 1943, FBI file 65-32550-21.

46 *Congressional Record*, February 1, 1943, 474-486.

47 "Memorandum for Mr. Tolsen," February 24, 1943, FBI file 65-32550-23.

48 "Hoover to SAC," New York, March 2, 1943, FBI file 65-32550-24.

49 *Un-American Propaganda Activities*, 3,383–97.

50 "Memo for Mr. Tolsen," April 26, 1943, FBI file 65-32550-27.

51 "Memorandum for the Director," May 3, 1943, FBI file 65-32550-28; "Memorandum for Mr. Tolsen," April 23, 1943, FBI file 65-32550-34.

52 "Memorandum for Mr. Tolsen," May 10, 1943, FBI file 65-32550-33; Karr's Selective Service file contained a letter dated May 7, 1943 stating that he had taken a job as a war correspondent for *Il Progresso Italo-Americano* and left the OWI with a letter from Generoso Pope requesting a deferment for him. Karr then wrote to the SSS that he had returned to the OWI to await approval of his correspondent status. See "Report Made at Washington, D.C.," March 14, 1951, FBI file 65-32550-94.

53 *The Rubicorn*, August 31, 1942; "To Mr. Abraham Feller from Allan Cranston," September 8, 1942, OWI papers.

54 Correspondence among Karr, Green, et al., OWI papers.

55 The most reliable account of Tresca's life and death is Dorothy Gallagher, *All the Right Enemies* (New Brunswick, NJ: Rutgers University Press, 1988). The quotation is from p. 240. She concludes that the most likely scenario is that Tresca was killed by Mafioso Carmine Galanti, in large part because of his hostility to Pope and one of Pope's Mafia contacts. Elmer Davis to Norman Thomas, January 23, 1943, OWI files, RG2080WI, box 1070. Letters between Luigi Antonini, August Bellanca, Elmer Davis, and Alan Cranston are in the OWI papers.

56 "Report to the President," Office of War Information, June 13, 1942– September 15, 1945, OWI papers, National Archives.

57 "To Elmer Davis from Alan Cranston," January 26, 1943, OWI papers.

58 Office of Personnel Management; "Report Made at Washington, D.C.," March 14, 1951, FBI file 65-32550-94.

59 The affidavit is located in FBI file 65-32550-42.

60 "Report of Investigation," July 10, 1943, Westbrook Pegler papers, box 49, subject file, Drew Pearson, Herbert Hoover Presidential Library.

61 "To John Kerr from Clinton Anderson," June 22, 1943, Kerr Committee file, box 856, Clinton Anderson papers, Manuscript Division, Library of Congress; Haynes and Klehr, *Venona*, 113–14, 181–83,186–88, 342, 343; Haynes, Klehr, and Vassiliev, *Spies*, 207–212.

62 "Kerr to Gore," June 23, 1943, Kerr Committee file, box 856, Clinton Anderson papers.

63 "Jackson to Karr," May 6, 1942, Gardner Jackson papers; "Karr to Anderson," July 1, 1943, "Anderson to Mintzer," November 5, 1943, Kerr Committee file. ADL file on David Karr, "Report re: Walter Steele."

64 "Karr to Davis," July 29, 1943; "Davis to Karr," August 26, 1943, OWI papers.

65 *Congressional Record*, December 19, 1950, 16744-45.

66 "Memorandum for Mr. Glavin," November 18, 1943, FBI file 65-32550-44; "Hoover to Herbert Gaston," February 4, 1944, FBI file 65-3255-47; "To the Civil Service Commission from Gaston," March 22, 1944, FBI file 65-32550-48.

67 "To OWI from Eva Abramson," March 24, 1944; "Harvey to Abramson," March 30, 1944, Karr file, Office of Personnel Management.

68 See, for example, the thirty-three-page report on German refugee organizations, labeled "Confidential," that clearly had been written by someone within the OWI in Reel 24, Henry Wallace Vice Presidential Papers, FDR Library.

69　"Barnett Hodes to Harold Young," August 30, 1943, box 50; "Young to Karr," September 8, 1943, box 2, Henry Wallace papers, FDR Library.

70　"Burdick to Karr," October 18, 1943; "Young to Burdick," October 29, 1943; "Burdick to Young," February 23, 1944, box 15, Henry Wallace papers, FDR Library.

71　Appendix to the *Congressional Record*, February 18, 1944, A815.

CHAPTER 2: INVESTIGATIVE JOURNALIST

1　Department of State Passport Office; "In the Matter of the Application of David Karr," September 30, 1955; "To Mr. Tolsen from Mr. Nichols," May 30, 1944, FBI file 65-32550-49.

2　Spencer Klaw, "Dave Karr in the President's Chair," *Fortune*, 157.

3　Haynes, Klehr and Vassiliev, *Spies*, 160–61; Oliver Pilat, *Drew Pearson: An Unauthorized Biography* (New York: Harper's Magazine Press, 1973).

4　Interview with Jack Anderson, Washington, D.C., March 23, 1990; "Schlesinger to Klehr," April 18, 1990.

5　Haynes and Klehr, *Venona*, 234–36.

6　The account is drawn from "Lange to Harold Young," July 2, 1944; "Lange to Young," July 3, 1944; "Dorothy Sheinfeld to Young," July 6, 1944; "Bert Hoselitz to Young," July 6, 1944, all in Henry Wallace papers, FDR Library.

7　Ibid.

8　"Memo of telephone conversation between Lange and Young," July 3, 1944; "Young to Lange," July 3, 1944 in ibid. The FBI's file on this investigation, 47-32546, was provided under the FOIA, but the original microfiche was reproduced so poorly as to be virtually unreadable. It appears that Lange demanded that the second column be suppressed, and the Censorship Office was consulted.

9　Ibid.

10　"David Karr," February 11, 1946, FBI file 65-32550-57 contains a summary of the interview; the complete report of the interview with Wallace is in 47-32546-9x2 but large portions are unreadable. The information about Young paying Karr is in "To Director FBI," August 16, 1944, 47-32546-17.

11　"David Karr," February 11, 1946, FBI file 65-32550-57; "Lange to Hoover," July 5, 1944, FBI file 47-32546-8; "Memorandum for Mr. Hoover," August 5, 1944, 47-32546-10; "To Mr. Tamm from A. Rosen," August 16, 1944, FBI file 47-32546-16.

12　"To Director from Guy Hottel," August 16, 1944, FBI file 47-32546-16; the admission is in Department of State Passport Office; "In the Matter of the Application of David Karr," September 30, 1955.

13　"To Mr. [unreadable] from Mr. Smith," August 19, 1944, FBI file 47-32546-19.

14　See Harvey Klehr and Ronald Radosh, *The Amerasia Spy Case: Prelude to McCarthyism* (Chapel Hill: University of North Carolina Press, 1996), 100–103. In Karr's FBI file, most of the details of his relationship with Roth are blacked out. See "David Harold Karr," February 11, 1946, FBI file 65-32550-57. But the material about his contact with White is in "Report Made at New York City," February 20, 1949, Alger Hiss FBI file 74-94-1960.

See also "Statement of David Karr, Conference Notes, Saturday December 12, 1953," in Pearson v. King Features Conferences, container F174, 1 of 2, Drew Pearson papers, LBJ Library; "Report Made at Los Angeles," January 12, 1951, FBI file 65-32550-84.

15 Venona 998, KGB New York to Moscow, July 15, 1944.

16 The FBI had followed Karr on his visit to California and observed his meetings. See "To the Director from D. M. Ladd," March 8, 1948, FBI file 65-32550-64. Large portions of the report are blacked out, but the FBI conceded that there was no evidence Karr was a Communist. See "Report Made at Washington, D.C.," May 26, 1946, FBI file 100-17493-5490, 301–2 for the Karr-Lee conversation.

17 Klehr and Radosh, The Amerasia Spy Case, 67.

18 Berle testimony, HUAC, August–September 1948 Hearings, 1,291–1,300.

19 "Report Made at Washington, D.C.," May 26, 1946, FBI file 100-17493-5490.

20 Ibid.; Report Made at Washington, D.C., January 8, 1951, FBI file 65-32550-69. There is no indication that Karr ever actually endorsed the book.

21 Oliver Pilat, Drew Pearson, 13.

22 Ibid.

23 "David Karr's Soviet Connection," Business Week, May 19, 1975, 143.

24 "Wallace Here for Rally," L.A. Times, April 18, 1946, A2; "Karr to Norman Corwin," November 14, 1946; "Dr. G. F. Hinman to Karr," December 3, 1946, in David Karr #1 folder, container G83, 2 of 3, Drew Pearson papers, LBJ Library.

25 "Karr to Lawrence Kraus," May 22, 1947; "Karr to Robert Kenny," July 12, 1947; "Karr to Joel Fisher," August 8, 1947; "Karr to Bartley Crum," September 2, 1947 in David Karr #2 folder, Drew Pearson papers, LBJ Library.

26 Richard Harris Smith, The OSS: The Secret History of America's First Central Intelligence Agency (Berkeley: University of California Press, 1972), 117; see also "To the Order of AHEPA, August 18, 1947," an angry attack on Vournas by dissidents in AHEPA. Westbrook Pegler papers, box 49.

27 "Memo signed by John Maragon," April 17, 1947 in Westbrook Pegler papers, box 49; Pearson's letter to Ruth Shipley requesting a passport for Vournas and the rejection letter are in Drew Pearson papers, container F126, no. 1, Pegler Lawsuit NY, vol. 1.

28 "To the Director from D. M. Ladd," March 8, 1945, FBI file 65-32550-64; Memorandum, July 20, 1949 signed by Cutler, in "Pearson v. King Features" (two cases), container F174 1 of 2, Drew Pearson papers.

29 "Charles Rohrer to Pearson," May 6, 1947; "Karr to Rohrer," May 27, 1947; Drew Pearson papers, David Karr #1 folder, container G83, 2 of 3, LBJ Library; "From Vournas by Phone," Pegler notes in Drew Pearson—David & Madeline Karr, box 49, Westbrook Pegler papers, Herbert Hoover Library.

30 "Madeline Karr Conference, February 18, 1954," in DP v. WP (two cases), Drew Pearson papers.

31 "Madeline Karr to William F. Buckley," September 18, 1953 in DP v. WP (two cases), Madeline Karr, Drew Pearson papers; Madeline Karr Conference, February 15, 1954.

32 "Karr to Leon Goldstein," April 25, 1947, David Karr #1 folder, Drew Pearson papers.

33 "Karr to Marcantonio," May 29, 1948; "Karr to DuBois," October 22, 1948 in ibid.; telephone interview with Oscar Brand, June 13, 1990.

34 See the memos in "Friendship Train" folder F1174-f6, Drew Pearson papers.

35 See thank-you letters in "Misc. Friendship Train Data," F117, 6 of 6, Drew Pearson papers; "Karr to Paul Ramsey," November 20, 1947; "Pearson to Ruth Shipley," December 9, 1947 in "Friendship Train, Administrative," F1174-f6.

36 "Confidential Report to Harry Warner," "European Friendship Train Report," in Friendship Train—Administrative folder, container F117, 2 of 6, Drew Pearson papers; "To Mr. C. Holland from Pearson," April 9, 1948 in Friendship Train—Distribution Criticisms, Drew Pearson papers.

37 See "Karr to H. M. Warner," December 3, 1947; "Karr to Warner," January 29, 1948; David Karr folder, box F22, 2 of 3, Drew Pearson papers.

38 "Pearson to Hoover," April 10, 1947 in "Andy Older," box F165, 3 of 3, Drew Pearson papers.

39 Tyler Abell, ed., *Drew Pearson: Diaries 1949–1959* (New York: Holt, Rinehart and Winston, 1974), 75.

40 "Memorandum for Mr. Tolsen from J. Edgar Hoover," March 3, 1948, FBI file 65-32550-63.

41 "Karr to Frank Lee," September 15, 1948 in "David Karr 1948," container G83 1 of 1, Drew Pearson papers.

42 "Karr to Burton," October 20, 1948; "Karr to Breitel," October 20, 1948 in David Karr folder, box F22, 2 of 3; "Karr to Breitel," October 25, 1948; "Karr to Keller," October 22, 1948; in David Karr, 1948, Drew Pearson papers.

43 "Report #8, July 11, 1950, Pearson v. King Features," G.R. Investigation Reports, container #174, 1 of 2, Drew Pearson papers.

44 "To the Director from D. M. Ladd," December 30, 1950, FBI file 65-32550-71.

45 "Karr to Nathan Strauss," May 18, 1948, "Karr to Jackson Lighter," May 19, 1948 in David Karr folder, box F22, 2 of 3, Drew Pearson papers; Department of State Passport Office; "In the Matter of the Application of David Karr," September 30, 1955 where he describes Crum as "one of the most untruthful men I have ever known in his dealings with clients and newspapermen." Crum, who remained sympathetic to the left—he served as a lawyer for the Hollywood Ten—may have blackballed Karr because of his perceived political shift.

46 Interview with Jack Anderson, March 23, 1990.

47 Ibid.

48 Ibid.

49 *Drew Pearson Diaries 1948–1959*, 518; Karr Conference, January 14, 1954 in Drew Pearson papers; "To Mr. Heinrich from Mr. Lamphere," April 11, 1951, FBI file 65-32550-98; "Drew Pearson to Morris Katz," November 29, 1949 in David Karr 1949 in container G83 1 of 3; "Karr to Clinton Anderson," June 3, 1948, David Karr folder, box F22, 2 of 3, Drew Pearson papers.

50 "Memo of October 13, 1947 to DP from DK, Thank You Train Data," in Drew Pearson papers.

51 Pegler's columns are in the "David Karr" folder in the J. B. Matthews papers, box 306, Manuscript Department, Duke University. Madeline Karr had applied for a job with G-2 in 1947. General Vaughn wrote to its head to "heartily recommend against" her employment "in any position where confidential or secret information would be available." "Vaughn to Brig. General C. B. Ferenbaugh," May 26, 1947, Papers of Harry Truman, official file.

52 *Un-American Propaganda Activities*, 3,383–97; Rushmore testimony, Judiciary Ct., 798–99.

53 *Congressional Record*, December 15, 1950, 16,634–38.

54 Ibid., 16,640–41.

55 *Congressional Record*, December 19, 1950, 16,744–46.

56 *Congressional Record*, September 15, 1950, 16,646; September 19, 1950, 16,746–47.

57 "To the Director from D. M. Ladd," December 20, 1950, FBI file 65-32550-85.

58 "To Mr. Tolsen from L. B. Nichols," December 30, 1950, FBI file 65-32550-72.

59 "To the Director from D. M. Ladd," December 30, 1950, FBI file 65-32550-71; "To Mr. Tolsen from L. B. Nichols," December 30, 1950, FBI file 65-32550-77.

60 "To Mr. Tolsen from L. B. Nichols," January 3, 1951, FBI file 65-32550-75. When I interviewed him nearly forty years later, Forster was far more positive about Karr, noting that he was "totally trustworthy" on issues of Nazis and fascists, topics on which he and the ADL traded information, and "was one of the good guys." "Interview with Arnold Forster," New York, June 26, 1989.

61 "To Mr. Tolsen from L. B. Nichols," January 4, 1951, FBI file 65-32550-74; "To Mr. Tolsen from L. B. Nichols," January 5, 1951, FBI file 65-32550-75.

62 "To Mr. Tolsen from L. B. Nichols," January 5, 1951, FBI file 65-32550-75; one week later, Karr called Nichols and said that a group called the Committee on the Present Danger had approached the Weintraub Agency to act as its PR firm and he wanted to know if his association with it might cause problems. Nichols was noncommittal. Karr ended the discussion by saying that "he was seeing the Army today and in all probability would be in uniform before long." "To Mr. Tolsen from L. B. Nichols," January 12, 1951, FBI file 65-32550-86. Since he had been rejected for the armed services during WWII for medical reasons, this was likely just another example of Karr's efforts to impress someone with his patriotism.

63 *Congressional Record*, January 22, 1951, 508–9; April 24, 1951, 4,268–70.

64 "To Mr. Tolsen from L. B. Nichols," January 27, 1951, FBI file 65-32550-91; "To Nichols from M. A. Bones," February 6, 1951, FBI file 65-32550-92; "To Mr. Tolsen from L. B. Nichols," January 26, 1951, FBI file 65-32550-93; "To Mr. Heinrich from Mr. Lamphere," April 11, 1951, FBI file 65-32550-98. Wakefield's affidavit claimed that "to the best of my knowledge, David Karr has never been a member of the staff or employed in any capacity by the *Daily Worker*." He sent it to Karr along with a letter denouncing "the unprincipled attacks on yourself," and lauded Karr as one of the most "consistent, intelligent and effective opponents of communism" in the country. "Wakefield to Karr," January 12, 1951, in Drew Pearson papers.

CHAPTER 3: PUBLIC RELATIONS FLACK

1 "Lewis Rosenstiel," Wikipedia; "Lewis Rosenstiel, Founder of Schenley Empire, Dies," *New York Times*, January 22, 1976, 37.

2 Anthony Summers, *Official and Confidential: The Secret Life of J. Edgar Hoover* (New York: G. P. Putnam's Sons, 1993); Nicholas von Hoffman, *Citizen Cohn: The Life and Times of Roy Cohn* (New York: Doubleday, 1988).

3 Spencer Klaw, "Dave Karr in the President's Chair," 261.

4 "Independent Confidential Report," in folder 8, J. B. Matthews papers, Duke University Library.

5 Ibid.; David Karr, *Fight for Control* (New York: Ballantine Books, 1956), 3.

6 Telephone interview with Norman B. Norman, May 24, 1990.

7 Telephone interview with George Biderman, May 15, 1990; telephone interview with Christopher Cross, May 23, 1990.

8 "The Katyn Forest Massacre," *Hearings*, 2,186–88, 2,278.

9 A copy of Pegler's column, published on September 18, 1953, is in Karr's FBI file 65-32550-A not recorded. Madeline Karr wrote a letter to William F. Buckley, then employed at Henry Holt, her publisher, denying the charges and emphatically stating "I am not now and never have been a member of the Communist Party. I have never been a member of any Communist Front organization nor have I written for any Communist paper at any time." "Madeline Karr to William Buckley," September 18, 1953 in DP v. WP Madeline Karr, Drew Pearson papers. There is a suggestion in one interview with Madeline that Buckley had informed her that due to "the circumstances of the time," presumably the Pegler article, the book was being withdrawn. See D&MK-Conference-home, Monday, February 8, 1954, DP v. WP, (two cases), David Karr, Drew Pearson papers.

10 Department of State Passport Office; "In the Matter of the Application of David Karr," September 30, 1955; independent confidential report, J. B. Matthews Papers, Duke University Library.

11 Conference DK & MK, January 21, 1954, in DP v. WP (two cases) folder, Drew Pearson papers.

12 Westbrook Pegler, "Former Partners Now on the Outs," in "David Karr" file, folder 8, box 306, J. B. Matthews papers, Duke University Library; "Lanham to Karr," November 23, 1954, box 13, Charles T. Lanham papers, Princeton University Library; "Market Relations 1954–1955" folder; "Pegler to Lanham," January 24, 1952, January 2, 1953, "King Feature Syndicate" folder, box 11, Charles T. Lanham papers.

13 "Lanham to Karr," April 24, 1954, May 11, 1953; "Lanham to Karr," November 23, 1954, box 13, "Market Relations" folder, Charles T. Lanham papers, Princeton University Library; Westbrook Pegler, "Former Partners Now on the Outs," in "David Karr" file, folder 8, box 306, J. B. Matthews papers, Duke University Library.

14 "Agreement Between David Karr and C. T. Lanham," October 5, 1954; "General Lanham to Head Market Relations Network," December 1, 1954, box 13, Charles T. Lanham papers.

15 "Lanham to Karr," November 18, 1954, in box 13, Charles T. Lanham papers.

16 http://www.seth-smith.org.uk/familytree/familystories/jacksonleighter.html has information on Leighter supplied by his goddaughter; "Lanham to Leighter," February 23, 1955, in box 13, Charles T. Lanham papers.

17 "Office Memorandum," March 9, 1955; "Hansen to Lanham," March 17, 1955 in box 13, Charles T. Lanham papers.

18 "Aide Memoire," April 22, 1955; "Aide Memoire," May 2, 1955; "Memorandum to Mr. Karr," May 20, 1954 in ibid.

19 "Lanham to Karr," May 27, 1955; "Karr to Lanham," May 27, 1955 in ibid.

20 Lanham, "Memorandum for the Record," April 4, 1961; "Klaw to Lanham," March 29, 1961; "Lanham to Klaw," March 30, 1961; "Lanham to Panuch," July 24, 1958; "Lanham to Sulzberger," August 24, 1955; "Lanham to Pegler," November 11, 1955 in ibid.

21 "Karr to Lanham," August 17, 1956 in ibid.

22 "Panuch to Lanham," January 31, 1958; "Lanham to Panuch," February 2, 1958 in ibid.

23 "FBI Washington Field Office to Director and SAC New York," September 16, 1955, FBI file 65-32550-100; the complete affidavit, without the exhibits, was released to me by the State Department under the FOIA.

24 Department of State Passport Office; "In the Matter of the Application of David Karr," September 30, 1955.

25 "To Director from SAC Washington," October 20, 1955; "To Miss Frances Knight from J. Edgar Hoover," November 10, 1955, FBI file 65-32550-101; "To Mr. L. V. Boardman from Mr. A. H. Belmont," November 4, 1955, FBI file 65-32550-102.

26 Details about her life are in Elizabeth Cooke, *Life Savors* (Troy, New York: The Troy Book Maker, 2011).

27 Ibid., 124.

28 Ibid., 124–25, 130–31.

29 David Karr, *Fight for Control* (New York: Ballantine Books, 1956), 15.

30 Ibid., 86–88. Buffy Karr related in her autobiography that for their first Christmas, she gave David two copies of the book "bound in antique leather," but he was less than thrilled; she later learned that he had not written the book. Cooke, *Life Savors*, 124.

31 Cooke, *Life Savors*, 127; Karr, *Fight for Control*, 86, 126.

32 Daniel Seligman, "Battling Art Landa," *Fortune*, June 1958, 146–48, 206, 208–12.

33 The best portrait of Landa is in Diana Henriques, *The White Sharks of Wall Street: Thomas Mellon Evans and the Original Corporate Raiders* (New York: Scribner, 2000), from which I have drawn much of what follows.

34 Ibid.; Seligman, "Battling Art Landa," 148, 206.

35 "Concerning the Activities of Alfons Beaumont Landa in Reference to the Penn-Texas Company," in "Alfons Landa" folder, container F159, 2 of 3, Drew Pearson papers.

36 Henriques, *The White Sharks of Wall Street: Thomas Mellon Evans and the Original Corporate Raiders*, 128–30. A family-inspired history of Fruehauf

maintains that it was David Karr who dug up dirt on Kolowich, implying that he and Landa had been working together prior to 1956; see https://www.singingwheels.com/harvey's-double-cross-and-the-proxy-battle.html.

37 Ibid., 88–89, 119–22, 157–58.

38 "Memorandum for the Record," April 4, 1961; "Memorandum to Mr. Karr," May 20, 1955; "Silberstein to Lanham," June 10, 1955; "Lanham to Silberstein," November 5, 1954; in box 13, Charles T. Lanham papers.

39 Lawrence Armour, "Corporate Cinderella," *Barron's*, May 6, 1963, 5, 17–19; "Lanham to General Alfred Gruenther," March 14, 1956, in box 13, Charles T. Lanham papers.

40 *Congressional Record*, House of Representatives, February 6, 1957, vol. 103, part 2, 1,611–12, 3,809–10. The SEC had investigated Penn-Texas. A memo found in the Drew Pearson papers outlines a series of secret findings that rebuked Silberstein for a variety of shady moves allowing relatives and friends to make profits on buying Fairbanks, Morse shares. See "Memo" in Leopold Silberstein file, container G298, 1 of 3, Drew Pearson papers.

41 "To Drew Pearson from David Karr," February 14, 1957 in Pennsylvania #4 folder, container G241, 1 of 3, Drew Pearson papers.

42 "Burnt Fingers," *Barron's*, December 2, 1957, 1; Armour, "Corporate Cinderella," *Barron's*, May 6, 1963, 17.

43 Armour, "Corporate Cinderella," 18.

44 "Telephone Conversation between Drew Pearson and General Lanham," January 30, 1957; "Lanham to Silberstein," April 5, 1957, in box 13, Charles T. Lanham papers. There are a series of "Memorandum for the Record," written by Lanham that recount in great detail the maneuverings of the next few months.

45 "Memorandum for the Record," July 24, 1957; "Memorandum for the Record," July 30, 1957; "Memorandum for the Record," August 5, 1957, in ibid.

46 "Broken Empire," *Forbes*, April 15, 1958, 24.

47 "Penn-Texas Landa-Slide," *Forbes*, July 15, 1958, 20; Klaw, "Dave Karr in the President's Chair," 262.

48 "Panuch to Lanham," September 13, 1957; "Lanham to Panuch," December 26, 1957; "Panuch to Lanham," January 31, 1958; "Lanham to Panuch," February 2, 1958; "Lanham to Panuch," February 8, 1958 in Charles T. Lanham papers.

49 "Panuch to Lanham," February 25, 1958; "Lanham to Panuch," February 26, 1958; "Panuch to Lanham," March 18, 1958; "Lanham to Panuch," March 19, 1958; "Panuch to Lanham," May 8, 1958; "Panuch to Lanham," June 9, 1958; "Lanham to Panuch," July 24, 1958 in Charles T. Lanham papers; Armour, "Corporate Cinderella," *Barron's*, May 6, 1963, 18.

50 Armour, "Corporate Cinderella," *Barron's*, May 6, 1963, 18; "To Director FBI, From SAC, New York," October 22, 1958, FBI file 65-32550-104.

51 *Wall Street Journal*, May 4, 1959, 32; "Troubles at Fairbanks-Whitney," *Forbes*, June 15, 1962, 15; "Lanham to Panuch," November 12, 1958; "Lanham to Panuch," November 24, 1958 in Charles T. Lanham papers.

52 Westbrook Pegler, "Little Davey—from Red to Capitalist," *New York Journal-American*, July 10, 1959 in FBI file 65-32550-107.

53 "Karr to Eisenhower," November 8, 1957; "Karr to Eisenhower," January 13, 1958; "Karr to Eisenhower," March 3, 1959; "Karr to Eisenhower," June 23, 1959; "Karr to Eisenhower," February 2, 1960 in White House Central File, Alphabetical File, Dwight David Eisenhower Library.

54 Cooke, *Life Savors*, 135.

CHAPTER 4: CEO

1 "Memorandum for Mr. Tolsen, Mr. DeLoach, from J. Edgar Hoover," July 23, 1959, FBI file 65-23550-108; "To: Mr. J. Edgar Hoover," August 4, 1959, FBI file 65-23550-109.

2 "To Director FBI, From SAC, New York," March 11, 1960, FBI file 65-32550-113.

3 "To Director FBI, From SAC, New York," February 11, 1960, FBI file 65-32550-110.

4 "Report: David Karr," April 6, 1960, FBI file 65-32550-118; "Report on David Karr," June 15, 1960, FBI file 65-32550-125.

5 Cooke, *Life Savors*, 126; Interview with Elizabeth Cooke, September 17, 2015. If Cooke's memory is accurate, it is entirely possible that Karr had concocted this story and his alleged membership card.

6 "Report on David Karr," June 15, 1960, FBI file 65-32550-125.

7 "To Office of Special Investigations Air Force, From John Edgar Hoover," October 21, 1960, FBI file 65-32550-132.

8 "To Mr. Herbert Lewis, From John Edgar Hoover," February 14, 1961, FBI file 65-32550-133; "To Director FBI, From SAC, New York," February 4, 1961, FBI file 65-32550-134; "To Director FBI, From SAC, San Francisco," March 10, 1961, FBI file 65-32550-136; "David Karr," March 15, 1961, FBI file 65-32550-137.

9 "To Director FBI, From SAC, New York," March 15, 1961, FBI file 65-32550-138; "David Karr," March 30, 1961, FBI file 65-32550-143.

10 "To Director FBI, From SAC, New York," March 10, 1961, FBI file 65-32550-139.

11 A copy of the April 25, 1961 issue is located in the FBI files 65-32250-A not recorded, after 65-32550-146.

12 "Fairbanks-Whitney Net in Half Hit $1,178,000," *Wall Street Journal*, July 13, 1959, 7.

13 Scott Schmedel, "'Counter Raids' & Clausewitz," *Wall Street Journal*, March 23, 1962, 1, 20; "Trouble at Fairbanks Whitney," *Forbes*, June 15, 1962, 15.

14 Henriques, 216–32; Scott Schmedel, "'Counter Raids' & Clausewitz," 1, 20.

15 "Fairbanks-Whitney Net in Half Hit $1,178,000," *Wall Street Journal*, July 13, 1959, 7.

16 Drew Pearson, "Sea Yields Cheap Fresh Water," *Washington Post*, March 29, 1961, D13.

17 Herbert Freeden, "Zarchin's Break-Through on the 'Water Front,'" *AJR*

Information (Association of Jewish Refugees in Great Britain, v. XV, n. 2, 1960), 1, 897–99; "Salt Water into Fresh," *Time*, September 3, 1956; *Christian Science Monitor*, January 27, 1961, 12; Seth Siegal, *Let There Be Water: Israel's Solution for a Water-Starved World* (New York: Macmillan, 2015), 106; Yaakov Morris, *Master of the Desert; 6,000 Years in the Negev* (New York: Putnam, 1961), 243.

18 Freeden, "Zarchin's Break-Through on the 'Water Front,'"; "US Firm is Partner in Zarchin Project," *Jerusalem Post*, December 11, 1959, 1.

19 "Israel's Commercial Desalination Plant Seen as Ready by 1961," Jewish Telegraphic Agency, May 12, 1960; "The Well That Never Runs Dry," Fairbanks Whitney Company, 1961, enclosed with "David Karr to Ralph Dungan," June 21, 1961, John F. Kennedy White House Central Name File, box 822; "Fairbanks-Whitney Claims Low Cost Way for Desalting Water," *Wall Street Journal*, January 11, 1960, 5.

20 Dan Sachs, "Zarchin Plant to be in Full Operation by End of 1961," *Jerusalem Post*, May 12, 1960, 3; "Ground Broken in Eilat," *Jerusalem Post*, March 30, 1961, 1.

21 Casimir Lanowick, "The Greatest Scientific Breakthrough," *The Herald of Christ's Kingdom*, v. XLIV, n. 9, September/October 1961; Klaw, "Dave Karr in the President's Chair," 155; "Ground Broken," *Jerusalem Post*, 1.

22 "Zarchin May Air Contract Terms," *Jerusalem Post*, March 11, 1960, 3; "Ministry of Development contract with Fairbanks Whitney," February 2, 1965; "Karr to Zarchin," January 13, 1961, Israel Ministry of Development Archives; Jesse Zel Lurie, "Zarchin vs. Flash Process," *Jerusalem Post*, July 14, 1961, 7.

23 "Karr to Jacob Adari," September 11, 1962; "Karr to Bader," November 13, 1962 in Ministry of Development Archives; "BLH Awarded Contract," *Wall Street Journal*, November 13, 1962, 15.

24 "First Desalinization Plant in Israel Starts Operation in Eilat," *Jewish Telegraphic Agency*, January 2, 1964; "Drought and Water," *Jerusalem Post*, June 4, 1963, 1; Siegal, *Let There Be Water*, 106; "Israeli Firm Reports Successful Test for US Built Desalinization Plant," *Jewish Telegraphic Agency*, August 19, 1966. Zarchin himself blamed the failure on the inability or refusal of engineers to follow his specifications. He sued the Israeli government, claiming that he was owed royalties on all investments in desalinization projects, not only those using his methods. See Carl Alpert, "Israel: Inventor Raises Fury," and "The Zarchin Case," *Jewish Advocate*, June 17, 1965, A2, and May 29, 1969, A2.

25 Nathan Berkman, "Back in the Old Days," at http://www.ildesal.org.il/main.php?location=education&action=history.

26 Rivka Borochov, "Israel Leads Way in Making Saltwater Potable," *Water Online*, February 2, 2012, 1; Drew Pearson, "Rules Committee Clash on Rights," *Washington Post*, July 7, 1964, B25.

27 "Fairbanks Whitney Net Rose in Third Quarter," *Wall Street Journal*, October 27, 1959, 16; "Fairbanks Whitney Says Its Sales Have Climbed Sharply in Past 6 Weeks," *Wall Street Journal*, November 2, 1960, 6; "Fairbanks Whitney Had 3rd Period Loss, Sharp Drop in 9-Month Profit," *Wall Street Journal*, November 9, 1960, 24.

28 Vartanig Vartan, "Fairbanks Pay Boosts Arouse Ire at Meeting," *New York Herald Tribune*, May 5, 1960, 37; "Fairbanks Whitney Says Sales Trail '60 Pace," *Wall Street Journal*, March 20, 1961, 27; "Fairbanks-Morse Says Profit in 1st Period Will Trail '60," *Wall Street Journal*, April 20, 1961, 5; Kenneth Smith, "Meeting Is Lively for Tool Maker," *New York Times*, May 3, 1962, 43.

29 Klaw, "Dave Karr in the President's Chair," 155; "Trouble at Fairbanks Whitney," *Forbes*, June 15, 1962, 16.

30 "Fairbanks Whitney Expects Profit in First Half," *Wall Street Journal*, March 29, 1962, 25; "Landa and Finkelstein Resign as Officers of Fairbanks Whitney," *Wall Street Journal*, May 31, 1962, 16.

31 "Landa and Finkelstein Resign as Officers of Fairbanks Whitney," 16; Leslie Gould, "D-Day Near for Karr," *New York Journal-American*, May 25, 1962, 30.

32 "Vice President Quits Fairbanks Whitney in Promotion Dispute," *Wall Street Journal*, June 1, 1962, 7; Lawrence Armour, "Corporate Cinderella," *Barron's*, May 6, 1963, 18–19; "James Bruce Leaves Fairbanks-Morse Board," *Wall Street Journal*, June 26, 1962, 28.

33 Klaw, "Dave Karr in the President's Chair," 156; "Lanphier, President of Fairbanks Whitney Subsidiary, Resigns," *Wall Street Journal*, August 3, 1962, 9; Lawrence Hughes, "Personal Leadership Sparks 'New' Fairbanks Morse," *Sales Management*, June 2, 1961, 59–62.

34 "Fairbanks Whitney President Says He Cut His Key Men's Pay to Put Firm in Black," *Wall Street Journal*, August 8, 1962, 26.

35 "Director Quits Board of Pratt-Whitney: Says He Was 'Kept in Dark,'" *Wall Street Journal*, August 30, 1962, 5; "George Lessner, et al. v. Alfons Landa, et al," United States District Court, Southern District of New York, "David Karr" file, LBJ Library; "Stockholder Tells SEC He Plans Proxy Fight at Fairbanks Whitney," *Wall Street Journal*, January 11, 1963, 4.

36 "Fairbanks Whitney Names G.A. Strichman President, Chief Officer," *Wall Street Journal*, October 16, 1962, 10; "Cleaning up the Mess," *Forbes*, April 15, 1963, 39; Armour, "Corporate Cinderella," 5.

37 "Karr out as Fairbanks Whitney Chairman; Management Policies at Issue for a Year," *Wall Street Journal*, February 6, 1963, 32.

38 "David Karr Resignation at Fairbanks Whitney Could Lead to Others," *Wall Street Journal*, February 8, 1963, 8; "Lawyer Drops Plan for Fairbanks Whitney Proxy Fight, Wins Seat on Firm's Board," *Wall Street Journal*, March 8, 1963, 5; "Fairbanks Whitney Had $849,000 Deficit in First Quarter," *Wall Street Journal*, May 8, 1963, 4; Scott Schmedel, "Fairbanks Whitney, Two Former Officers Settle Contracts; Two Others Spurn Offer," *Wall Street Journal*, July 19, 1963, 20; "Fairbanks Whitney, 4 Former Officers Set a Contract Settlement," *Wall Street Journal*, February 25, 1964, 15.

39 Lawrence Armour, "Corporate Cinderella," 5; "Cleaning up the Mess," *Forbes*, 39; Cooke, *Life Savors*, 153.

CHAPTER 5: HOLLYWOOD AND BROADWAY INTERLUDE

1 Cooke, *Life Savors*, 133–34.

2 Ibid., 131–33; Interview with Frank Karr, Atlanta, September 17, 2015.

3 Evans, *Nemesis*, 131–32, 273.

4 Cooke, *Life Savors*, 136, 147, 148.

5 Ibid., 160–69.

6 Telephone interview with Max Youngstein, June 30, 1990.

7 A detailed description of the Loew's fight is in Louis Nizer, *My Life in Court* (Garden City, NY: Doubleday & Co., 1961), 427–524.

8 Cooke, *Life Savors*, 131; Interview with Elizabeth Cooke, September 17, 2015.

9 "Karr to Walter Jenkins," December 2, 1963, name file, David Karr, container #30, Drew Pearson papers, LBJ Library; "How President Slashes Red Tape," *Los Angeles Times*, December 3, 1963, A6.

10 "To the President from Karr," February 19, 1964, name file, David Karr, container #30, Drew Pearson papers, LBJ Library; "Max Youngstein—David Karr Unite; Their Diversified Films, Inc. Dealing," *Variety*, February 19, 1964, 5.

11 "Max Youngstein—David Karr Unite," 5; Milt Freudenheim, "Max Youngstein, 84; Helped Run United Artists," *New York Times*, July 11, 1997, 20.

12 Telephone interview with Max Youngstein, June 13, 1990.

13 Although Karr was not listed in the credits for the play, a letter from him to Drew Pearson, dated September 1, 1966, indicates he had put together the financing; Pearson was one of the investors. "Karr to Pearson," September 1, 1966, "David Karr" file 1964–1969, personal papers of Drew Pearson, LBJ Library.

14 Betty Martin, "Duo Slated for 5 Pictures," *Los Angeles Times*, January 21, 1966, C6; Betty Martin, "Vaughn Will Cry Havoc," *Los Angeles Times*, January 31, 1967, D8.

15 "Karr to Pearson," September 14, 1964, "David Karr 1962–1969" folder, container G83, 1 of 3, Drew Pearson papers, LBJ Library.

16 FBI file 65-32550-125, 5.

17 Telephone interview with Max Youngstein, June 13, 1990; James Gladstone, *The Man Who Seduced Hollywood: The Life and Loves of Greg Bautzer, Tinseltown's Most Powerful Lawyer* (Chicago: Chicago Review Press, 2013), 73–76; Dennis Hevesi, "Buff Cobb, TV Host of Early '50s Talk Show," *New York Times*, July 23, 2010, B9.

18 Dennis Hevesi, "Buff Cobb," B9; "Buff Cobb," Wikipedia.

19 "Buff Cobb," Wikipedia; interview with Elizabeth Cooke, September 17, 2015; interview with Max Youngstein, June 13, 1990; interview with Denise Karr, June 5, 1990.

CHAPTER 6: DEAL-MAKER

1 "David to Dear Mother," undated; "Feenie to Dearest Mom," August 17, 1967; Feenie Ziner papers, University of Connecticut.

2 "Feenie to Dearest Mom," August 4, 1967 in Feenie Ziner papers, University of Connecticut; Betty Martin, "Film Pact for Doris Day," *Los Angeles Times*, May 9, 1967, D17; David McClintick, *Indecent Exposure: A True Story of Hollywood and Wall Street* (New York: William Morrow & Co., 1982), 323.

3 "Karr to Pearson," undated, "Karr to Pearson," June 4, 1967, in "David Karr" file 1964–1969, Drew Pearson papers; "Feenie Ziner to Dearest Mom," June 30, 1967, Feenie Ziner papers.

4 I am indebted to Preminger's son, Aner, for information about his father.

5 A number of the émigrés became involved in the Red Orchestra, the U.S.S.R.'s famous espionage ring that worked against the Nazis in World War II, most notably its leader, Leopold Trepper, who embodied both its heroism, its blind ideological fervor, and the dead end that anti-Zionist Jews in Palestine faced. Born in Poland, Trepper had immigrated to Palestine in the 1920s and become an activist in the PCP. He was expelled by the British in 1929 and worked as a Communist in both France and the U.S.S.R., where he was recruited by the KGB in the late 1930s and sent back to Europe to build an extensive espionage network filled with former PCP comrades living in France and Belgium. Activated after the Soviet Union was attacked, the Red Orchestra, as it was known, was slowly but surely dismantled by the Nazis and most of its members executed. Trepper was captured and pretended to cooperate with the Germans but managed to escape and remain in hiding until the liberation of Paris. He returned to Moscow but was imprisoned in the Lubianka on suspicion of having been a Nazi collaborator. Convicted of treason in 1947, he was not released and rehabilitated until 1954, and then allowed to return to his native Poland in 1957, where he became a functionary in the now-tiny Jewish community. Horrified by the Polish Communist Party's anti-Semitic campaign in 1967, he demanded to be allowed to leave the country. Harassed for several years, he was finally allowed to emigrate in 1973 after a worldwide campaign on his behalf. He died in Israel, from which he had been expelled forty-four years earlier, in 1982, still a convinced Communist. See Leopold Trepper and H. Weaver, *The Great Game: Memoirs of the Spy Hitler Couldn't Silence* (New York: M.W. Books Ltd., 1977).

6 Dalia Karpel, "A Revolutionary Life," *Haaretz*, December 9, 2004. Another PCP militant, Lukasz (Gideon) Hirszowicz, like Preminger, had arrived in Palestine in 1939. He returned to Poland in 1948, where he became a respected figure at the Institute for History of the Polish Academy of Sciences. Forced to leave Poland in the anti-Semitic campaign of 1967, he settled in England where for many years he edited the *Bulletin of Soviet and East European Jewish Affairs*; Chimen Abramsky, "Lukasz Hirszowicz 1920–1993," *East European Jewish Affairs*, v. 23, n. 2, 1993, 5–7.

7 The meeting with Preminger is described in David Ben-Gurion, *War Diaries* (1947–1949), edited by Gershon Rivlin and Elhanen Orren, Hebrew; *Jerusalem: Israel Defense Ministry*, 1983, v. 1, 315–16. I am indebted to Gideon Remez for locating and translating this material. For Preminger's expulsion see *Kol Ha'am*, February 14, 1949, 1.

8 "Knesset Communist Joins Mapam," *Jerusalem Post*, August 16, 1949, 1.

9 CIA database CREST with stories on Preminger. See, for example, https://www.cia.gov/library/readingroom/docs/CIA-RDP80-00809A000700210058-0.pdf. When Oren was finally released and returned to Israel in 1956, he remained loyal to the Soviet Union.

10 "Aner Preminger to Klehr," October 24, 2016; confidential communication.

11 Harvey Klehr, John Earl Haynes, and David Gurvitz, "The Two Worlds of a Soviet Spy," *Commentary*, March 2017, 27–33; "David Katz to Klehr," March 3, 2017; "Aner Preminger to Klehr," March 3, 2017.

12 Some of this information about Preminger comes from a documentary film made by his son, Aner Preminger, *On My Way to Father's Land*. Also, see "Aner Preminger to Klehr," September 12, 2012.

13 "Aner Preminger to Klehr," November 3, 2012.

14 "Pearson to Harriman," May 10, 1968; "Pearson to Karr," May 10, 1968; "Karr to Pearson," June 26, 1968; "Karr to Pearson," January 20, 1969; and "Pearson to Karr," January 28, 1969 in "David Karr" folder, G24, 1 of 3, Drew Pearson papers, LBJ Library.

15 "Pearson to Karr," August 21, 1968, in "David Karr" folder, G24, 1 of 3, Drew Pearson papers; Scott Stossel, *Sarge: The Life and Times of Sargent Shriver* (Washington, D.C.: Smithsonian Books, 2004), 573.

16 Roy Rowan, "The Death of Dave Karr, and Other Mysteries," *Fortune*, December 3, 1979, 99; "Michael Johnson to Harvey Klehr," March 13, 1990. *Variety* did report that Karr was coproducing an adaptation of a Dashiell Hammett story, "The Big Knockover," in 1967 and an Alain Resnais film for MGM in 1968. *Variety*, February 1, 1967, 21; *Variety*, March 20, 1968, 3. It is not clear if either was ever produced.

17 Rowan, "The Death of Dave Karr," 99.

18 Abel Green, "Karr as Paris Deal-Maker," *Variety*, September 25, 1968, 3, 55.

19 Rowan, "The Death of Dave Karr," 99; "Forte to Klehr," June 29, 1990; "Feenie to Dearest Mom," March 8, 1969 in Feenie Ziner papers.

20 Peter Evans, *Nemesis: Aristotle Onassis, Jackie O, and the Love Triangle That Brought Down the Kennedys* (New York: HarperCollins, 2004), 70, based on an interview of Evans with David Karr.

21 "Dear Mr. President from David Karr," March 26, 1968; "Memorandum for James Jones," April 3, in diary backup, April 3, 1968, LBJ Library.

22 "Pearson to Karr," April 5, 1968, "Karr to Pearson," April 20, 1968, "David Karr" file, "Personal Papers of Drew Pearson," G24, 1 of 3, LBJ Library; "Dear David from LBJ," May 6, 1968, name file: David Karr, LBJ Library; Evans, *Nemesis*, 170, 184.

23 Evans, *Nemesis*, 100–117.

24 Ibid., xv.

25 Ibid., 156; George Jonas, *Vengeance: The True Story of an Israeli Counter-Terrorism Team* (New York: Simon & Schuster, 2005). Hamshari is a major character in Steven Spielberg's film *Munich*.

26 Evans, *Nemesis*, 166.

27 For an excellent counterargument debunking the conspiracy theories, see Mel Ayton, "Did the PLO Murder Robert Kennedy," reprinted at HNN.us/node /10781.

28 Evans, *Nemesis*, 274–75, 299–300.

29 Ibid., 230, 238–40; interview with Elizabeth Cooke, September 17, 2015.

30 Evans, *Nemesis*, 235–39; George Jonas, *Vengeance: The True Story of an Israeli Counter-Terrorism Team.*

31 "Evia Karr to Harvey Klehr," July 24, 2011. According to Doug Karr, David's grandson, his father, Andrew, wanted to sue Evans for his claims in the book. Since you cannot libel a dead person, the idea went nowhere. Interview with Doug Karr, New York, August 7, 2011.

32 "Karr to Pearson," June 4, 1967, in "David Karr" file 1964–1969, Drew Pearson papers.

33 Carl Blumay, *The Dark Side of Power: The Real Armand Hammer* (New York: Simon & Schuster, 1992), 313; Roy Rowan, "The Death of Dave Karr," 94.

34 "David to Dear Mom," undated, Feenie Ziner papers; interview with Arnold Forster, June 26, 1989; "David Karr to Scoop Jackson," February 5, 1971, in Henry M. Jackson papers, accession number 3560-4, box 6, folder 41, University of Washington Library; "Shriver Denies Support for Rogers Plan," *Jerusalem Post*, December 14, 1970, 8.

35 "Aner Preminger to Klehr," September 23, 2012; "From the Testimony of Nina Admoni," http://www.yadvashem.org/righteous/stories/sugihara/admoni -testimony.

36 Evans, *Nemesis*, 248.

37 "Karr to Pearson," April 14, 1969, July 2, 1969, "David Karr" file, G24, 1 of 3, Drew Pearson papers; "Michael Johnson to Harvey Klehr," March 13, 1990; Evans, *Nemesis*, 131–32, 273.

38 Stossel, *Sarge*, 570–74.

39 Daniel Yergin, "The One-Man Flying Multinational, Part 2," *The Atlantic*, July 1975, 62.

40 The best biography of Hammer, from which most of the following is taken, is Edward J. Epstein, *Dossier: The Secret History of Armand Hammer* (New York: Random House, 1996).

41 John Earl Haynes, Harvey Klehr, and Alexander Vassiliev, *Spies: The Rise and Fall of the KGB in America* (New Haven, CT: Yale University Press, 2009), 456–72.

42 Quoted in Steve Weinberg, *Armand Hammer: The Untold Story* (Boston: Little, Brown, 1989), 259.

43 Stossel, *Sarge*, 574–75.

44 Epstein, *Dossier*, 295, 310–11.

45 Ralph Blumenthal, "Armand Hammer's Maze of Skullduggery," *New York Times*, October 14, 1996, C11, 18; Victor Nikolaev, "The Affair of Lenin's Letters," *Pravda*, April 18–21, 1996, 4. The two lawyers, representing the Meade Corporation, were Stanley Pottinger, who had served as assistant attorney general of the United States from 1973 to 1977, and Armistead Gilliam. Pottinger also told the *Times* that he recalled Karr's "hinting of more damaging information" about Hammer that he called "an atom bomb."

46 Jonathan Braun, "Olympics Promoters Name Kosygin Kin as Sharing in Deal," *Jewish Week*, September 3, 1978, 1; Blumay, *The Dark Side of Power*, 220; Roy Rowan, "The Death of Dave Karr," 105.

47 Interview with Jean Guyot, Paris, June 4, 1990.

48 "David Karr's Soviet Connection," *Business Week*, May 19, 1975, 142.

49 Rowan, "The Death of Dave Karr," 94.

50 "To Mr. Kazlovski, Minister of Geology, From David Karr," March 7, 1978, Jeff Gerth material.

CHAPTER 7: SOVIET AGENT

1 Rowan, "The Death of Dave Karr," 94.

2 Yevgenia Albats, "Senator Edward Kennedy Requested KGB Assistance with a Profitable Contract for his Businessman-Friend," *Izvestia*, June 24, 1992, 5.

3 "Confidential source to Harvey Klehr," September 5, 2010. Although wary of information that cannot be publicly attributed, I believe that this information, coinciding as it does with other information about Karr's ties to the KGB, is credible.

4 Albats, "Senator Edward Kennedy," 5.

5 Stossel, *Sarge*, 577–81.

6 Ibid., 619–23.

7 Ibid., 627–40.

8 FBI files, http://vault.fbi.gov/robert-sargent-shriver-jr/robert-sargent-shriver-part-01-of-02/view.

9 "Henry Jackson to David Karr," November 23, 1942; "David Karr to Scoop," November 9, 1943; "Henry Jackson to Personnel Assistant," June 1, 1944; "John Salter to David Karr," July 25, 1944, in Henry M. Jackson papers, accession number 3560-2, box 4, folder 36, University of Washington Library.

10 "David Karr to My Dear Scoop," February 5, 1971; "David Karr to My Dear Scoop," June 10, 1971, in Henry M. Jackson papers, accession number 3560-4, box 6, folder 41, Henry M. Jackson papers, accession number 3560-5, box 6, folder 3; Robert Kaufman, *Henry M. Jackson: A Life in Politics* (Seattle: University of Washington Press, 2000), 242–83.

11 "David Karr to Dear Scoop," April 2, 1975; "David Karr to Senator Henry Jackson," July 3, 1975, Henry M. Jackson papers, accession number 3560-5, box 6, folder 3.

12 "David Karr to Dear Scoop," April 2, 1975; "David Karr to My Dear Scoop," December 24, 1974, Henry M. Jackson papers.

13 Jeff Gerth, "US Entrepreneur's Soviet Ties," *New York Times*, October 5, 1979, D9; Jeff Gerth, "Gov. Brown Supporting Projects That Aid a Mexican Contributor," *New York Times*, March 11, 1979, 1, 18; Joe Scott, "Brown May Lose a Bundle Because of This," *L.A. Herald Examiner*, July 15, 1979; Chase Davis, "Brown's 1979 'Special List' Highlights Eclectic Relationships," *California Watch*, accessed June 20, 2011, http://californiawatch.org/money-and-politics/brown-s-1979-special-list-highlights-eclectic-relationships-5397; Laurie Becklund, "US Financier Tells Plans for Major Projects in Baja," *L.A. Times*, October 14, 1978, SD-A1. Bustamante died in 2011 at the age of ninety-five. One of his sons, Carlos, was the mayor of Tijuana.

14 Christopher Andrew and Vasili Mitrokhin, *The Sword and the Shield: The Mitrokhin Archive and the Secret History of the KGB* (New York: Basic Books, 1999), 290–91.

15 Fedora, "Kennedy's Comrade: Hunting a KGB Mole in the Democratic Party,"
     October 23, 2006, *Free Republic*, accessed June 20, 2011, http://freerepublic.
     com/focus/f-news1724508/posts?page=170.

16 "Nation: Olympics: To Go or Not to Go," *Time*, January 28, 1980
     at http://www.time.com/time/magazine/article/0,9171,923893,00.
     html#ixzz1RoNKz9Nd; "The Market Turns Bearish for Moscow Games
     Merchandiser Stanford Blum," *People*, February 11, 1980.

17 Andrew and Mitrokhin, *The Sword and the Shield*, 291.

18 Albats, "Senator Edward Kennedy," 5. The memo is reproduced in Yevgenia
     Albats and Catherine Fitzpatrick, *The State within a State* (New York: Farrar,
     Straus and Giroux, 1999), 249–50.

19 Vasily Mitrokhin, "The KGB in Afghanistan," Woodrow Wilson
     International Center for Scholars Working Paper, 2002.

20 Peter Robinson, "Ted Kennedy's Soviet Gambit," *Forbes*, August 27, 2009;
     Paul Kengor, *The Crusader: Ronald Reagan and the Fall of Communism* (New
     York: Harper, 2007), 215–20, 317–20.

21 Vladimir Bukovsky and Pavel Stroilov, "A Phenomenon Called Senator
     Kennedy," *National Review*, November 27, 2006, at https://www
     .nationalreview.com/2006/11/phenomenon-called-senator-kennedy
     -vladimir-bukovsky-pavel-stroilov/.

22 Tim Sebastian, "Teddy, the KGB, and the Top-Secret File," *Sunday Times*,
     February 2, 1992.

23 "Marsh to Karr," October 21, 1974; "Marsh to Karr," November 5, 1974 in
     WHCF, FG/6-11-1, Gerald Ford Library.

24 "Sonier to Nessen," September 24, 1974, "Nessen to Karr," October 3, 1974,
     "Nessen to Karr," October 18, 1974 in Ron Nessen papers, box 158, Personal
     Correspondence File K, Gerald Ford Library.

25 "Karr to Marsh," October 8, 1974, "Marsh to Karr," October 24, 1975, "Marsh
     to Karr," November 5, 1974 in WHCF—name file, "David Karr" folder, Ford
     Library.

26 "Karr to Ted Marrs," October 9, 1974, "Marrs to Karr," October 21, 1974,
     "Sonier to Marrs," October 10, 1974, WHCF—name file, "David Karr" folder,
     Ford Library.

27 "Karr to Marsh," November 18, 1974 in WHCF, box 42, FG/6-11-1, Ford
     Library.

28 "Marsh to Karr," January 23, 1975, "Karr to Marsh," February 13, 1975 in
     WHCF—name file, "David Karr" folder, Ford Library.

29 "Russ Rourke to Jack Marsh," April 21, 1975, "Jack Marsh to Russ Rourke,"
     April 23, 1975, "Russ Rourke to Bud McFarlane," April 28, 1975 in WHCF—
     name file, "David Karr" folder, Ford Library.

30 "Memo," May 19, 1975, WHCF, box 44, FG/6-11-1 (General), Ford Library;
     "David Karr's Soviet Connection," *Business Week*, May 19, 1975, 144. Karr
     was not happy with the article. He objected to claims that he had been on the
     Daily Worker staff, wrote speeches for Gvishiani, and had failed at Fairbanks
     Whitney. He once again referred to his book, *Back Stage in the Board Room*,
     which he promised would soon be published. Karr telex to Mr. Lewis Young,

May 15, 1975, accession number 3560-5, box 6, folder 3, in Henry M. Jackson papers.

31 "Karr to Nessen," May 5, 1975, "Nessen to Karr," May 13, 1975, Ron Nessen papers, box 158, Personal Correspondence Folder K, Ford Library.

32 "Memorandum for Ben Evans," May 22, 1975, redacted and released under the FOIA by the CIA.

33 "Memorandum for the Record," May 23, 1975, released under the FOIA by the CIA; FBI files 65-32550-19, 32250-150; Rob Roy Ratliff Facebook entry.

34 "Karr to Nessen," June 23, 1975, "Karr to Ford," June 23, 1975 in WHCF, box 51, CO158, Ford Library.

35 Ibid.

36 Interview with Jack Anderson, Washington, D.C., March 23, 1990; telephone interview with Lee Falk, July 9, 1990.

37 Vladimir Poytapov, "Onassis's Millions," *Pravda*, February 4, 1992, 5; Evans, *Nemesis*, 303.

38 Poytapov, "Onassis's Millions," 5.

39 Nigel Dempster, *Heiress: The Story of Christina Onassis* (New York: Grove Weidenfeld, 1989), 101–12; Oleg Kalugin, *The First Directorate* (New York: St. Martin's Press, 1994), 263–66. Yevgenia Albats, "Senator Edward Kennedy," 5; Evia Karr says that she introduced Karr to Christina at the Berkeley Hotel in London. "Evia Karr to Harvey Klehr," July 24, 2011.

40 "The Death of a Pimpernel," *Daily Express*, August 24, 1979, 17; Jeff Gerth, "U.S. Entrepreneur's Soviet Ties," *New York Times*, October 5, 1979, D1; "Mark Kramer to Harvey Klehr," October 6, 2016.

41 Kalugin, *The First Directorate*, 193–94.

42 Epstein, *Dossier*, 311–12; Judith Miller, "How Is Occidental Run?," *New York Times*, February 13, 1979, D1. More than twenty years ago, I requested a copy of Karr's testimony from the SEC under the FOIA. I was informed that because of pending lawsuits by Occidental, its release was impossible. In 2010, I renewed my request, but was told that after a thorough search, the SEC could not locate the requested records. "Jeff Ovall to Klehr," December 29, 2010.

43 USA v. Leo Henzel (Penn-Lee Products); Leo Henzel v. State of Florida (June 18, 1968); District Court of Appeal of Florida, Third District; 296 F. 2d 650, Leo Henzel, Appellant, v. United States of America, Appellee.

44 608 F. 2d 654: Leo Henzel, Plaintiff-appellant, v. Richard Gerstein et al., Defendants-appellees, Robert L. Shevin, Attorney General et al., Defendants; 475 F. 2d 1271: Leo Henzel, Petitioner-appellant, v. State of Florida, Respondent-appellee.

45 Weinberg, *Armand Hammer*, 247–48; *Billboard*, October 16, 1976, 14.

46 Jonathan Braun, "The Times Tried to Cut in on Big Soviet Promotion," *The Jewish Week*, July 2–15, 1978, 1.

47 "Hard-Selling the Moscow Olympics," *TV Guide*, March 10, 1979; Gerth, "US Entrepreneur's Soviet Ties," *New York Times*, October 5, 1979, D4; United Euram Corp. v. Occidental Petroleum Corp., 123 Misc. 2d 574, 474

N.Y.S. 2d 372, NY Sup., 1984; for a report on a congressional investigation of the jockeying for the broadcast rights that mentioned Karr, see "Olympic Tales: Networks Detail Negotiations with the Soviet Union," *Broadcasting*, October 10, 1977, 58, 61, 62, 64.

48 Rowan, "The Death of Dave Karr," 106.

49 United Euram Corp. v. Occidental Petroleum Corp., 123 Misc. 2d 574, 474 N.Y.S. 2d 372, NY Sup., 1984; Weinberg, *Armand Hammer*, 248.

50 Braun, "Olympic Promoters," 1.

51 United Euram Corp. v. Union of Soviet Socialist Republics, 61 F. Supp. 609 S.D.N.Y., 1978.

52 Interview with Arnold Forster, New York, June 26, 1989.

53 Rowan, "The Death of Dave Karr," 106; interview with Charles Simonelli, Greenwich, CT, August 10, 1989; Jonathan Braun, "Mystery Death Refocuses on Fees to Soviet Favorites in Olympics," *Jewish Week*, November 25, 1979, 1.

54 Rowan, "The Death of Dave Karr," 95.

CHAPTER 8: BY PERSONS UNKNOWN?

1 "Evia Karr to Klehr," July 24, 2011; interview with Elizabeth Cooke, September 17, 2015; Cooke, *Life Savors*, 205.

2 Interview with Luvie Pearson, Washington, D.C., March 23, 1990; interview with Elizabeth Cooke, September 17, 2015; interview with Frank Karr, September 17, 2015; Cooke, *Life Savors*, 206.

3 Interview with Charles Simonelli, August 10, 1989; interview with Jean Guyot, June 4, 1990; telephone interview with Lee Falk, July 9, 1990; telephone interview with Max Youngstein, June 13, 1990; interview with Michette Karr, Paris, June 5, 1990.

4 "Feenie to Dearest Mom," June 10, 1969 in Feenie Ziner papers.

5 Interview with Frank Karr, September 17, 2015.

6 Ibid.

7 Interview with Elizabeth Cooke, September 17, 2015; Cooke, *Life Savors*, 203–205; Evans, *Nemesis*, 238. Evans based his comments on a story told him by one of Onassis's aides, who claimed to have heard it from Karr.

8 Interview with Frank Karr, September 17, 2015; Cooke, *Life Savors*, 208.

9 Cooke, *Life Savors*, 206.

10 "To Denise Karr from David Karr," undated but signed on June 28, 1978, in "David Karr" file, New York County Surrogate's Court Records Department, 31 Chambers St., rm. 402, New York, NY 10007, file no. 3359/79.

11 Ibid.

12 Interview with Elizabeth Cooke, September 17, 2015; telephone interview with Max Youngstein, June 13, 1990.

13 "David Karr and Evia Freiberg Karr," Superior Court of California, County of San Diego, case number D132342, in Surrogate's Court file; interview with Elizabeth Cooke, September 17, 2015; "Evia Freiburg," April 28, 1979 in Surrogate's Court file; Philippe Bernert, "La Ténébreuse Affaire Karr" [The Mysterious Karr Affair], *Enquête*.

14 This description is based on the account in Rowan, "The Death of Dave Karr," 95–96.

15 "Evia Karr to Harvey Klehr," July 31, 2011; "Proceeding for Letters of Administration, Estate of David Karr; Affidavit of Evia Freiberg Karr," in Surrogate's Court file; Jacques Lesinge, "Mon Mari a Été Assassiné," Aurora, August 16, 1979; holographic will signed by David Karr, June 26, 1979 in Surrogate's Court file.

16 "Proceedings for Letter of Administration, Evia Karr Affidavit," Surrogate's Court file.

17 Ibid.

18 "Evia Karr Affidavit," January 20, 1982; "Proceeding for Letters of Administration"; "Personal Effects," July 7, 1979, Surrogate's Court file.

19 "Complaint Against Person or Persons Unknown," Paris, September 20, 1979; "Evia Karr to Klehr," July 31, 2011.

20 "Death of David Karr and Message for White House from Son," American Embassy Paris to Secretary of State, Washington, D.C., July 10, 1979.

21 "From American Embassy Moscow to American Embassy Paris," October 1975.

22 "Death of David Karr and Subsequent Developments," American Embassy Paris to Secretary of State, Washington, D.C., July 30, 1979.

23 Ibid.; "Mort Mystérieuse d'un Homme d'Affaires Américain," Le Matin, July 23, 1979; "A Most Embarrassing Corpse," L'Express, July 27, 1979; Jacques Lesinge, "Mon Mari a Été Assassiné," L'Aurore, August 16, 1979.

24 Ibid., Bernert, "The Mysterious Karr Affair," Enquête; "From American Embassy Paris to Secretary of State," Washington, D.C., August 17, 1979.

25 "From American Embassy Paris to Secretary of State Washington," July 30, 1979; "Wrap-up for Karr Autopsy Report but Not for Rumors," American Embassy Paris to Secretary of State Washington, D.C., August 1979; "David Karr: Death Controversy Remains on Back-Burner in Paris," American Embassy Paris to Secretary of State Washington, D.C., September 1979.

26 Jacques Lesinge, "Un 'Accident' Bien Bizarre [A Very Bizarre Accident]," L'Aurore, August 21, 1979, 16; Jacques Lesinge, "La Mort Très Étrange du Millionaire U.S. [The Very Strange Death of the U.S. Millionaire]," L'Aurore, August 7, 1979, 7.

27 "Le Mort Du David Karr [The Death of David Karr]," Le Monde, August 29, 1979, 7; Phillippe Bernert, "The Mysterious Karr Affair," Enquête; "The Death of a Pimpernel," Daily Express, August 24, 1979, 17; "Wrap-up for Karr Autopsy Report but Not for Rumors," American Embassy Paris to Secretary of State Washington, D.C., August 1979; "David Karr: Death Controversy Remains on Back-Burner in Paris," American Embassy Paris to Secretary of State Washington, D.C., September 1979.

28 Lesinge, "Mon Mari a Été Assassinéé," L'Aurore, 1; "Evia Karr to Klehr," August 7, 2011.

29 "Complaint Against Person or Persons Unknown," September 20, 1979 in Jeff Gerth material.

30 "Death of David Karr: Estate Case and French Investigation of Cause of

Death," American Embassy Paris to Secretary of State Washington, D.C., November 8, 1979.

31 Ibid.

32 Ibid.

33 "Evia Karr to Judge Millard Midonick," February 6, 1980, Surrogate's Court file. Chapman had met with Evia several times between July and November 1979 and wrote most of the dispatches about the case sent to the State Department. In her letter Evia said he used the alias Ernest Fisher, implying that he worked for the CIA. There is no evidence for that claim. He was the target of an assassination attempt by Lebanese radicals in 1981. For an extensive interview of Chapman about his long and distinguished career (he does not mention David Karr), see http://www.adst.org/OH%20TOCs/ Chapman,%20Christian%20A.toc.pdf.

34 "Evia Karr to Judge Millard Midonick," Surrogate's Court file; "Recent Developments on Aftermath of David Karr's Death," American Embassy Paris to Secretary of State Washington, D.C., August 17, 1979.

35 "Evia Karr to Klehr," August 7, 2011.

36 Rowan, "The Death of Dave Karr," 99–100.

37 Ibid.; Genoble Prevost, "Plaza Athenee: Coup Bas Contre la Participation [Plaza Athenee: Low Blow Against the Shareholders]," *Les Echos*, August 1, 1979, 5; Jean-Pierre Montespan, "Pas Finie L'Affaire du Plaza [The Affair of the Plaza is Not Finished]," *Minute*, August 8, 1979.

38 Interview with Elizabeth Cooke, September 17, 2015. After checking with two CIA officers who served in Paris in the 1970s, I was unable to confirm this story.

39 Rowan, "The Death of Dave Karr," 94.

40 Patrick Marnham, "No Hiding Place for Amin," *Spectator*, December 22, 1979, 14–15. The alleged documentary evidence never surfaced.

41 "Le Ministre des Affaires Étrangèrs A-T-Il Reçu Des 'Cadeaux' De Moscou? [Did the Minister of Foreign Affairs Receive 'Gifts' from Moscow?]," *Minute*, August 22–28, 1979; "Moscow's Gifts?," *Le Monde*, August 23, 1979.

42 Roy Rowan, "The Death of Dave Karr."

43 David Krivine, "The Saga of the Gadot Chemicals Group," *Jerusalem Post*, September 16, 1982, 6; "Aner Preminger to Klehr," September 26, 2012.

44 "Order to Show Cause to Stay Issuance of Letters Testamentary," July 31, 1979, Surrogate's Court file.

45 Mark Stout, "The Pond: Running Agents for State, War, and the CIA," *Studies in Intelligence*, v. 48, n. 3.

46 "Robert Nedelkoff to Klehr," May 19, 1996.

47 John Grombach, "Red Ties to Olympic Graft," *The American Mercury*, spring 1980, 16–20. Although Grombach's article avoided the anti-Semitism, a 1974 article in the same magazine by Colonel X, "Secrets of the Hidden Hand," *The American Mercury*, fall 1974, 21–23, did not bring up the Soviet espionage angle, but denounced Karr as a shill for the Anti-Defamation League, who smeared patriotic Americans on behalf of Communist and Jewish causes.

CHAPTER 9: THE WILL

1 "Stipulation Discontinuing Action," Surrogate's Court file.

2 "Notice of Cross-Petition to Recognize Respondent's Rights as the Surviving Spouse under the Laws of France, Decedent's Domicile and for Discovery of Assets; Affidavit of Evia Freiberg Karr," January 13, 1982, Surrogate's Court file.

3 "Death of David Karr and Subsequent Developments," American Embassy Paris to Secretary of State Washington, D.C., July 30, 1979.

4 David Karr's handwritten letter, June 26, 1979, in Surrogate's Court file.

5 "Affidavit of Evia Freiberg Karr," January 13, 1982, Surrogate's Court file.

6 Nicholas von Hoffman, *Citizen Cohn* (New York: Doubleday, 1988), 459; "Examination of Evia Freiberg Karr," February 3, 1982, Surrogate's Court file. Shuman's affidavit is not in the Surrogate's Court records, nor are transcripts of portions of Evia Karr's testimony. It appears that Shuman may have argued that absent his original affidavit, the copy in Evia's possession had been either forged or altered. An alternative explanation is sloppiness.

7 "David Karr Will and Codicil," Surrogate's Court file.

8 "Proceeding for Letters of Administration, Estate of David Karr," August 7, 1979; "Colloquy," Surrogate's Court file.

9 "Proceeding for Letter of Administration, Estate of David Karr; Affidavit of Evia Freiberg Karr," August 8, 1979 in Surrogate's Court file.

10 "Proceeding for Letters of Administration," July 12, 1979, Surrogate's Court file.

11 "Notice of Cross-Petition to Recognize Respondent's Rights as the Surviving Spouse under the Laws of France, Decedent's Domicile and for Discovery of Assets; Affidavit of Evia Freiberg Karr," January 13, 1982, Surrogate's Court file.

12 Ibid.

13 "Gouriou to Pikna," January 8, 1982; "Filing of the Holographic Will of David Karr," June 6, 1980, Surrogate's Court file.

14 Interview with Jacques Elis, Paris, France, June 5, 1990.

15 "Evia Karr to Judge Millard Midonick," February 6, 1980, Surrogate's Court file.

16 "Midonick to Evia Karr and Maitre Danielle Gouriou," March 7, 1980, Surrogate's Court file.

17 "Henry Lowet to Evia Karr," March 10, 1980, Surrogate's Court file.

18 "Affidavit in Opposition to Motion for Reargument," January 31, 1980, Surrogate's Court file.

19 "Evia Karr to Judge Millard Midonick," February 6, 1980, Surrogate's Court file.

20 "Henry Lowet to Evia Karr," March 10, 1980, Surrogate's Court file. Although Evia claimed it was worth in excess of $1,000,000, the *Ottelia* was sold for $300,000, which did go into the estate.

21 Midonick, "Estate of David Karr," April 23, 1981; "Order Denying Election," June 8, 1981, Surrogate's Court file.

22 "Order Denying Election," June 8, 1981, Surrogate's Court file.

23 "Colloquy," January 26, 1982, Surrogate's Court file.

24 Ibid.

25 "Affidavit in Opposition to Motion for Reargument," Surrogate's Court file.

26 "Compromise Agreement," June 4, 1981, Surrogate's Court file.

27 "Notice of Cross-Petition," January 13, 1982; "In the Matter of the Application," January 26, 1982, Surrogate's Court file.

28 "Colloquy," January 26, 1982, Surrogate's Court file.

29 "Guardian Ad Litem's Affirmation of Services," May 6, 1982, Surrogate's Court file.

30 "Vaneria to Goldfarb," May 6, 1982; "Examination of Evia Freiberg Karr," February 3, 1982, Surrogate's Court file. This latter transcript is the only portion of Evia's testimony in the voluminous and disorganized Karr probate file.

31 "Stipulation of Settlement," February 5, 1982, Surrogate's Court file.

32 Matter of Pikna, 101 A.D. 2d 588 (1984); 108 A.D. 2d 130 (1985); U.S. v. Pikna, 880 F. 2d 1578 (1989).

33 Ruth Beers and Louis Ahrensfeldt v. Richard Pikna, U.S. District Court, Southern District of NY, 84 Civ. 7234; USA v. Richard Pikna, Ruth Beers et al., United States Court of Appeals, Second Circuit, no. 1267, docket 89-6046. Karr's probate records are replete with filings and counter-filings trying to sort out the mess created by Pikna.

34 "Compromise Agreement," June 4, 1981, Surrogate's Court file.

35 "Petition for an Order," December 3, 1982; "Agreement," December 16, 1985, Surrogate's Court file.

36 "In the Matter of the Judicial Settlement of the Final Account," Surrogate's Court file.

CONCLUSION

1 http://today.uconn.edu/2013/01/professor-emerita-of-english-florence -feenie-ziner-dies/.

2 Douglas Martin, "Madeline Amgott, Television Producer, Dies at 92," *New York Times*, July 22, 2014, B9.

3 Elizabeth Cooke, *Life Savors* (Troy, NY: Troy Book Makers, 2011); *How to Game People without Even Trying* (Bloomington, IN: Archway Publishing, 2015).

4 "Andrew Karr to Klehr," May 9, 2010, June 2, 2010, October 4, 2016; interview with Doug Karr, August 7, 2010; Cooke, *Life Savors*, 232; "Jean-Michel Karr to Klehr," September 18, 2015.

INDEX